ASSESSING

21st Century

SKILLS

To Riley, for whom all things are possible

ASSESSING
21st Century
SKILLS

A guide to evaluating mastery and authentic learning

LAURA
GREENSTEIN

CORWIN
A SAGE Company

CORWIN
A SAGE Company

FOR INFORMATION:

Corwin
A SAGE Company
2455 Teller Road
Thousand Oaks, California 91320
(800) 233-9936
www.corwin.com

SAGE Publications Ltd.
1 Oliver's Yard
55 City Road
London EC1Y 1SP
United Kingdom

SAGE Publications India Pvt. Ltd.
B 1/I 1 Mohan Cooperative Industrial Area
Mathura Road, New Delhi 110 044
India

SAGE Publications Asia-Pacific Pte. Ltd.
3 Church Street
#10-04 Samsung Hub
Singapore 049483

Acquisitions Editor: Hudson Perigo
Associate Editor: Allison Scott
Editorial Assistant: Lisa Whitney
Permissions Editor: Adele Hutchinson
Project Editor: Veronica Stapleton
Copy Editor: Alan Cook
Typesetter: C&M Digitals (P) Ltd.
Proofreader: Wendy Jo Dymond
Indexer: Gloria Tierney
Front Cover Designer: Lisa Riley
Back Cover Designer: Rose Storey

Printed in the United States of America.

Library of Congress Cataloging-in-Publication Data

Greenstein, Laura.

Assessing 21st century skills : a guide to evaluating mastery and authentic learning / Laura Greenstein.

pages cm
Includes bibliographical references and index.

ISBN 978-1-4522-1801-4 (pbk.)

1. Educational tests and measurements—United States. I. Title.

LB3051.G715 2012
371.26--dc23   2012008928

This book is printed on acid-free paper.

12 13 14 15 16 10 9 8 7 6 5 4 3 2 1

Contents

List of Figures

Preface

Without a doubt, we live in complex times. Recently, I was sorting through the stacks of studies, reports, and reviews on 21st century education I've read, trying to make sense of the diversity of studies, perspectives, and opinions found there. While doing so, I heard an unexpected and most straightforward comment: "When times get complicated, people look for simple answers." The speaker was Ira Glass (2010), the producer of *This American Life* on National Public Radio. He continued to explain that it is difficult for people to face the world's complexities; as a result of this tendency to oversimplify things, a "fact gap" exists. His idea rings true to me, because many sectors in education are seeking simple answers to very complicated problems.

Over the years, I have seen a steady stream of initiatives in education. I am still amazed at how these proposals become popular and then fade away. From open classrooms and whole language, to charters and common core, we repeatedly seem to grab on to the latest reform in hope that it will provide an easy fix, only to discard it when it doesn't work and wait for the next "best thing" to come along. These initiatives fail because of oversimplification, uneven implementation, inconsistent monitoring, and other reasons. Rarely is quality assessment incorporated in the blueprint, yet it must be an essential component of any formula for reform.

Along with complexity, there are a number of current tensions in education. Some say that our schools must undividedly focus on literacy and numeracy. At the same time, there is strong support for college and career readiness. In reality, no one is ready for college and career without a robust foundation in core skills and knowledge. But those foundations must also incorporate 21st century skills: critical thinking, actions for success, and the ability to genuinely apply these in a global society. For the sake of today's students who will be competing in a rapidly changing world, we must extend learning beyond the core and provide relevant and challenging real-world connections throughout their education.

These two ideas—*core* and *21st century*—are not in opposition to each other. 21st century skills do not replace content knowledge, but complement it. Meaningful content, combined with quality instruction and valid assessment, is the starting point for expanding learning opportunities. Embedding 21st century skills, along with relevant assessments connected to real learning, into all parts of the curriculum, is one of the central tasks of teaching in our time. Some might say we've always done this. Progressives in the 1800s were strong supporters of critical intelligence and applied learning. Contemporary figures such as Ted Sizer and Dennis Littky embraced and implemented these ideas. Nonetheless, I contend that we have rarely assessed the outcomes of these practices in a practical and consistent manner.

The research and the voices of authority that are reported on in the book convey an imperative: We must intentionally change both what we are teaching (from simple content to complex thinking) and how we are teaching (from delivery of information to student engagement and building of knowledge). Changes to assessment must follow: We must shift from reliance on traditional selected-choice and completion instruments to a greater emphasis on alternative measures of authentic learning. This requires a refocus from once-a-year, large-scale measures of literacy and numeracy to multiple and local models of assessing higher-level thinking, creativity, collaboration, digital skills, and global understanding.

In a dream, I'm standing at a crossroads in educational assessment. The signpost points me in contradictory directions and forces me to make difficult choices. Should I head down the road toward standardized tests or toward alternative assessments? Is content knowledge more important than critical thinking? Do I really have to choose between summative and formative assessment, large scale and local? And then there's that aha! moment when I wake up with clarity. There are decisions to be made, and as I take the first steps, I feel elated and relieved. I can no longer wait for the engines of education to decide the path for me. The guidepost at the beginning asks, "What is it that we want and need students to know, understand, and do to be successful in the world of today and tomorrow?" I see the path we need to take. It is one that focuses on 21st century outcomes. And I start down it.

In this book, you'll find recommendations for action along with strategies for assessment in the 21st century classroom. The ideas extend basic content knowledge into a model of 21st century knowledge and skills, the need for which is driven by current forces such as globalization, technology, and changes in the demands of the workplace. To respond to these circumstances effectively, we must ask ourselves such questions as these:

Can our students question and critically evaluate the information they view? Are they able to work together to solve problems? What do they do when faced with new problems? Are they able to understand and synthesize multiple perspectives?

Chapters 1 through 4 provide an introduction to current perspectives on education, a summary of several 21st century learning paradigms, fundamentals of assessment, and a variety of strategies for assessing authentic learning. A synthesized model of 21st century skills incorporating insights from all the varying schools of thought provides the foundation for the rest of the book. This straightforward view includes three groups of skills: *thinking*, *acting*, and *living*.

The model provides the foundation for developing appropriate and meaningful assessments. Chapters 5 through 8 offer a spectrum of strategies for assessing thinking, acting, and living skills. A range of educational outcomes are cross-referenced with 21st century skills and aligned with strategies for measuring those outcomes. Each section includes explicit examples that can easily be adapted to classrooms in multiple content areas and grade levels.

In its conclusion, the book recognizes that assessment must be a key part of any proposal for reform of education. Recommendations are made for changes to policy and practice. These recommendations may not be a panacea, but they can refocus the debate toward an emphasis on the learning outcomes that really matter for our children—both today and for our kindergarteners, who will be retiring in the 2070s. This refocusing requires that we decide in the present what we want and need our students to know, understand, and do in the future. It requires us to identify new ways to recognize when these changes happens and to develop new strategies and metrics to achieve these outcomes.

Reading this book, you will meet teachers who are using these strategies and see examples of them in action. This book is by and large about teachers and students, about teaching and learning. It focuses more on day-to-day classroom assessment than on large-scale assessment. Educational theories and strategies will evolve to ensure that all learners are prepared to be productive citizens of the 21st century. The world continues to change; there will always be disequilibrium. It is this disequilibrium that leads to transformation. Amid the complexity, there are clear steps that can be taken to guide the change.

Next you will find the first of many charts, tables, and diagrams that have been included in this text to facilitate understanding and to aid in immediate implementation of the strategies. Figure P.1 not only gives you an overview of this book's aims, but it also explains what this book is not. If you are looking for a book about radical reform, this isn't it. If you are interested in thoughtful, informed, and reasonable change, please read on.

Figure P.1   About the Book

What This Book Is About	What This Book Isn't About
Recognizing and keeping what's good in education	Demolishing the current system of education
Incorporating 21st century skills throughout teaching and learning	Exchanging core skills and knowledge for 21st century skills and knowledge
Assessment for learning: informs and engages students in assessment	Assessment of learning: Producing final test scores and measuring students for reporting purposes
Modifying current practices for better compatibility with 21st century practices	Replacing current practices with entirely new practices and paradigms
Considering a spectrum of 21st century skills and knowledge: some closer to traditional, others more remote	Stipulating and mandating specific skills and knowledge
Broad-based standards that guide complex learning for all grades and content areas	Narrowly focused outcomes defined solely by national standards
Description rather than prescription	Prescription rather than description

> *Not everything that counts can be counted, and not everything that can be counted counts.*
>
> — Albert Einstein

Acknowledgments

T his book would not be possible without the ideas and encouragement of many remarkable people:

The supportive and insightful teachers, administrators, and board members in Montville and East Lyme, Connecticut, who generously shared their insights and enthusiasm. Special thanks go to Margo, Jen, Carolyn, Tim, and Sue for their robust morning conversations.

The faculty of the Johnson and Wales Educational Leadership program, especially Ralph Jasparro, for their steadfast endorsement.

My students, who have graciously and with good humor allowed me to practice the strategies in the book; especially the students in the Capstone program, who endured many lessons about metacognition and habits of mind.

My family near and far: my husband Eric, our daughter Casey, our son Andrew, and his remarkable wife Catherine, who show me what it means to continuously love, learn, create, and persist.

And the many people whose ideas I have borrowed and built on: Doug Reeves, Heidi Hayes Jacobs, Linda Darling-Hammond, Lori Shepard, Craig Jerald, Elena Silva, and so many others whom I have met and have yet to meet.

A special thank you to the folks at Corwin: Hudson Perigo, who saw the potential of the first draft, Allison Scott who nurtured and polished that draft, Cathy Hernandez who took over the work in midstream, Lisa Whitney, editorial assistant, Veronica Stapleton, project editor, and the many other production and copy editors.

> *Coming together is a beginning. Keeping together is progress. Working together is success.*
>
> — Henry Ford

PUBLISHER'S ACKNOWLEDGMENTS

Corwin wishes to acknowledge the following peer reviewers for their editorial insight and guidance.

Gary J. Benton
Professor Emeritus
Mississippi State University, Meridian Campus
Meridian, MS

Cindy Corlett
Teacher
Cimarron Middle School
Rowlock Way, CO

Janice L. Hall
Associate Professor of Secondary Education (Retired)
Grace, ID

Julie Prescott
Assessment Coordinator
Vallivue High School
Caldwell, ID

About the Author

Laura Greenstein has been an educator for three decades. The spectrum of ideas on assessment and 21st century learning presented in this book reflect her experiences as a teacher, school leader, adjunct professor, school board member, and consultant. She has a BS from the University of Connecticut, an MS from the State University of New York at Oneonta, a 6th year in Educational Administration from Sacred Heart University, and her EdD in Educational Leadership from Johnson and Wales University. Her interest in assessment emerged as she worked on her dissertation on teacher's assessment practices. During this process, she came to the conclusion that assessment drives everything in education—or at least that it should.

Laura and her husband, Eric, live in East Lyme, Connecticut, and spend as much time as feasible with their children who live on the West Coast. In her leisure time, she enjoys traveling, global cooking, and kayaking. She can be reached at lauragteacher@hotmail.com. You can find more information on assessment at her website www.assessmentnetwork.net.

1

Introduction

This book is both timely and urgent. It mirrors the rapid change in the world in general and in education specifically. As early as 1965, Intel cofounder Gordon Moore (1965) noted that the capability of computer circuits had doubled every year since their invention; his prediction that this trend would continue and have broader applications has become known as Moore's Law. Buckminster Fuller, in his book *Critical Path* (1982), describes the "knowledge-doubling curve," explaining that new knowledge, which had doubled every century until 1900, is now estimated to double every 18 months. And the pace of growth is increasing.

At times, it can be difficult to comprehend that rate of change and the amount of new information. As schools grapple with this, many are still teaching content from the 20th century. Yet most students are growing up in a very different world. If Rip Van Winkle were to wake up in the middle of Times Square today, he would be awestruck by the multimedia messages and the pace of the world around him. If he were to wake up in a classroom, he might notice that the blackboard is now white, but otherwise feel relatively comfortable in the surroundings.

POISED FOR THE 21ST CENTURY

In education, most of the change has focused on teaching and learning. Some are calling for a corresponding change in educational assessment. This view of assessment as the driver of educational change is of great importance; combined with the traditional focus on teaching and learning, it produces is a strong and emerging imperative to alter our long-held conceptions of these three areas.

But we still have much to accomplish. Twenty-first century skills must build on the core literacy and numeracy that all students must master. No longer will measures of disconnected vocabulary or isolated facts suffice. Students will need to think critically and creatively, to communicate and collaborate effectively, and to work globally to be productive, accountable citizens and leaders of their world. A measure of those skills merely provides a number; assessment guides a response.

The challenge lies in reformulating curriculum, reformatting standards, developing instructional strategies to deliver them, and designing assessments that measure these skills while incorporating the psychometrician's goals of validity, reliability, and fairness. The challenge has been presented; the question is not whether, but how, we can meet it. Mike Schmoker (2011) urges teachers to focus on what to teach and how to teach it. I urge educators to add a third part to his formula: a focus on how to assess it.

This book is intended to spur change based on the best information available in an informed, purposeful, and strategic way. It considers the best ideas of Heidi Hayes Jacobs, Laurie Shepard, Linda Darling-Hammond, Cheryl Lemke, Craig Gerald, Margaret Heritage, John Hattie, Chris Dede, Donald Leu, Elena Silva, and many more. It is a book about teaching, learning, and assessing in the 21st century, locally and globally, with an eye on preparing students for world we cannot yet see.

> *Make assessment a vision worth working toward.*
>
> — Thomas Angelo

End of Stagnation

In the more than 25 years since the National Commission on Excellence in Education (1983) issued *A Nation at Risk*, the most significant change in education has been the reauthorization of the Elementary and Secondary Education Act in 2002. This bill, called No Child Left Behind, did not become the panacea it was predicted to be. The demand for accountability morphed into a system of sanctions and consequences for schools that could not meet the requirements of Annual Yearly Progress (AYP). Greater accountability was equated with standardized testing. School choice and reconstitution became catchphrases for change.

Presently, there are calls for another "Sputnik moment" by increasing investments in education and technology. International measures put the United States behind many other countries, including China, South Korea, Finland, Australia, and Canada. Whether you believe this is due to their better-trained teachers, more highly motivated students, or lower levels of poverty, it is a wake-up call for the United States.

In its report, *A Nation Accountable* (2008), the U.S. Department of Education continued the work of *A Nation at Risk*. Since then, graduation rates for high school and college have shown only small improvements, and international test score comparisons rank the United States as average (Organisation for Economic Co-operation and Development, 2009).

More than a decade into the 21st century, the call for school reform continues. Comprehensive reform models are numerous. In states, communities, and schools across the nation, there is ongoing exploration of policies and practices that are intended to reduce the gap between students of different backgrounds and to raise overall achievement. Research on those policies has shown mixed results, difficulty bringing effective programs to scale, and little conclusive evidence.

Changing for the Future

The path we are on is not the same one we walked 20, or 50, or 100 years ago. The world is different, and the following data explain why test scores haven't changed much in very many years. They also demonstrate the necessity for change.

SAT Scores

- In the 1920s, when the SAT was first widely given, 8,000 students took it (Lawrence, Rigol, Van Essen, & Jackson, 2002).
- In 1960, that number was 137,000, with an average verbal score of 534 and an average math score of 509 (Jacobsen, 2011).
- In 2011, 1.5 million students took the test, with an average verbal score of 497; the average math score was 514.

Population

- In 1900, 74,000 Asians immigrated to the United States; in 2000, the number was nearly 3 million (Gibson & Lennon, 1999).
- In 1990, Hispanic Mexican, Central American, and Caribbean immigrants numbered 70,000; in 2000 the number was 6 million (Gibson & Lennon, 1999).
- In 2010, 38% of the people under the age of 18 in the United States were of African, Asian, or Hispanic descent. (Lapkoff & Li, 2007)

Family and Income

- Single-parent families, which typically have a higher rate of poverty, have increased dramatically; 25% of white children and 60% of black children will grow up in a single-parent household.
- In 2010, the poverty rate for children rose to 25%, with rates higher for black and Hispanic children.

- Poverty is associated with low birth weight, lower rates of school readiness, lower school success, and higher dropout rates. (National Center for Children in Poverty, 2012)

These statistics clearly indicate that the students we are educating today are not the same as those we were teaching a generation or two ago. There is no blame being placed in that statement: Simply, the world has changed and so must education. As Einstein said, "We can't solve problems using the same kind of thinking we used when we created them." Applied to education, we can't educate today's children using the same methods we used yesterday.

Policy

The divergence of viewpoints between educators and policy makers is another consideration. Educators focus on strategies that will change instruction such as curriculum, class size, instructional resources, and professional development. Policy makers, from Washington, D.C., to local boards of education, emphasize accountability, generally through large-scale testing. As government has increasingly inserted itself in education, numerical accountability has taken precedence over responsive assessment. Diane Ravitch (2002, p. 2), in "A Brief History of Testing and Accountability," makes the comparisons shown in the following table.

Policy Makers	Professional Educators
Endorse the standards and testing approach	Reject standards and testing as the sole measure of learning
Want high-stakes tests to motivate schools and students	Recognize that intrinsic motivation does not come from external mandates
Support charters and vouchers	Are skeptical about the claims made for these schools
Reward teachers with merit pay for test score improvement	Recognize that other teacher factors need to be considered in teacher evaluation

As educational research has become more grounded in scientific methods, there are more data on what truly works in education. The works of Robert Marzano, John Hattie, Doug Reeves, Linda Darling-Hammond, and others illuminate this. More of their work will be included in later chapters, but for now, if we know what works in education, why are their voices the quietest in the mix of corporate and policy formulations? A review of the research on effective instructional strategies shows numerous common threads: viable curriculum, high yield instruction, clear goals, higher-order questioning strategies, informative feedback, differentiated instruction, and engagement with content. Policy must support these best practices.

If we used the data available and followed research-based practices in our schools, assessment would look much different. Teachers and students would have multiple ways to measure competencies. A balance of formative, summative, and alternative assessments would be the norm. Tests would be taken over time as students showed readiness and mastery of content. Test scores would show growth rather than merely comparisons to others once a year. As students demonstrate mastery, they would move on to higher levels of thinking and performing. Those who need additional help would continue to develop the basics. The growth of the student would be the focus.

History has taught us a lot about what does and doesn't work. There's adequate evidence that any reform works best when both policy makers and educators are at the table solving the problems together. And there's enough expert knowledge, as well as emerging research and data, on what is effective and what isn't.

Reflection

- What do you think are the biggest changes in education over the last several decades?
- What are the biggest challenges facing education today?
- What is your vision of the future of education? What will it look like 20 or 50 years from now?
- What are three steps that can be taken today to make this happen?

FOUNDATIONS: BUILDING ON THE WORK OF OTHERS

The research base for defining, developing, and applying 21st century learning is promising. There was little research when Henry Ford developed assembly line production or when Bill Gates created a computer in his garage. These forward-thinking inventors turned to existing knowledge and critical information in tangential areas of thought, and combined these with their own critical thinking, problem solving, and creativity.

Current Initiatives

In an investigation of key research on defining 21st century skills, a few initiatives stand out.

Partnership for 21st Century Skills

The Partnership for 21st Century Skills (p21.org) has emerged as a major advocate for 21st century skills. This coalition of public, private, nonprofit, and educational groups has created a framework that defines expectations, content, strategies, and outcomes. The four main components of the model are (1) core subjects, (2) learning and innovation skills, (3) information, media and technology skills, and (4) life and career skills. Each of these is then refined as explained in Figure 1.1.

Figure 1.1   Partnership for 21st Century Skills

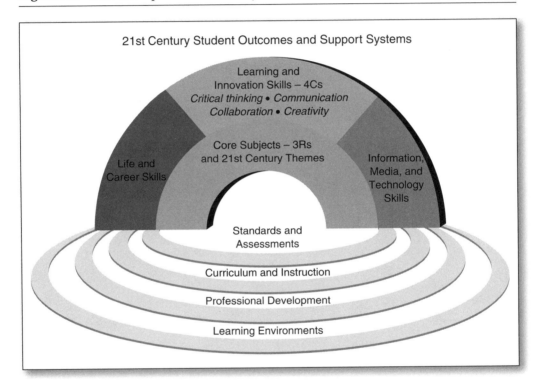

- Core subjects include English, reading, and language arts; world languages; arts; mathematics; economics; science; geography; history; and government and civics.
- Learning and innovation skills are those possessed by students who are prepared for the 21st century and include creativity and innovation, critical thinking and problem solving, and communication and collaboration.
- Information, media, and technology skills are needed to manage the abundance of information and also contribute to the building of it. These include information literacy; media literacy; and information, communications, and technology (ICT) literacy.

- Life and career skills are those abilities necessary to navigate complex life and work environments. These include flexibility and adaptability, initiative and self-direction, social and cross-cultural skills, productivity and accountability, and leadership and responsibility.

Assessment and Teaching of 21st Century Skills

The Assessment and Teaching of 21st Century Skills project (atc21s .org) has its headquarters at the University of Melbourne in Australia, where an international group has been working at defining essential 21st century skills and developing ways to measure them. Founding countries include Australia, Finland, Portugal, Singapore, the United Kingdom, and the United States. Their core belief is that alignment of goals with learning and assessment is essential to policy and practice. They emphasize the importance of balanced assessment systems that incorporate 21st century goals.

In this theoretical model, 21st century skills are organized into four groups, each comprising three to four competencies:

- Thinking includes creativity, critical thinking, problem solving, and metacognition.
- Working involves communication and collaboration.
- Information and technology literacies are the tools for working.
- Citizenship, life skills, and personal responsibility are necessary for living in the world. (Binkley et al., 2010)

Center for Public Education

Craig Jerald, in a report for the Center for Public Education (CPE), uses workplace data to support the imperative to transform education. Reports from 431 employers showed that "while employers still view basic skills like reading comprehension to be fundamental to success on the job, some broader competencies such as the ability to communicate, collaborate, think critically, and solve problems are considered even more valuable" (2009, p. 47).

The CPE's conception and organization of 21st century education is shown in Figure 1.2. The sphere is composed of layers, with foundational skills at the center. Each layer builds on the preceding one. Then the literacies are applied to these skills. Finally competencies for success are described.

Organisation for Economic Co-operation and Development

In a 2009 paper, the Organisation for Economic Co-operation and Development (OECD) described skills and competencies that young

Figure 1.2   Center for Public Education

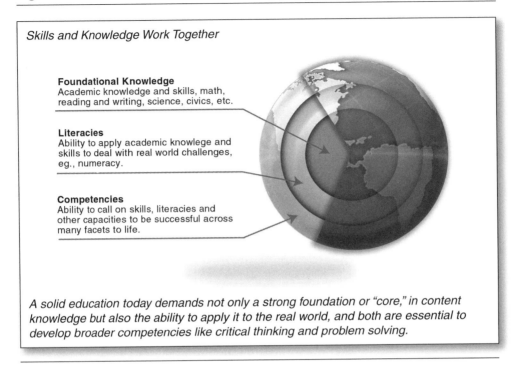

Skills and Knowledge Work Together

Foundational Knowledge
Academic knowledge and skills, math, reading and writing, science, civics, etc.

Literacies
Ability to apply academic knowlege and skills to deal with real world challenges, eg., numeracy.

Competencies
Ability to call on skills, literacies and other capacities to be successful across many facets to life.

A solid education today demands not only a strong foundation or "core," in content knowledge but also the ability to apply it to the real world, and both are essential to develop broader competencies like critical thinking and problem solving.

Source: Jerald (2009). Used with permission.

people require in order to benefit from and contribute to a rapidly changing world. The OECD distinguishes these by defining *skills* as the ability to perform tasks and solve problems. Skills include critical thinking, responsibility, decision making, and flexibility. They define *competencies* as the ability to apply skills and knowledge in a specific context such as school or work. The OECD framework for 21st century skills and competencies has three dimensions:

- Information: This dimension includes accessing, selecting, evaluating, organizing, and using information in digital environments. Use of the information involves understanding the relationships between the elements and generation of new ideas. The competencies necessary to effectively use information include research and problem-solving skills.
- Communication: This dimension includes the ability to exchange, critique, and present information, and also the ability to use tools and technologies in a reflective and interactive way. The requisite skills are based on sharing and transmitting information to others.
- Ethics and Social Impact: This dimension involves a consideration of the social, economic, and cultural implications of technologies, and an awareness of the impact of one's actions on others and the larger society. Skills and competencies required for this are global understanding and personal responsibility.

Metiri/NCREL

A report by the Metiri Group in partnership with the North Central Regional Educational Laboratory (Lemke, Coughlin, Thgadani, & Martin, 2003) explains that 21st century skills are built on basic literacies of language and numeracy, which are then applied to thinking, communicating, producing, and using technology. The report refers to principles and recommendations from many sources and concludes that "educational decision makers must acknowledge that the academics of yesterday are not sufficient for today. To adequately prepare students, they must learn content within the context of 21st century skills" (p. 4). Figure 1.3 graphically illustrates their ideas.

Figure 1.3   enGauge 21st Century Skills

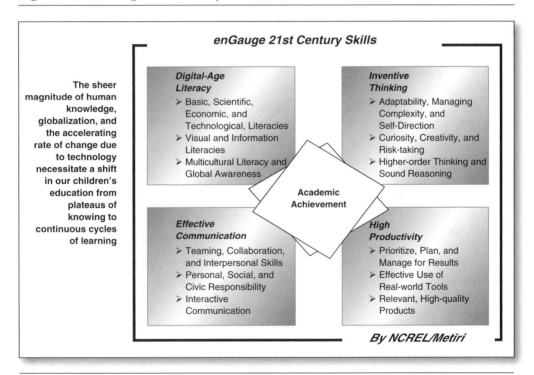

Source: Metiri Group (2003).

- Digital-age literacy comprises three areas: basic (linguistic and mathematical), scientific, economic, and technological literacies; visual and information literacies; and multicultural and global literacies.
- Inventive thinking includes adaptability, self-direction, curiosity, creativity, risk taking, higher-order thinking, and sound reasoning.
- Effective communication emphasizes collaboration, interpersonal skills, personal responsibility, social and civic responsibility, and interactive communications.

- High productivity means prioritizing and planning, use of real-world tools, and the ability to produce relevant high quality products.

Knowledge Works Foundation

The *2020 Forecast* from the KnowledgeWorks Foundation (2008) presents a multidimensional vision of the future in the realms of knowledge, the economy, changes in society, resilient systems, amplified organizations, and the individual. They consider the major forces that will reconfigure learning to include

- Knowledge: information proliferation and data management through visualization;
- Economy: a maker economy in which anyone can design knowledge and promulgate it;
- Society: new civic discourse where all constituents and parties can contribute;
- Systems: flexible systems that change with needs and demands; and
- Self: extended human capacities through technologies and advances in neuroscience.

They believe that the forces of globalism, networking, collaborative media, portable learning, and transliteracies will remake learning. In plain language, these forces will enable people to work together at any time and any place.

Earlier Roots

The designation of certain abilities as 21st century skills may be new, but the essential ideas of this movement have roots that go back many decades.

Habits of Mind

The habits of mind were synthesized from the work of others by Art Costa and Bena Kallick in the 1980s (Costa & Kallick, 2000). They are not intellectual tools but instead are dispositions that people use when they are faced with new and challenging problems. They are not measures of intelligence but rather behaviors that people choose in response to real-life questions and challenges. Costa and Kallick cite the research of Ames, Ennis, Glatthorn, Goleman, Sternberg, and others in explaining these essential qualities. Figure 1.4 summarizes and explains them.

Figure 1.4   Habits of Mind

Persisting: *Stick to it.*	**Managing impulsivity:** *Take your time.*	**Listening with understanding and empathy:** *Try to understand others.*	**Thinking flexibly:** *Look at it another way.*
Using Metacognition: *Think about your thinking.*	**Striving for accuracy and precision:** *Check it again.*	**Questioning and problem posing**: *Ask "How do you know?"*	**Applying past to new situations.** *Use what you learn.*
Thinking and communicating with clarity and precision: *Be clear.*	**Gathering data through all senses:** *Use your natural pathways.*	**Creating, imagining, and innovating:** *Try a unique and different way.*	**Responding with wonderment and awe:** *Have fun figuring it out.*
Taking responsible risks: *Try something new Venture out.*	**Finding humor:** *Laugh a little.*	**Thinking interdependently:** *Work together for better results.*	**Remaining open to continuous learning:** *Learn from experiences.*

Source: Adapted from Costa and Kallick (2000).

In practice, teachers can incorporate the habits in multiple ways. Students can read biographies of well-known people and identify the habits they used to achieve success. Applying the past to the present is an integral part of an introduction to a new topic. Managing impulsivity can be incorporated into classroom management. And, of course, humor can quickly diffuse the tension and stress in any classroom.

Triarchic Intelligence

As early as the 1970s, Robert J. Sternberg was redefining intelligence and emphasizing elements of today's 21st century skills. He defined intelligence as "mental activity directed toward purposive adaptation to, and selection and shaping of, real-world environments relevant to one's life" (1985, p. 45). This definition incorporates not only core knowledge but also how an individual applies that knowledge throughout his or her life. Sternberg's concept of intelligence has three aspects:

1. *Analytic* or *componential intelligence* comprises the macro components of intelligence used in problem solving and decision making.

2. *Experiential intelligence* relates to how well a task is performed in relation to our prior experience with it.

3. *Practical* or *contextual intelligence* uses three processes: adaptation, shaping, and selection to create a fit between the individual and their environment.

Bloom's Taxonomy

Going back even further, Benjamin Bloom introduced his taxonomy in the 1950s (Bloom, 1956). This hierarchy of skills illuminates the spectrum of thinking from early acquisition of knowledge through synthesis and creative applications. The classification is a tiered model of thinking and learning that builds on prior learning. The original taxonomy was revised in the 1990s, primarily to reflect a change from thinking of the skills as nouns to thinking of them as action verbs and to place more emphasis on creativity. Figure 1.5 relates Bloom's taxonomy to teaching, learning, and assessing in the 21st century.

Most educators focus on the cognitive aspect of Bloom's work, but he also developed taxonomies in the affective and psychomotor domains. The affective domain incorporates the 21st century skills of communication and collaboration. Working independently, accepting responsibility, planning, and problem solving are also included in this domain.

In the psychomotor domain, physical movement and coordination are the focal points. Actions for success are part of this domain. Following directions and applying and practicing skills as one works toward competence at such tasks as assembling a robot or baking a cake are important 21st century applications.

The domains cannot be separated from each other in everyday practice in schools or in the workplace. For example, how one perceives his coworkers on a project will affect his contribution to the project. How one feels about her stature, build, or strength will influence her participation in physical education. And how one feels about his academic achievement will guide his educational choices.

Critical Thinking: Edward Glaser

The foundations of 21st century skills can be traced back even further in history. In 1941, Edward Glaser explained that the ability to think critically involves three things:

1. An attitude of being disposed to consider in a thoughtful way the problems that comes within the range of one's experiences

2. Knowledge of the methods of logical inquiry and reasoning

3. Skills in applying those methods

In his account, critical thinking requires persistence of effort and examination of information in the light of facts and evidence. Glaser believed that problems could be solved and solutions discerned through the use of relevant information. The ability to interpret data, evaluate arguments, recognize relationships between ideas, draw conclusions, and

Figure 1.5 Applying Bloom's Taxonomy in the 21st Century

Bloom's Taxonomy	21st Century Skill	21st Century Application
Knowing/ Remembering List, define, describe, name, locate, find, label, identify	• Embedding learning in memory • Retrieving and recalling information and knowledge	• Label a diagram. • Draw a picture of it. • Search and bookmark.
Comprehending/ Understanding Interpret, summarize, paraphrase, classify, give an example, estimate	• Fitting into prior learning • Organizing prior knowledge into a graphic • Constructing meaning	• Summarize the story/illustrate your ideas. • Define the problem. • Give an example of each idea. • Make a rainbow to illustrate things you know about this. • Include it in a blog or Tweet.
Applying Carry out, use, modify, discover, demonstrate, show, produce	• Using learning/knowledge in multiple, novel, and personalized ways • Implementing ideas	• Construct a theory as to why it happened that way. • Brainstorm ways to use this information, and try one. • Show a classmate how to do it using Google Docs or other application.
Analyzing/Comparing Organize, outline, infer, distinguish, integrate, break down, differentiate, attribute to	• Making meaning by exploring and questioning so that its structure and parts can be understood, related, and connected • Distinguishing between components	• Take a position and compare it to others. • Figure out what others need to know to complete the task and help them. • Explain a choice the character made and why you think they did this. Would you do the same? • Map your ideas; create a mash-up.
Synthesizing/Evaluating Hypothesize, critique, compile, devise, plan, reorganize, appraise, defend	• Combining/putting ideas together • Judging the ideas based on criteria and standards • Testing hypotheses	• Evaluate other's solutions to a problem. • Self- and peer review of work • Create a flyer on your topic using multiple sources. • Post an editorial on your blog. • Network with others; combine ideas.
Creating Reorganize, innovate, invent, adopt an unusual approach, plan and produce, generate something new	• Generating something new • Putting elements into a coherent whole • Reorganizing ideas into new patterns	• Create a new ending. • Design another way to convey the message of the story. • Come up with a new way to do, prepare, or fix something. • Create digital products: film, simulation, game, podcast.

make generalizations is essential. All of this is based on the propensity to comprehend and use language with accuracy, clarity, and discrimination. Seventy years later, we are building the foundations of 21st century learning on his core ideas.

Reflection	
Several trends are emerging in the 21st century, and the pace of change is increasing every day. In the table below, a number of significant influences on education are listed. For each driver of change, you are invited to consider how it is influencing education. Reflect on the process you used, your thoughts during the process, and the effectiveness of your strategy.	

Driver of Change	Influences in Education
Example: Instant access to information	Less time researching, more time evaluating and synthesizing information
Information amplification	
Technology	
Globalization of economies	
Personalized learning	
Social/professional networking	
Reformulated workplace skills	
Preparation for college and career	
Multiple platforms for communicating	

Developmental Perspectives

As you read this book, you'll notice an emphasis on the secondary level. There is no doubt that all students can benefit from the inclusion of 21st century skills, and examples at all levels will be included. Of course, communication and collaboration are important even among our youngest students. There are opportunities to solve problems and sort information at all levels. But a solid foundation in literacy and numeracy is essential. During the elementary grades, it is reasonable to introduce critical thinking and concepts such as comparing, synthesizing, and reflecting. At the secondary level, it is more feasible and realistic to expand these building blocks to include higher-level thinking, metacognition, media literacy, and global awareness.

The value of incorporating children's development in teaching and learning is incontrovertible. The National Council for the Accreditation of Teacher Education calls for teachers to understand theories of development, and most teacher preparation programs include a class in educational psychology or human development. For example, Piaget's stages of cognitive development provide a good foundation for reflecting on the developmental process. The sequence from the preoperational stage through concrete operations to formal operations supports the progressive mastery of 21st century skills.

Due to developmental differences, a unit on immigration would look different in a third grade as compared to tenth grade classrooms. Both could be based on a formative Know/Want to Know/How to Learn (KWL) activity followed by teacher-planned delivery of essential content. After demonstrated mastery of content knowledge (i.e., traditional quiz, compare/contrast graphic organizer, learning log), third graders would create headlines and news stories about immigrants' experiences and assemble their work into a class newsletter on the immigration experience of different groups. This supports their concrete operational ability of classifying and sorting information and builds digital literacy/technology skills. High school students can use research data or interviews to compare the differences in immigration through the generations. Each small group would use technology—perhaps a wiki, a glogster, or an original video—to present a synthesis of their findings followed by a Socratic Seminar on current immigration laws. This would support the formal operational ability to apply abstract ideas. Learning would be assessed through multiple measures such as portfolios of work, checklists and rubrics, peer review, and teacher conferences.

Robert Marzano's (2007) and John Hattie's (2008) research supports and extends practical applications of much of the developmental research. As children mature, they make meaning, organize information, put parts and wholes together, and make social and emotional connections in more complex ways. Marzano's and Hattie's high yield strategies of clear goals, questioning, summarizing, and feedback, can be used to support these learning outcomes. Sarah Blakemore and Suparna Choudhury at University College London found that adolescents become "more self aware and more self-reflective, and develop the capacity to hold in mind more multidimensional concepts and are thus able to think in a more strategic manner" (2006, p. 296). Carol Dweck's research on motivation builds on the earlier work of Edward Deci and leads to the understanding that over time, extrinsic rewards become meaningless (Dweck, 2006). Establishing a learning mind-set is essential. Priming the brain for learning, helping it make meaning from new learning, and intrinsically recognizing the value of learning led Daniel Pink (2009) to his conclusion that autonomy, purpose, and mastery are the foundations of motivation and are best exemplified in student-focused classrooms. Synthesis, creativity, problem solving, and metacognitive skills can be developed over time and Pink believes it is these right-brained thinkers who will be most successful in Thomas Friedman's (2005) "flat world."

Assessment must also match developmental abilities. I recently saw a second grader present his story about heroes and heroines. His reading was followed by a statement, "Upon reflection, the next time I write a story I will add more detail about the place where it happened." The audience was very impressed with this 7-year-old's ability to reflect on his work. On checking with the teacher, it was discovered that with prompts and scaffolds all students were able to make recommendations for how they could improve their work. Over time, less support will be needed for this student to reflect on his work independently.

TRANSFORMING ASSESSMENT

When the best ideas from effective practices, cognitive development, and neurological functionality are combined, some important principles stand out.

Responsive Assessment

Assessment in the 21st century will incorporate multiple methods and will be responsive to the individual student's abilities. Measurement of core skills can be the starting point but not the target. Many visionary educational theorists, John Dewey among them, advocated changes in assessment of student learning away from standardized testing and toward more relevant and authentic measures of learning.

There is evidence that 21st century learning and assessment can boost student engagement. Reports from Suzanne Morse (2006); John Bridgeland, John Dilulio, Jr., and Karen Morison (2006); William Hart and Dolores Albarracin (2009); Lannie Kanevsky and Tracey Keighley (2003); and the Center for Evaluation and Education Policy (2009) show that students are frequently bored, disengaged, and find the work meaningless. An achievement mind-set was strengthened by engaging work. Factors that support engagement include control, choice, challenge, complexity, and caring. These are some of the same characteristics that are found in 21st century teaching, learning, and assessing.

Most students would benefit from an approach that would better prepare them for the 21st century than standardized tests currently do. Here's the story of one of such student. I first met Aaron as a high school senior in my section of the Senior Capstone Project. He was a special education student with a shock of red hair and freckles. As I got to know him, I learned that he had been teased throughout his life and thus was very reticent. As he became more comfortable with the other students in the class, he talked more about his ideas for a project. These included some of the traditional type of projects: do some volunteer work, learn to cook, or save the world. During the planning process, each time Aaron shared his experience with playing music, participating in a drum and bugle corps, and working at a summer camp for children interested in music, his eyes grew wide and his enthusiasm became more evident. His classmates encouraged him to develop a project that would allow him to pursue this passion. He was paired up with a mentor, wrote a proposal, and began his project. His plan was to write a few songs for trumpet, baritone, and tuba. During the semester, his modest project became a full-blown symphony. His passion, dedication, and confidence grew. By the end, this shy student was willing to go on stage and conduct the school orchestra in a performance of his symphony. This student who believed he was not capable of attending college is now majoring in music education.

STANDARDS AND SKILLS

Starting With Standards

The Common Core State Standards (CCSS) are available through the U.S. Department of Education (www.corestandards.org). They were written in partnership with the Council of Chief State School Officers (CCSSO) and the National Governor's Association (NGA). Their purpose is to "ensure that all students are college and career ready no later than the end of high school." When these standards were released in 2010, the response from political and educational sectors ranged from strong support to robust opposition.

The connection between CCSS and 21st century skills is at times subtle and at other times strong. For example, one might suppose that "Reason with shapes and their attributes" was a higher-level skill, but this geometry standard is included at the kindergarten level. The standard for high school statistics is more clearly connected to 21st century skills; it requires that students be able to "make inferences and justify conclusions from sample surveys, experiments, and observational studies." To succeed in today's world, students need to master core skills and knowledge. They also need the skills necessary for personal and career success. In blending the two together, the core is honored and the 21st century skills are embedded.

Large-scale assessments will be based on CCSS. Timeliness and fairness in scoring while maintaining validity and reliability are important considerations. But equally important is assessment that determines a student's ability to use information and apply skills in real world situations. These types of assessment are more complex to administer and assess. Students should have multiple opportunities in the classroom to display their ability to solve problems, create, collaborate, and demonstrate leadership and global understanding. Teachers will need the skills and knowledge to assess them.

Connections to the Common Core State Standards

A review of the CCSS reveals a mixture of traditional skills and 21st century skills. Many are intended to build a foundation in literacy and numeracy. The list below shows some that connect the basics with 21st century skills. After that, Figure 1.6 shows how the common core foundational skills extend into higher-level analysis and evaluation.

K–12 anchor standards in speaking and listening:

- Participate effectively in a range of conversations and collaborations with diverse partners, building on other's ideas and expressing their own.

K–12 anchor standards in presentation of knowledge and ideas:

- Present information, findings, and supporting evidence such that listeners can follow the line of reasoning and the organization, development, and style are appropriate to the task, purpose, and audience.
- Make strategic use of digital media and visual displays of data to express information and enhance understanding of presentations.

K–12 anchor standards in writing:

- Text types: Write arguments to support claims in an analysis of substantive topics or texts, using valid reasoning and relevant and sufficient evidence.
- Production and distribution: Use technology, including the Internet, to produce and publish writing and to interact and collaborate with others.
- Research: Gather relevant information from multiple sources, assess the credibility and accuracy of each source, and integrate the information.
- Draw evidence from literacy or informational texts to support analysis, reflection, and research.

K–12 anchor standards in reading:

- Key ideas: Analyze how and why individuals, events, and ideas develop and interact over the course of a text.
- Craft and structure: Assess how point of view or purpose shapes the content and style of a text.
- Integration of knowledge and ideas: Delineate and evaluate the argument and claims in a text, including the validity of the reasoning as well as the relevance and sufficiency of the evidence.

Agreement among all stakeholders on what is important for students to know and be able to do will guide best practice in measuring them. When we start with these core skills and extend them into 21st century skills such as creating and solving authentic problems, then assessments can be designed to sustain those skills.

Figure 1.6   Extending Foundational Skills

CCSS Foundational Skills/Grade	CCSS Extension of Skills
Reading, writing, speaking, and listening/K–5: • Write narratives using effective techniques. • Write informative texts to convey ideas.	• Engage in collaborative discussions
Reading/6–12: • Determine the theme or central idea. • Determine an author's point of view.	• Analyze how style and content contribute to the text.
Writing/6–12: • Produce clear and coherent writing.	• Write arguments to support claims with valid reasoning and relevant evidence.
Speaking and Listening/6–12: • Prepare for and participate in a range of conversations and collaborations.	K–12 Anchor • Evaluate a speaker's reasoning and use of evidence.
Literacy in Social Studies and Science/6–12 • Cite specific textual evidence to support analysis of sources.	Grades 6–8 • Distinguish among fact, opinion, and reasoned judgment in a text. High School • Integrate and evaluate multiple sources of information.
Math Grade 3: Number and Operations • Understand fractions as numbers.	• Solve problems involving measurement and estimation of intervals of time, liquid volumes, and masses of objects.
Math Grade 5: Measurement and Data • Convert like measurement units.	• Represent and interpret data.
Math Grade 7: Geometry • Draw and describe geometrical figures.	• Solve real-life problems involving angles, area, and volume.
Math High School: Statistics • Understand random processes underlying statistical experiments.	• Make inferences and justify conclusions from surveys, experiments, and observational studies.

21st Century Skills

Standards, assessment, and technology are all driving change. National standards are driving local decisions. Instruction is moving away from traditional seat time to an engaged and collaborative model with the teacher as facilitator rather than deliver of learning. Assessment at all levels, from standardized tests to minute-by-minute classroom formative assessment, is being transformed. Technology is becoming the platform for learning as students have instant access to real-time information and use this to generate new ideas. Clearly, the task of infusing 21st century skills into this milieu is both exciting and challenging.

I recently saw a presentation to a board of education on a learning collaboration between the local school and a school in Tanzania. These fifth-grade students used technologies to share information on their country's government, geography, climate, natural resources, schools, and family life. Grounded in language arts, math, and social studies, this exchange brought an understanding of the similarities and differences between the countries and awareness that people around the world are alike in many ways. In their presentation, the students were eloquent in their use of music, art, dance, and food to explain how each of these reflected life in their country. Through the use of technology, collaborative learning, and critical thinking, the students' worldviews were expanded. Throughout the project, students kept journals, self-assessments, and rubrics to measure progress.

There is no shortage of groups and organizations, locally and globally, that have been working to define 21st century skills. Readers will find many commonalities and patterns in each of their formats and descriptions. Yet each has its own unique approach. Some are very simply written and displayed, and others are highly complex and intricate. Some are newer and others have been available for decades. Upon reading and reviewing them, the common elements become clear. It's also evident that terminology varies with each source. A review of basic vocabulary and multiple perspectives on 21st century learning is a good starting point for the patterns and models in the next chapters.

It is in fact nothing short of a miracle that the modern methods of instruction and assessment have not yet entirely strangled the holy curiosity of inquiry; for this delicate little plant, aside from stimulation, stands mainly in need of freedom; without this it goes to wrack and ruin without fail.

— Albert Einstein

Reflection

If you were to select three of the most relevant skills for you and your students from the various models of 21st century skills, what would they be?

- Compare your selections to those of others in your learning community.
- Collaborate to create one list of the three most important.
- Begin to think about ways to include them in teaching and learning.
- What would be a relevant first step to make this happen?
- Envision and describe instruction that is refocused on 21st century skills.

2

A Synthesis of 21st Century Skills

S ome 21st century skills, such as digital literacy and global awareness, may be new, but others are enduring ideas that are being renewed and reconfigured. Globalism, technology, social networking, information proliferation, and the pace of change are making it necessary to change teaching, learning, and assessing. All the models and frameworks in Chapter 1 are built on core knowledge in reading, writing, math, science, and social studies. Once the foundations are built, the 21st century skills support, enable, and facilitate the application of those foundational skills. Used together, they will enable students to be capable and successful contributors to their rapidly changing world.

Educational and professional groups are increasingly attentive to 21st century skills as they update their curricula, policies, and practices. The American Association of School Librarians and the National Councils of Teachers of English, Math, Science, Social Studies, and Technology are embracing the ideas described in this chapter. The Educational Testing Service, the International Society for Technology Education, and the U.S. Department of Labor's Secretary's Commission on Achieving the Necessary Skills are also thoughtfully engaged in dialogue, as are regional school accreditation organizations and those focused on teacher preparation and evaluation.

The implementation of these ideas requires a strong foundation, thoughtful scrutiny, and intentional application. One of the first steps is to recognize the common components. Collectively, there is a pattern in the remarkable work of the visionary individuals and groups summarized in Chapter 1. When synthesized into one design, their ideas form a matrix of skills that is shown in Figure 2.1.

Figure 2.1   21st Century Crosswalk of Skills

SKILL \ SOURCE	Partnership for 21 C. Skills 2004	ATC21S Univ. of Melbourne 2010	Center for Public Education, Craig Jerald 2009
THINKING Critical and higher level	Critical thinking AND Problem solving	Critical thinking	Critical thinking
THINKING Problem solving		Problem solving and decision making	Problem solving
THINKING Creativity		Creativity	Creativity
THINKING Metacognition		Metacognition Learning to learn	Thinking about thinking
ACTING Communication and collaboration	Communication AND collaboration	Communication and collaboration	Collaboration
ACTING Information and communication technology	Digital and visual literacy	Information literacy	Applied literacy
	Information media, and technology literacy	ICT	ICT
ACTING Flexibility and initiative	Flexibility Initiative Self-direction	Flexible Self-directed	Adaption to change Self-sufficiency
LIVING IN THE WORLD Global Understanding	Global skills	Citizenship Global understanding	Global skills
LIVING Civic	Civic literacy	Citizenship	Civic engagement
LIVING Leadership and responsibility	Leadership and responsibility	Personal and social responsibility	Personal responsibility
LIVING College and career readiness	Productivity and accountability	Life and career skills	

Figure 2.1   (Continued)

Organisation for Econ. Co-operation & Development 2009	enGauge-Metiri Group 2003	Costa and Kallick: Habits of Mind 1980s	Robert Sternberg Triarchic Intelligence 1970s	Edward Glaser Critical Thinking 1941
	Higher-order thinking and sound reasoning		Analytical	Knowing how to think critically
Problem solving	Producing real-world products	Questioning and posing problems	Problem solving	Recognize and solve problems Appraise evidence and evaluate arguments
	Creativity, curiosity	Creating, imagining, innovating	Creative: Synthesize existing knowledge	
		Metacognition Applying past knowledge to new situations		Make inferences Render accurate judgments
Communication AND collaboration	Communication, collaboration, interpersonal skills	Listening with understanding Communicating clearly Thinking interdependently		Comprehend and use language with accuracy/ clarity
Searching, selecting, evaluating, and organizing info Interpreting info	Digital and visual literacy			Gather pertinent information Interpret data
Functional and applied ICT	Technology skills			
Restructuring and developing new goals	Adaptability Self-direction	Thinking flexibly Self-awareness		(Note: These are included in Leadership)
	Global awareness Multicultural literacy			
Civic and social engagement	Personal, social, and civic responsibility			
Ethical and social impact Responsibility	Self-direction Social and civic responsibility			
	Plan Prioritize High productivity	Continuous learning Accuracy and precision Past to present	Practical/Applied	

As a first step, consensus and clarity on 21st century skills are required before educators can begin to teach and measure these skills. Educators in each content area and at each grade level can then decide how to align curriculum, instruction, and assessment. The following section provides clarification of the three components of 21st century skills and knowledge: thinking, acting, and living. Most of the descriptors are compilations and syntheses from the organizations and individuals discussed in Chapter 1, but when the precise terminology used is borrowed from those sources, it has been noted. In some sections, the ideas are grouped by main ideas; in others, you will discern a sequence of skills and knowledge.

THINKING

Critical Thinking

Uses/Applies (information, experience, past to present/future)

Seeks and uses information and data to strengthen conclusions and analysis

Uses information and experience across disciplines and in real-world situations

Objectively reviews evidence and data to support statements

Applies past experiences and learning to future planning

Manages complexity through multiple approaches

Proposes additional options

Revisits, reviews, and reconstructs patterns of beliefs based on new evidence

Evaluates (a decision, an experiment, an argument, a product)

Recognizes and considers multiple perspectives

Compares and contrasts ideas

Interprets information and draws conclusions

Evaluates evidence for claims and beliefs

Connects facts and information to viewpoints and ideas

Analyzes (a problem, an argument, causes and connections)

Analyzes how parts interact and produce a whole compilation of knowledge, ideas, and beliefs

Seeks relationships and patterns

Grasps complex, abstract, and symbolic images, objects, and text

Reasons and makes judgments, draws conclusions/generalizations about an issue or topic

Uses multiple types of reasoning including inductive and deductive

Identifies gaps and deceptions in an argument

Analyzes assumptions and biases

Attends to contradictions and ambiguities

Recognizes unstated assumptions

Synthesizes (knowledge, skills, beliefs, dispositions)

Connects multiple pathways of thinking and learning

Combines evidence, arguments, claims, and beliefs

Links together facts and parts into larger understandings

Looks for and sees patterns and relationships among the elements

Problem Solving

Understands and applies a system for responding to unfamiliar problems

Identifies and applies the steps in the problem-solving process

Describes a problem with clarity and supporting evidence

Gathers necessary and relevant information regarding the problem

Uses multiple strategies

Generates multiple solutions

Considers alternative solutions and possibilities in a given problem

Thoughtfully selects from multiple possible solutions to a problem

Evaluates the outcome in relation to the problem; adjusts accordingly

Assigns relative value to the elements of a problem and uses those values to rank elements in meaningful ways (enGauge)

Uses inductive and deductive reasoning in applied situations

Solves a variety of types of problems in the real world

Recognizes the complexity of each part of a problem in relation to the whole

Recognizes that sometimes there is no right answer

Creating

Possesses fundamental curiosity and inquisitiveness

Demonstrates knowledge of the creative process

Uses multiple types of creative techniques including fluency, elaboration, and originality

Questions to find deeper meaning

Displays an answer-seeking approach to living in the world

Demonstrates originality and inventiveness (www.p21.org)

Creates original, new, and unique ideas and products

Generates a number of new ideas that are fresh and unusual

Elaborates and adds details

Is flexible in considering new ideas

Designs, computes, and produces original works, performances, and presentations

Creates with complexity and intricacy

Generates layered and multifaceted ideas

Is able to see new patterns in existing works

Thinks both divergently and convergently

Applies creativity to real-world problems

Is open to diverse ideas, and uses these to support the creative process

Continuously improves the creativity of one's work through a reflective process

Works with others to develop, implement, and communicate new ideas.

Tolerates ambiguity; accepts the messiness and unpredictability of the creative process

Recognizes the impact of new innovations on existing paradigms

Realizes barriers to innovation and creativity

Frames creativity in the context of responsible risk taking

Metacognition

Reflects on one's thinking

Monitors one's thinking

Is flexible in one's thinking

Recognizes the diversity of learning styles

Knows one's own learning strengths and styles

Is willing to learn through multiple modalities that may not be one's primary modality

Responsive to learning through all sensory pathways

Is able to select an approach that aligns with strengths and styles of learning

Is aware of the effect of feelings on thoughts and deeds

Considers the effects of one choices and actions on others

Acts mindfully

ACTING

Communicating

Defines various types of verbal communication (i.e., conversation, discussion, debate)

Identifies various types of written communication (formal, informal, scientific)

Applies skills in a variety of forms and contexts

Engages in constructive dialogue with others

Demonstrates receptive communication skills in multiple settings and through varied media

Reads, views, and listens to a variety of sources

Understands the tenets of written language including basic grammar and style

Reads and understands various types of text

Listens effectively to understand the intent and content of written and verbal communications

Discerns the intent and information in still and video images

Produces effective communication through multiple medium and technologies

Articulates thoughts and ideas effectively using oral, written, and non-verbal communication (www.p21.org)

Communicates clearly and effectively so that others can understand the message

Communicates for a variety of purposes such as informing and persuading

Communicates in multiple settings

Collaborating

Works productively with others

Actively participates and contributes

Balances listening and speaking, and leading and following, in a group

Demonstrates flexibility and compromise

Works collegially with diverse types of people

Respects the ideas of others

Demonstrates perspective-taking skills

Commits to advancing the aims of the group

Considers the interests and needs of the larger group

Values the contributions of each member of the group

Recognizes and uses the strengths of others

Matches tasks and assignments to individuals' strengths and abilities

Works together to solve problems and create new ideas and products

Assumes shared responsibility for completing the work

Prioritizes needs and goals, both individual and group

Works with others to make decisions that include the views of multiple individuals

Identifies areas of agreement and disagreement

Participates respectfully in frank discussion, debates, and disagreements

Monitors one's own emotions

Contributes to conflict resolution within the group

Digital Literacy

Accesses information from multiple sources

Efficiently and effectively selects information

Searches, sorts, and collects information for multiple purposes

Determines what information is needed for a specific purpose

Prioritizes sources for importance, credibility, and depth

Evaluates information critically for relevance and accuracy

Understands the importance of evidence in building a base of knowledge

Appreciates the purpose and use of media messages

Recognizes the persuasive constructs of media messages

Examines the personal interpretation of media messages

Considers the effect of messages on humans and the influence of media on beliefs, behaviors, and values

Uses the information to learn, produce, and create

Manages the flow of information from a wide variety of sources (www .p21.org)

Recognizes individual and cultural differences in accessing, interpreting, and using information

Acknowledges and complies with ethical and legal rules in accessing and using information

Technology Literacy

Understands primary computer functions

Uses multiple types of electronic software, programs, and applications

Selects from a variety of technologies to meet a specific purpose

Creates media products using appropriate and purposefully selected technologies

Uses technology to access, gather, manage, integrate, and create information (www.atc21s.org)

Uses technology as tool to research, organize, evaluate, and communicate information (www.atc21s.org)

Applies technology to communicate and network with others

Applies technology to create and innovate in various contexts

Uses a variety of technologies in effective ways to increase creative productivity (enGauge)

Uses technology to present, graph, and track data

Uses technology to identify and solve complex problems in real-world contexts (enGauge)

Understands and considers legal and ethical issues in relation to the use of electronic technologies

Continuously learns and critically evaluates emerging technologies

Flexibility and Adaptability

Adjusts to changes in assignments, responsibilities, schedules, and locations

Makes appropriate changes in response to inputs and evidence

Accommodates and adjusts to changing situations and settings

Modifies one's thoughts, attitudes, and behaviors in response to new information

Negotiates to seek acceptable conclusions and solutions

Considers personal biases in learning and acting

Accepts and deals with both praise and criticism

Commits to continuous change and growth

Initiative and Self-Direction

Establishes priorities

Plans strategically and purposefully

Sets goals and takes active steps to achieve them

Manages time to maximize productivity and goal attainment

Works independently to complete tasks

Recognizes that hard work and perseverance breed success (enGauge)

Develops a positive self-image through the use of selected strategies and actions

Perseveres rationally to task completion

Demonstrates effective self-management

Delays gratification

Monitors own performance (enGauge)

Realistically faces obstacles and works to overcome them

Stretches beyond basic mastery to develop expertise

Learns from past experiences to build toward future success

Note: Although both of the preceding two skill areas fall under the category of Acting in the matrix, to avoid redundancy in this book, they have been merged with the Leadership and Responsibility skill area. That skill area falls under the Living in the World category of the matrix, and is discussed in Chapter 7.

LIVING IN THE WORLD

Civic Responsibility and Citizenship

Understands the political structure and process of a democratic form of government

Compares this to the governmental structures of other countries

Is willing to participate in the democratic process

Actively engages in the democratic process

Uses personal skills to contribute to the democratic process

Makes connections at the community, local, state, national, and international levels

Understands the structure, function, and processes of democratic institutions

Develops core civic dispositions: justice, equality, and personal responsibility

Respects the diversity of perspectives on justice and personal responsibility

Works toward improving the quality of life for all individuals

Recognizes the role of institutions in policy making

Knows how to access and interface with policy-making groups

Knows of and acts on the rights and obligations of citizens

Compares these rights at the local, state, national, and global levels

Is aware of the global implications of local decisions

Acts in ways that demonstrate understanding of civic responsibilities

Accepts responsibility for actions that infringe on others' rights

Participates in the classroom through demonstrations of good citizenship

Contributes to the well-being of others

Global Understanding

Is familiar with ongoing and emerging global events, issues, and challenges

Learns from and works collaboratively with individuals representing diverse cultures, religions, and lifestyles in a spirit of mutual respect and open dialogue in personal, work, and community contexts (www .p21.org)

Is knowledgeable about the connectedness of the nations of the world historically, politically, economically, technologically, socially, linguistically, and ecologically (enGauge)

Recognizes, analyzes, and evaluates major trends in global relations (enGauge)

Identifies the interconnections of global cultures, geopolitics, and economies

Participates in and makes a contribution to global society

Understands the history and foundations of one's own and other cultures

Recognizes the symbols, icons, and traditions of cultures

Is sensitive to cultural differences

Demonstrates awareness of how cultural beliefs, values, and sensibilities affect the way people think and behave (enGauge)

Respects the ideas of people from a range of social, ethnics, religious, and cultural backgrounds

Is sensitive to the issues of bias, racism, prejudice, and stereotyping (enGauge)

Appreciates the differences and similarities between cultures

Incorporates the ideas of a variety of cultures to improve the quality of life

Is conversant in languages in addition to English

Takes the perspective of people from other cultures

Accepts the concept of human rights and equality (www.atc21s.org)

Leadership and Responsibility

Recognizes the role of the individual in contributing to the greater good

Uses interpersonal skills to work with and guide others toward a goal

Inspires and assists others in accomplishing a common goal

Influences others with integrity and ethics

Makes decisions that improve outcomes for the group

Takes personal responsibility for success and failure

College and Career Readiness

Develops a plan for personal and professional growth

Uses models of short- and long-term planning in relationship to life and career plans

Applies skills, knowledge, dispositions, and capacities to personal and professional roles

Sets goals independently

Establishes priorities

Balances goals and time management

Purposefully acts toward goal achievement

Manages short- and long-term projects

Adapts to the changing landscape of daily life, school, and the workplace

Demonstrates a commitment to development of mastery and ongoing learning

Contributes through meaningful productivity

Supports others toward successful productivity

Takes responsibility for quality and accuracy of products

CONCLUSIONS AND PARADIGMS

If information equivalent to 37,000 Libraries of Congress is produced annually and is growing at 30% each year (Lyman & Varian, 2003), then it is no longer feasible to teach every bit of content that today's students may need to know, especially as they have the world of information at their fingertips. This requires a transition from a curriculum based on mastery of factual knowledge to one based on understanding and application of knowledge. These changes in teaching and learning will, in turn, alter assessment practices.

In Mr. Ems's classroom, the day starts with students opening their running records from the previous class. They compare their progress to the learning tracker that every student receives at the beginning of the unit. Each student writes one or two goals for the day and then confers with others who are at a similar place in their learning. They confer on the progress they are making and plan the next steps to be taken. On some days, Mr. Ems selects student to work together in pairs or triads. His choices are based on student progress toward learning goals. As he identifies groups who are struggling to make the requisite progress and master core content, he works more closely with them to guide their next steps.

Kristy and Kaela are very quiet students when participating in a large group but work productively together. One girl does really well on tests, while the other is nervous about getting the "right" answer and therefore leaves questions blank. One is good at sequencing and organizing projects, while the other provides the creative inspiration. Early in the year, Mr. Ems worked hard to engage them in whole-class discussion and activities. Over time, he recognized their individual strengths and reorganized some of the projects so that they could work together successfully.

An observer who steps into this classroom shortly after the start of class will see two groups of students at computer pods. One group is using Google Docs or a similar application to sharing the articles they have found. Another group of students, who are slightly ahead in their work, is creating a Prezi (or similar presentation software) on the research that it has synthesized. Another group is at the electronic board showing a nearby group its progress on the project and receiving peer feedback. These groups are using rubrics to assess their products and to make revisions. The items on the rubric include mastery and application of content knowledge as well as collaboration, productivity, and use of technology. Explicit content knowledge can also be measured in more traditional ways. During class, Mr. Ems consults with each group, reviews progress, and makes recommendations for next steps. After class, he reviews the running records, leaves notes on their work, and makes further recommendations for how to proceed.

If you read this and wonder at what subject and grade level this is occurring, there is no answer. It is not likely that these are very young children. If they were, the steps would be more specific, and additional support would be built in to the learning process. For any subject, each teacher embeds their respective content in these types of engaged learning scenarios and then selects the applicable 21st century skills that align with their purposes

Schools can no longer explicitly teach all skills and knowledge: As a result, changes in assessment must follow the changes in pedagogy. In the words of Chris Dede, "At this point in history the primary barriers to altering curricular, pedagogical, and assessment practices are not conceptual, technical, or economic, but instead psychological, political, and cultural" (2009a, p. 12).

Reflection

- What common threads in the 21st century skills are relevant to you, your class, school, district, or group?
- How can you fit content into the context of 21st century skills? Think of some examples.
- Do you think some content areas have stronger links to 21st century skills than others? Explain how and why.
- If we can no longer teach all the content, what are your priorities for adjusting teaching and learning? How will you do that?

3

Assessment Fundamentals

There's an ancient Greek fable about Procrustes, an innkeeper who provided accommodations for weary travelers. He kept his inn by the side of a busy highway road where he invited guests for a pleasant meal and a night's rest. Procrustes had a very special bed for these guests that he promised had the unique property of being exactly the right length for whoever slept in it. What Procrustes didn't reveal was the method he used to achieve this. As soon as a guest lay down, he went to work making the adjustments. He either stretched guests on the rack if they were too short or chopped off their feet if they were too tall. The tale comes to a gory end when the hero Theseus adjusts Procrustes to fit his own bed.

In education we have been trying to adjust students to the tests for decades. We have tutored them, trained them, and offered test prep workshops. Few, if any, of these efforts have produced consistent, widespread success. We have adjusted curricula to align with test questions, and still scores have barely budged. Perhaps it is time to adjust the bed to fit the students: we should change our methods of instruction, encourage critical thinking, let students apply their skills in building right-sized beds, give them opportunities to create a variety of styles and sizes of beds, and encourage them to solve the problems that arise.

This chapter examines the potential and possibilities of 21st century assessment. It includes a review of quality assessment indicators and makes recommendations for maximizing 21st century outcomes.

CHANGEWORTHY

Dillon tries to sit quietly while his teacher talks about history from 150 years ago. It's almost the end of the school year, and it has taken longer than planned to get through the curriculum, so the teacher is spending a lot of time "covering" material. In Shania's class, students complete their science lab reports individually and submit them to the teacher for review, then wait for her to grade them. Matty doesn't even know that the way his classroom is arranged into neat and orderly rows is not preparing him for the work he will be doing and the life skills he will need in the 21st century.

Information abounds on 21st century skills and the unique needs of today's technologically savvy students. Stakeholders from a wide range of constituencies are proponents of changing current practices. They argue that schools can no longer teach the 20th century curriculum, but must prepare students for the 21st century. "We need to overhaul, update, and inject life into our curriculum and dramatically alter the format of what schools look like to match the times in which we live" (Jacobs, 2010, p. 2).

Time-honored assessment practices, whether at the classroom level or at a larger scale, have not been able to effectively judge students' ability to analyze, synthesize, and create. Traditional selected-response tests questions typically test the lower-level cognitive skills of memory and recall. Inquiry, questioning, and supporting a position raise this to a higher level, but less common are assessments that ask students to evaluate, produce, or devise. It is not necessary to abandon measuring content knowledge, but rather to move toward assessing more complex skills such as organization, collaboration, and originality as well.

Traditionally, assessment comes at the end of instruction, both in its administration to students and in the instructional planning process. With the recent emphasis on formative assessment, more thought has been given to incorporating assessment during instruction, and more consideration has been given to using the assessment data to guide instructional decisions. This trend will serve 21st century learning well. Elena Silva clarifies this idea by stating,

> Assessment is a curious driver in the 21st century skills debate. But it may well be one of the best opportunities to bridge the skills-content divide that has emerged from the push and push-back of the 21st century skills movement. (2009, p. 630)

QUALITY ASSESSMENT: FUNDAMENTAL PRINCIPLES

I recently asked a group to teachers to respond to this prompt: "Good Assessment Is Good Assessment." Their task was to brainstorm indicators of quality assessment. Their lists included ideas related to formative

Figure 3.1 Assessment Fundamentals

Criteria and Requirements	In Practice
Responsive assessment identifies students' strengths and weaknesses so that strengths can be built on and gaps and problem areas can be addressed. • Student focused • Monitors progress • Used to improve student learning	Math teachers formatively assess students' prealgebra understanding of exponential functions before moving forward with instruction. Students track their own progress toward standards.
Assessment is integrated with instruction, meaning that teachers can continually take the pulse of learners and respond to that rhythm directly. It is the basis for providing relevant feedback, planning, monitoring instruction, and engaging students. • Instructionally purposeful • Ongoing and embedded in learning • Responsive to student needs • Identifies gaps and guides interventions	Spanish teachers routinely gather data on students' mastery of vocabulary and verb tense and adjust instruction accordingly, reteaching common errors and moving more quickly through selected vocabulary. Students post responses through an interactive whiteboard system that tracks progress.
Assessment serves educational outcomes in a practical manner by generating valuable information on a comprehensive range of targets and standards. • Fully aligned system of standards, curriculum, instruction, assessment • Evidence of learning is visible	All teachers at ABC Elementary School prepare lesson plans that show how assessment aligns with the objectives, standards, and instructional strategy. The assessment information is used to guide upcoming lesson plans and report outcomes.
Multiple measures are used to determine a student's strengths and weaknesses. They encompass and support the breadth and depth of the curriculum. • Uses a variety of measures and methods • Facilitates self-assessment	Mrs. Aleph is working on her professional goal of using projects, peer review, and journaling in additional to traditional selected choice and completion tests. Students have a choice of projects with aligned rubrics, checklists, and reflections.
Assessment necessitates the ability to distinguish between measurement that involves numerical expression of data and assessment that requires interpretation, judgment, and intervention. • Provides usable data for decision making	Although many students meet proficiency in writing on standardized tests, the language arts teachers identify that student skills in generating original ideas need further development. They develop a guide, exemplars, and checklist for students to use.

(Continued)

Figure 3.1   (Continued)

Assessment data are used to communicate to others. A range of constituents is aware of assessment outcomes from multiple methods and measures.	Teachers at XYZ High School use the same indicators of learning classroom in rubrics and other scoring as they do with report card grades.
Procedures should be fair: Fairness can be construed as meaning "without bias," but equally important in fairness is that students are aware of learning targets and how those targets will be assessed. • Targets and outcomes are clear to all	All the teachers at Lakeside Middle School are required to give their students a written overview of a unit that includes expected student outcomes, learning activities, and assessments that align with targets.
Procedures should be valid: Validity refers to how well an assessment measures the intended outcomes and the soundness of the decisions that are made as a result of the measure. • Purposefully and accurately assesses essential intended targets • Guides data-based decisions	Mr. Somes is trying a new post-test strategy. He asks students to note the hardest or most confusing question. He tallies their responses and then reviews the most prevalent to determine how well they align with instruction and whether they should be included or retaught before counting toward a summative grade.
Procedures should be reliable: Reliability relates to the errors in scoring that need to be considered when using assessment results. Assessments need to be consistent between users when making decisions about teaching and learning. • Routine checking for corroboration	Teachers at Valley High School use their Professional Learning Community to compare grading on common formative assessments and base instructional decisions on that data.

assessment: *integrated into instruction, responsive, usable feedback,* and *multiple measures.* They also identified qualities that bridge both formative and summative assessment, such as *measures targets, informs instruction,* and *monitors progress.* They overlooked a few others, such as *provides opportunities for improvement* and *engages students.* Overall, teachers know what good assessment is.

The big ideas in assessment come from many sources, including the Joint Committee on Standards for Educational Evaluation, the National Council on Measurement in Education, the National Research Council, the National Forum on Assessment, and the Council of Chief State School Officers. The same ideas are also advocated by the major organizations representing each of the content areas, including English, math, science, social studies, media, arts, and vocational subjects. These ideas can be synthesized into a common set of criteria and requirements for all assessments that represent the fundamentals of good practice. The descriptors in Figure 3.1 (pages 37–38) can be applied day to day in the classroom, in shared common assessments and large-scale measures.

The bottom line is that just about anything can be assessed. What matters is how the assessment is used. The method or strategy is less important than how well it aligns with specific learning targets. Tests that simply convey a numerical value are less important than are assessments that provide useful and actionable evidence of learning.

Reflection	
Select one or two fundamental indicators used your class, school, or district, and make recommendations to improve your practice.	
Assessment Fundamental	*Improvement to Your Practice*

STARTING AT THE END: STANDARDS, GOALS, OBJECTIVES, AND TARGETS

New teachers receive training on how to write instructional objectives. They learn that a well-written objective is composed from the student's perspective and is specific, actionable, and measurable. Objectives may also include strategies for achievement, selected resources, duration, and levels of proficiency.

Measuring these is best done in relation to the standard and desired outcome (criterion-referenced), rather than in relation to other students (norm-referenced). Regardless of whether an objective is content based or performance focused, and whether it is assessed with traditional or with alternative measures, those objectives need to be stated clearly in writing. Figure 3.2 contains some examples of 21st century standards that are generic to multiple content areas and can be customized for selected targets.

Figure 3.2 Standards Into Objectives

21st Century Skill	Objective
Questioning	Students are able to construct three guiding questions that will broaden and deepen their knowledge and reflect their analysis of web-based content.
Creativity	Students will be able to discern and construct original uses for outmoded products/ideas that will be evaluated through a peer-review process.
Information and Communication Technology	Students will incorporate three examples of products from technology-based assignments that are self-, peer, and teacher reviewed in an electronic portfolio.
Citizenship	For the duration of the school year, students will commit to participating, for at least one hour per week, in a school or community group that provides a service to others.

COMMON CORE STATE STANDARDS IN THE 21ST CENTURY

Common standards and normed outcomes have been part of education since early times. Examples of 20th century targets include the following: recognizing the causes of war; comparing mean, median, and mode; following lab safety rules; discerning the author's main idea; and using data to support a position. In the 21st century, outcomes include managing complex problems through multiple approaches, analyzing parts in relation to the whole, demonstrating inquisitiveness and originality, communicating through a variety of media and contexts, collaborating on the production of multimedia products, and contributing to the local and global community.

To support students in the 10th grade English standard of "analyzing how events and individuals develop and interact over the course of a text," a teacher typically would assign the required book, then read and discuss it with the class. In the 21st century, students would begin with a personalized search for historical fiction. Small groups would focus on the creation of concept maps that illuminate similarities and differences across texts. A 21st century wrapper would include reflective thinking through learning logs on how characters influence their environments. Assessment would be based on the ability to connect textual information to conceptual understanding using specific support. Communication and collaboration are recorded through teacher's anecdotal records, student logs, and checklists. There may well be a common summative assessment as required by the district, but in the 21st century, it would be included as part of a balanced system of data gathering and analysis. Figure 3.3 shows a few more examples of this adaptation.

Figure 3.3   20th Century Into 21st Century Standards

Common Core Standard	20th Century	Assessment	21st Century	Assessment
Writing: word analysis and writing for a purpose	Students write down the weekly words and their definitions and use the words in a sentence. They each post one of their sentences and read those written by their classmates.	Vocabulary quiz	"Borrow a line": Each student writes poems in a common format using words from a common vocabulary list. All poems are posted electronically. Students rewrite their poems, incorporating new words from another's with its definition.	Peer and teacher review based on a rubric for accuracy, mechanics, and creativity. Students e-log new vocabulary.
Reading: Determine central ideas and assess point of view.	Students compare and contrast two versions of the same news event.	Fill in a graphic organizer of each author's ideas and write a single summary of both.	Students read or view and then verify data related to news reports on a current issue from at least two diverse sources. Small groups synthesize each viewpoint. Debate the topic.	Accurate and data-based analysis of viewpoints (self, peer, and teacher) using a checklist Debate rubric.
Math: Solve real-world math problems.	Students are given teacher- or text-based problems to solve in class; may be completed individually or in a group.	End-of-unit test	Math challenge: Students create problems on ratios, fractions, angles, geometric shapes, etc. Class holds a mathematical decathlon that is produced as a webinar for other classes to use for review	Individual questions and group questions are graded for process and final answer in comparison to exemplars.

The ability to solve problems, to communicate effectively, or to be a good citizen requires a complex rather than a simple response. Quality multifaceted assessments make thinking transparent and support continuous improvement. Everything is measurable: It's easy to assign numbers to indicate achievement. The challenge is in the assessment: It's more difficult to analyze and use the information we obtain about students' learning.

For generations, selected-choice tests have measured recall and understanding. Other methods such as essays, case studies, and graphic organizers have been used to assess application, analysis, and synthesis. More complex and sophisticated strategies such as projects, performances, portfolios, and simulations will be required to effectively assess 21st century skills and knowledge.

Rather than replacing large-scale local, state, national, and international measures, 21st century assessment will be part of a larger system that supports student learning and is incorporated at all levels. In the past, educators valued what they measured rather than measuring what they value. It's time to reverse that equation. As Adlai Stevenson Jr. (1952) said, "If we value the pursuit of knowledge, we must be free to follow wherever that search may lead. The thinking mind is not a barking dog and cannot be tethered to a ten foot chain."

Reflection

Consider how your content standards can be translated into 21st century standards, How can progress toward achieving those standards be assessed?

20th Century Standard and Assessment	21st Century Standard and Assessment

21ST CENTURY ASSESSMENT FUNDAMENTALS

The ideas presented in this section encapsulate the key concepts for assessment in the 21st century. They build on established strategies and are a synthesis of ideas from the Partnership for 21st Century Skills, the Center for Public Education, the Organisation for Economic Co-operation and Development, Metiri/NCREL, and the University of Melbourne. You'll notice that they follow essentially the same sequence as Figure 3.1, with some fine-tuning.

Responsive

- Visible performance-based work generates data that inform curriculum and instruction. Teachers can adjust instruction, school leaders can consider additional educational opportunities for students, and policy makers can modify programs and resources.
- Processes for responding to assessments are thoughtfully developed, incorporating best practices in feedback and formative assessment.
- Feedback is to be targeted to the goal and outcome. Rather than a single test grade, students are informed of progress toward the goal. Self-reflection, peer feedback, and opportunities for revision will be a natural outcome.

Flexible

- Lesson design, curriculum, and assessment require flexibility, suppleness, and adaptability. Assessments and responses may not fit neatly into expected answers.
- Assessments need to be adaptable to students and settings. Rather than the uniform approach that works in traditional assessment, 21st century approaches are more elastic.
- As students' decisions, actions, and applications vary, the assessments and the system need to be flexible too.

Integrated

- Assessments are to be incorporated into day-to-day practice rather than as add-ons at the end of instruction or during a single designated week of the school calendar.
- Assessments are informed by awareness of metacognition. Assessment is about stimulating thinking, building on prior learning, constructing meaning, and thinking about one's thinking. It offers opportunities for students to consider their choices, identify alternative strategies, transfer earlier learning, and represent knowledge through different means.

Informative

- The desired 21st century goals and objectives are overtly stated and explicitly taught. Students display their range of emerging knowledge and skills. Exemplars routinely guide students toward achievement of targets.
- Learning objectives, instructional strategy, assessment methods, and reporting processes are clearly aligned.
- Complex learning takes time. Students have opportunities to build on prior learning in a logical sequence. As students develop and build skills, the work gets progressively more rigorous.

- Demonstrations of 21st century skills are visible and support learning. Students show the steps they go through and display their thought processes for peer and teacher review.

Multiple Methods

- An assessment continuum that includes a spectrum of strategies is the norm.
- Students demonstrate knowledge and skills through relevant tasks, projects, and performances.
- Authentic and performance-based assessment is emphasized. There is recognition of and appreciation for the processes and products of learning.

Communicated

- Communication of assessment data is clear and transparent for all stakeholders. Results are routinely posted to a database along with standards-based commentary, both of which be available and comprehensible at all levels.
- Students receive routine feedback on their progress, and parents are kept informed via access to visible progress reports and assessment data.
- The educational community recognizes achievement of students beyond standardized test scores.
- Large-scale measures incorporate and report on 21st century skills.

Technically Sound

- Adjustments and accommodations are made in the assessment process to meet student needs, and they are fair for all. Students demonstrate what they know and how they can apply that knowledge in ways that are relevant and appropriate for them.
- To be valid, the assessments must measure the stated objectives and 21st century skills with legitimacy and integrity.
- To be reliable, the assessment must be precise and technically sound so that users are consistent in their administration and interpretation of data. They produce accurate information for decision making in all relevant circumstances.

Systemic

- Twenty-first century assessment is part of a comprehensive and well-aligned assessment system that is balanced and inclusive of all students, constituents, and stakeholders and designed to support improvement at all levels.

BLENDING OF FUNCTIONS

Formative assessment requires a systematic and planned approach that illuminates learning and displays what students know, understand, and do. It is used by both teachers and students to inform learning. Evidence is gathered through a variety of strategies throughout the instructional process, and teaching should be responsive to that evidence. There are numerous strategies for making use of evidence before, during, and after instruction (Greenstein, 2010).

By comparison, summative assessments are administered at the conclusion of instruction. They provide a snapshot of a student's knowledge at a particular time. They can be given in the classroom, be used in common by an entire school or district, and be given at the state, national, and international level.

The integration of these strategies is at the core of effective 21st century assessment. For example, a curriculum goal may be to be able to explain the influence of genes and environment on behavior. Formatively, during instruction, students complete a graphic organizer, search for information on websites, or analyze a shared reading. Summatively, students personalize the information, using new vocabulary to describe how alleles influence their own phenotype and genotype, and how their families influence their behaviors and beliefs.

Assessment also extends learning. Consider an assignment in which students create an informational brochure or flyer, perhaps at the end of a unit on weather and climate change. As they synthesize their learning, they also extend it by building on earlier learning. A personal reflection on or peer review of their product, presentation, and process provides feedback. For the 21st century, these multiple purposes become blended and intertwined. Figure 3.4 illustrates the key concepts of 21st century assessment as they relate to formative and summative strategies.

Figure 3.4   Formative and Summative Indicators

Quality Indicator	Formative	Summative
Responsive	Formative strategies result in changes to instructional strategy: resources, pacing, depth, and sequence.	Additional scaffolds are provided to students who don't yet demonstrate proficiency.
Flexible	Students have choice of approaches to learning: read, view, listen. Then individual progress throughout the process is charted using chunking or color coding.	Progressive/adaptive tests that end when level of challenge becomes too difficult for individual student

(Continued)

Figure 3.4 (Continued)

Quality Indicator	Formative	Summative
Integrated	Formative strategies are used every day in every lesson: Bump in the Road, Corners, 3–2–1*	Revision is based on feedback on specific targets and encouraged until the very final assessment.
Informative	Learning is made visible through self-reflection and metacognition in an electronic learning log	Grades are connected to learning objectives through displays of data on student achievement of standards.
Multi-Method	Ongoing, during instruction, with application cards and ABC summary*	Unit test with selected choice, short answer, problem solving, and case studies
Communicated	Routine feedback: peer and teacher review of work in relation to standards and exemplars	Report cards contain achievement of CCSS and 21st century skills and knowledge.
Technically Sound	Work-along illuminates goals, standards, and learning strategies	Final assessment measures intended targets and displays achievement of goals and standards.

*Formative methods are described in Greenstein (2010).

CHALLENGES AHEAD

Traditionally, large-scale tests have been electronically scored. Answers to multiple-choice, true/false, and matching questions are bubbled into a scan sheet for easy scoring. In classrooms and schools, end-of-unit or end-of-year exams have followed this model. On a day-to-day basis, teachers may use more subjective assessment methods such as completion or essay tests. Most teachers do not use alternative types of assessment routinely. They are hard to craft and difficult to measure in an objective and fair way.

Effective assessment of 21st century skills presents numerous challenges, but these hurdles are not insurmountable. Here are a few of the issues that must be addressed:

- There is nominal consensus on what 21st century skills are, and limited agreement on which ones are explicitly teachable and assessable.
- We are still learning about how these skills develop, in what sequence, based on what requisite foundations, and at what levels of cognitive ability.
- Complex thinking is difficult to express. Accessing it and assessing it will require explicit processes and measures.

- Psychometrics have yet to be developed that support multiple answers, divergent responses, and original and unexpected ideas. It is a challenge to build capacity in teachers to assess this type of work at the classroom level and an even greater challenge to do so at the large-scale level.
- Altering a perception that 21st century skills are an add-on into a belief that they must be fully integrated into teaching and learning will take collective resolve.
- Intensive professional development is required at all levels of education: students, teachers, parents, school leaders, and policy makers.
- Transforming generations of traditionally trained teachers into 21st century teachers and learners will take commitment at all levels.
- Responding to assessment data consistently and accurately, and student by student, continues to perplex educators.

These challenges only skim the surface of the work ahead. But keep in mind that Lewis and Clark did not know the way to the Pacific when they started their journey, and Thomas Edison did now know how to invent a light bulb when he began the process. Today, we have maps and illumination to guide our process of discovery.

Reflection

Select three quality indicators and think about how you would adapt them for your subject or school.

Quality Indicator	Adjustment for the 21st Century	First Step to Take Toward This Change
Example: Assessment is integrated into instruction.	Review existing curriculum for opportunities for building 21st century assessment into teaching and learning.	Ask each Professional Learning Community for one idea.

4

Assessment Strategies

In Aesop's classic fable about the grasshopper and the ant, the grasshopper is portrayed as lazy and spends his summer singing and relaxing, while the ant is busy stockpiling food for the upcoming winter. When the cold weather comes, the grasshopper begs the ant for food and is rebuked for his idleness. He arrives at his reckoning point when winter arrives.

If instruction involves the busyness of conveying knowledge to the next generation, then assessment is sometimes the languid grasshopper. Curriculum is designed around standards, content, and instructional strategies. It is not uncommon for the assessment component to be added as an afterthought. In the 21st century, it is essential to motivate the grasshopper to lead the way for the ant.

Assessment of 21st century skills is a lens through which to view content knowledge. As we peer through the lens, we can see students working on literacy, numeracy, science, and social understanding in the context of higher-level thinking, collaboration, and applied technologies. It's complex and simple at the same time. Figure 4.1 shows the simplicity. This chapter begins to attend to the complexity.

Chapter 3 explained the fundamentals of assessment. In this chapter, three perspectives on assessment of 21st century skills and knowledge are considered. Multiple products of 21st century learning are categorized and cross-referenced with the skills. Alternative methods of assessing and measuring 21st century skills and knowledge are described. The final section offers illustrations, examples, and case studies of teaching, learning, and assessing selected skills in daily practice.

Figure 4.1   Teaching and Learning Through a 21st Century Lens

ASSESSING THE CONTINUUM OF SKILLS AND KNOWLEDGE

Figure 4.2 reflects a typical sequence of skills and knowledge from simple to more complex. The left column shows the more classic 20th century progression, the center refocuses these for the 21st century, and the right describes a technological application. In these apps, technology is the tool for learning, not its object.

Figure 4.2   21st Century Taxonomy

20th Century	21st Century	Applied Technology
Knowledge: recall of information	Mastery of core content	Bookmark important information
Understanding: making sense of content; describing and organizing it	Communication and collaboration: expressing ideas and working with others	Present a livecast, podcast, or webinar
Application: using the information	Applying past to new Problem solving	Create a wiki and invite people to help solve a community problem
Analysis: thoughtfully considering the information	Metacognition: learning and self-aware thinking	Blog your ideas with illuminations of your thinking
Evaluation: comparing, reasoning	Critical thinking Productivity	Yelp your ideas or contribute to another review/ratings website
Synthesis: combining ideas in a comprehensible and unique way	Leadership: responsibility and accountability Citizenship: contributing globally	Raise funds and social awareness of a global concern using social networking
Creation: production of original works, innovation	Creativity and innovation for applied purposes at work and in life	Design games, simulations, and virtual worlds

AUTHENTIC PRODUCTS AND ALTERNATIVE ASSESSMENTS

Alternative assessment encompasses a wide range of teaching and learning practices and activities. Generally, the literature describes alternative learning strategies rather than strategies for assessing their outcomes. Most definitions of alternative and authentic assessment include the idea that students demonstrate their knowledge and skills by performing real-world tasks. How assessment came to be considered something distinct from the skill or practice being assessed is worthy of discussion.

Traditionally, learning always took place in the real world. Children learned how to raise cattle and cook from their parents on the farm. A century ago, workers, many with eighth-grade educations, received on-the-job training so they could work on the factory production line. It wasn't until learning moved to the schoolhouse that it became necessary to include practical demonstrations as a distinct aspect of the learning process. This peculiarity has led educators full circle from natural learning in the world to cloistered learning in the classroom, and then back to developing new ways for students to demonstrate authentic mastery.

The ways in which alternative and authentic learning are implemented and measured in the 21st century are changing. Today, teachers are supporting students as they construct meaning and generate knowledge and products using planning, problem solving, collaboration, and technology. Figure 4.3 shows an array of ways for students to demonstrate authentic learning.

Figure 4.4 expands upon 4.3, showing links between these tools for authentic learning and 21st century skills. These tools are equally applicable across all content areas; they are presented here to provide a starting point for you to personalize and customize. You can fill in the blanks and adjust the grids to your specific needs.

In the remainder of this chapter, selected assessment strategies and examples of the skills to which they are applicable will be explored. Many of them require no special technologies or extensive training for teachers to use. You are encouraged to adapt them to your own grade level, subject, and school.

21ST CENTURY ASSESSMENT STRATEGIES

It may be possible to measure 21st century skills and knowledge with standardized tests, but most educators would agree that there are better strategies. Visible learning, metacognition, and creativity are more effectively assessed with thoughtfully matched measures such as those introduced next. Expanded and applied examples of these will be found in the following three chapters.

Figure 4.3   Examples of Authentic Learning

PRODUCTS Space capsule from one place for another Time capsule for the future Gift box from another time Design a board game Puzzles: Crossword, Scattergories Timeline of historical events, story board Science lab with results/report/analysis Scientific research Historical research with depictions and symbols Fund-raisers	*REPORTS/WRITING/PUBLISHING* Write a myth or fairy tale Write a play, TV show, soap opera, reality show Poem, haiku, cinquain, diamante Develop a catalog of twenty important factoids Create ten headlines Write a press release Letter to the editor Convey ideas with similes and metaphors Journaling Didactic journaling Journal article Policy reviews and recommendations Book and movie reviews Movie script Resume, cover letter Discussion board
ORIGINAL DESIGNS Artwork: painting, drawing 3-D: sculpture, glass, metal T-shirt, button, bumper sticker Fans, mugs or other consumer products Greeting card Cartoon or comic strip Book cover Bulletin board, poster Graph it or display it visually Illustrate it: poster, mural, collage, painting Graphic organizers: Venn diagrams, spiders, trees, maps Blueprints for homes, schools, designs Solutions to problems (i.e., transportation, environmental, economic) Replicas and mock-ups Photo editing	*DEMONSTRATIONS* Show how it works Explain how to do it Convey a solution Science lab *PRESENTATIONS* Puppet show Parody or satire Quiz show Programs such as Prezi, PowerPoint, Glogster
PERSUASION, POSITION, DEBATE, SPEECHES Debate Defend a position/Soapbox Advocate for a cause Election campaign materials Support a candidate Imagine a phone conversation/text exchange Advice column Socratic Seminar Editorial Soapbox Job interview	*DYNAMIC ARTISTRY; MUSIC AND DANCE* Music Song Rap Interpretive dance Skit Docudrama

TECHNOLOGY/MULTIMEDIA Photo essay Story board E-magazine Newscast Websites, programs, and software Video Podcast Webinar, videoconferencing Wiki Blog Online collaboration Create an electronic game Virtual games Gallery display, graphic display	SIMULATIONS Case study Interview someone—real or imaginary Reenact historical events Mock trial
	COLLABORATIONS On any of the above demonstrations of learning
	PORTFOLIOS Collection of any of the above artifacts over time and for a specific purpose

Rubrics

Rubrics are generally the most specific of the 21st century measures in that they are closely aligned with standards and outcomes and include explicit indicators of achievement at multiple levels. They are more descriptive than checklists and can be used by teachers and students as part of peer- and self-evaluation. *Rubric* is defined as a scoring scale used to assess student performance along a defined set of criteria. Analytic rubrics define levels of performance for each criterion, whereas holistic rubrics describe broader levels of performance. There are many examples of both types throughout the next three chapters and in the Appendixes.

Checklists

Checklists are most functional when they include a list of essential targets and desired outcomes. They can be used while students are in the process of learning or at the completion of an activity. They lend themselves to activities, such as participation in a group, that are difficult to assess with traditional measures. For this purpose, checklists may include traits such as *listens quietly when others speak, clearly and concisely shares ideas*, and *is respectful of divergent ideas*. Students can use the same checklists for self-assessment. Most rubrics can be converted to checklists. Figure 4.5 shows a checklist for student presentations.

Student Contracts

Learning contracts are agreements between students and teachers that describe the learning outcomes and strategies for achieving them. They give students choice over personal goals as well as over strategies and concrete steps for reaching them. They can be short or long term, can

Figure 4.4 Cross-Links Between Authentic Learning and 21st Century Skills

SKILL \ STRATEGY	Products	Writings	Original Designs	Demo Present	Persuasion/ Position	Dynamic Artistry	Multimedia	Portfolio
THINK Critical Thinking	Science lab analysis			Soapbox/ take a position	Debate		Blog	Collected examples
THINK Problem Solving		Case study analysis	Graphic organizer	Historical reenactment				
THINK Creativity	Board or virtual game	TV/movie script	Music and song			Interpretive dance	Wiki	Work in progress
ACT Communicating Collaborating		Press release			Socratic Seminar		Photo-story	
ACT Digital Literacy & Communication Technology	Website		Webinar	Teach others how to use technology			PowerPoint, Prezi	e-portfolio
LIVE Global Under-standing			Global menu		Campaign for global change	Multicultural artwork	Online global collaborations	
LIVE Civic/Citizenship	Fund-raiser	Letter to the editor			Attend a public hearing		Website	
LIVE Leadership and Responsibility				Teaching others		Plan a multicultural arts event		
LIVE College/Career		Resume	Prototype for a career interest	Work interview		College app. with original works		Electronic success plan

Figure 4.5   Checklist for a Presentation

Checklist for a Presentation		Comments
✓ if performance is satisfactory according to the standard NI if performance Needs Improvement based on the standard		
	Introduction captures the attention of the audience	
	Objectives are stated in the introduction	
	Content is clear and understandable	
	Presentation is logically sequenced	
	Projects voice so all can hear	
	Uses technology to effectively support message	
	Summary synthesizes main ideas	

provide for differentiation of learning and assessing, and can be used to hold learners accountable. At the same time, they can encourage a blending of core content and 21st century applications. Timelines, checkpoints, and accountability measures are essential components of student contracts. Figure 4.6 shows an abbreviated version of one.

Self-Assessment/Reflection

Self-assessment and reflection are important lifelong skills that can be developed and supported in the classroom. Younger students may need more structured approaches and support in mastering the essentials of self-assessment. Older students may be successful with open-ended prompts. Sometimes specific prompts work best, and other times a rubric or checklist can provide the foundation for more complex thinking. Self-assessment can be written or oral, daily or long term, and done individually or in small groups. Essential elements of self-assessment include the opportunity for reviewing learning, identifying lingering confusion,

Figure 4.6   Learning Contract

Student Learning Contract for (Name of Student)_____	Topic, Unit, or Goal_____ _____ _____	Date _____
Student's Responsibilities:	Completion Dates and Deadlines:	
Teacher's Responsibilities:	Evidence Required:	
Resources Recommended/Required:	Assessment of Learning (formative and summative):	
Student's Signature _____		
Parent's Signature_____	Teacher's Signature_____	

providing evidence of learning, evaluating progress, and defining explicit criteria for planning next steps and improving outcomes. An example is shown in Figure 4.7.

Figure 4.7   Self-Assessment/Reflection

Generic Questions

- What did I learn?
- What worked and what didn't?
- What's next (content, processes, lingering questions)?

Specific Questions

- What steps can I take to improve my writing?
- What three habits of mind did I use and how did I apply them?
- How well did I listen to the ideas of others and make a contribution to the group?
- If I were to do this again, here's what I would do differently:

Peer Review

Peer review, like self-assessment, varies in its structure and application. It is important to help students understand the process and function of nonjudgmental peer review and to make such review a regular and positive part of the learning process. A structure such as a checklist, which pinpoints specific learning outcomes, can help students stay focused. Peer feedback gives students alternative ways to view and process information. For example, the plot of the myth that Katie originally wrote was enhanced by the feedback of others. Grace's idea of planning a concert to raise money for MADD (Mothers Against Drunk Driving) was improved through feedback suggesting she find sponsors to maximize profits. In a fourth-grade class, students reviewed each other's contribution to a group project with a rating scale as shown in Figure 4.8.

Figure 4.8 Peer Assessment

Peer Assessment of Our Group Project	
4 = strongly agree 3 = agree 2 = disagree 1 = strongly disagree *Explain your ratings.*	*Score*
All members contributed to the group equally and fairly. Explanation:	
Members of the group worked well together. Explanation:	
When we disagreed, we were able to settle it promptly without hurting each other's feelings. Explanation:	
Group members encouraged each other toward achievement of goals. Explanation:	

Observations

Observations can be of students' thinking, actions, or engagement in learning. A teacher may observe a group of students discussing a book or debating a current news report. The activities observed can be informal, such as in a group discussion, or more formal, as in a Socratic Seminar. These observations can provide an assessment of student understanding and ability to use 21st century skills. The assessment can be anecdotal, or it can be combined with a checklist or rubric and aligned with selected standards. For example, in a Socratic Seminar on deforestation, the teacher may observe the group in order to assess content knowledge, noting the use of web-based reference materials, actively listening to other's contributions, building on other's ideas, and adding original ideas to the discussion. Figure 4.9 shows notes on a discussion that a teacher can use as the basis for conferences with students after the activity.

Figure 4.9   Observation of Learning

Evidence of Discussion Components	
4 = strongly agree 3 = agree 2 = disagree 1 = strongly disagree Provide evidence for your ratings.	Score
Presents a fact-based analysis of the problem Evidence:	
Uses text and data to support position Evidence:	
Respects a diversity of ideas on the topic Evidence:	
Responds thoughtfully to other's statements Evidence:	

Logs

Learning logs help students track their work toward a target. They can be structured to track specific knowledge, skills, and beliefs. They can be used by teachers and students to show progress toward benchmarks. They can also support metacognition as students reflect on their learning and plan their next steps. They work well for daily use or for long-term projects. As students assemble electronic portfolios, they can track their own progress, set schedules, and post messages to other students. Assessment can be based on evidence of progress, documented adherence to a planned schedule, and metacognition on the process that includes reflection on the course of learning and learning outcomes.

A simple tracker is shown in Figure 4.10.

Figure 4.10   Project Progress Log

Date	Progress	Evidence
	What goals have I worked toward?	
	What have I learned?	
	What are my next steps? What's the timeframe?	
	Whom can I collaborate with to improve my work?	
	How have I used my critical thinking skills?	
	How would I assess my progress so far?	

Anecdotal Records

Teachers can use anecdotal records in a planned manner to monitor learning outcomes and progress being made and to note specific accomplishments. To capture a complete picture, notes can be taken in an abbreviated manner, perhaps with symbols or acronyms. Some schools use handheld devices for this purpose. Running records track ongoing learning and identify areas in need of improvement. They can be triangulated to check alignment with other assessment data. When used in addition to traditional data, they can provide an enriched view of what is happening day by day in a classroom. Some teachers use then when they intuit that something is amiss but can't identify the problem precisely. The running record can pinpoint specific times during the day, certain student groupings, or particular learning strategies that may be a problem for some students. In response, interventions such as grouping or assistive technologies can be implemented.

Concept Maps

Graphic organizers are generally used as an instructional tool, but they can also be used to assess student's knowledge, understanding, and critical thinking. They can be simple or intricate webs and diagrams that display connections, processes, and relationships. Students can use shapes to represent categories of knowledge and different types of connectors to represent the types of relationships. Assessment can be based on depth of knowledge, accuracy of connections, ability to sort and organize information, and other learning targets. There are many software programs that support the creation of concept maps. The one shown in Figure 4.11 is based on a very simple design in Microsoft Word Smart Art. Inspiration, bubbl.us, and MindMeister also support such maps. A design that contains only partial information can be given to students so that they can fill in the details with teacher support.

Figure 4.11   Concept Maps

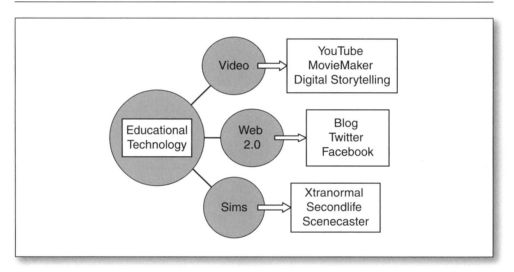

Journals

Journals can provide a window into a student's thinking and learning. A journal entry generally begins with a response to a question or an open-ended prompt such as "Compare a decision you had to make to the one faced by the character in the story" or "Describe two things you learned from this assignment/activity." Some teachers find journal assignments more useful when their focus is specific, such as "How will you use your new knowledge in your next blog posting?" Daily journals can be used for students to express creative ideas on a topic or to make entries written with a specific audience in mind (for example, retelling a story to a humanoid on another planet). They are useful in allowing students to assimilate new content and describe lingering points of confusion or to reflect on controversial issues. Journaling can be supported with wikis and other sharing software. Usually, the information recorded in journals lends itself to formative assessment. Teachers can make use of this information to respond to students' perceptions and gaps in learning.

Questioning

Formal and informal questions can be used to move students forward with their learning and to move them beyond the level of recall to higher cognitive levels. Formally, they can be planned and incorporated into assessment such as a 3–2–1 closure at the end of a lesson. In informal settings, a series of questions ranging in cognitive complexity from under-standing to application, analysis, and synthesis can add depth to a lesson. Rather than simply identifying responses as correct or incorrect and moving on, the teacher can use student responses to shape additional questions. Questioning can be used at the beginning of a lesson to review previous learning and establish a foundation and mind-set for new learning. Questions can be used during teaching and learning to engage students and assess progress toward goals.

Conferences

Student–teacher conferences generally focus on student progress. They are an opportunity for students to explain their emerging knowledge and skills and for the teacher to question and probe further. Peer-to-peer con-ferences are also possible. Graphic organizers such as KWL or compare/contrast charts can be used to provide a platform for discussion that illu-minates the student's present status and plans for future steps. During conferences, teachers and students work together to discuss progress, review emerging knowledge, and plan next steps. They can be held on a predetermined schedule but must also be flexible enough for students to request a conference when they need extra help. A strong metacognitive component is important, so that in addition to content knowledge, think-ing about one's thinking is emphasized. Parents can also be included in the conference; video applications such as Skype can facilitate their inclusion.

Portfolio Review

Portfolios for assessment of 21st century skills include a range of student work. In a nutshell, the assessment elements include clearly stated goals and standards, identification of the target audience for the portfolio, and purposeful selection of items. Portfolios can be used to demonstrate processes and growth in relation to the selected learning objectives. They can also be used to display 21st century skills such as problem solving, creativity, and information literacy. To be objective and comprehensive, assessment of student portfolios should be based on contracts, rubrics, and peer/self-assessment. In addition to assessing the individual items, the portfolio can also reflect strengths and weaknesses, time management skills, and metacognitive abilities. E-portfolios are growing in popularity. The outcomes of portfolio review serve to inform and guide instruction.

The Cube

The skills, products, and assessments described so far can be thought of as forming the three dimensions of a cube such as that shown in Figure 4.12. The interior of the cube contains each point at which a desired skill can be demonstrated through a specific product and assessed through a selected strategy. It is at these junctions that 21st century assessment takes place. In the next four chapters, examples of these points of intersection are illuminated.

Figure 4.12   Triad of 21st Century Assessment

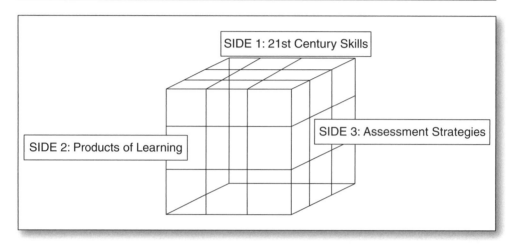

Reflection			
Consider your own standards, make a connection to a 21st century skill, identify an authentic product, and describe a way to assess it.			
Chosen Standard	*21st Century Skill*	*Authentic Product*	*Correlated Assessment*
Common Core State Standards: Grades 6–12 Write arguments to support claims with clear reasons and relevant evidence	Digital literacy Ability to analyze information Ability to synthesize ideas Technological competency	Create a digital brochure on global climate change that uses data to support or refute the idea	Technology—use checklist Rubric for critical thinking Peer review

5

Assessing Thinking Skills

"There is no use trying," said Alice. "One can't believe impossible things." "I daresay you haven't had much practice," said the Queen. "When I was your age, I always did it for half an hour a day. Why, sometimes I've believed as many as six impossible things before breakfast."

—Lewis Carroll

CRITICAL THINKING

The first step in assessing critical thinking is to understand what the term means. Somewhat paradoxically, it takes critical thinking to understand the complexity of critical thinking and to contemplate its application to teaching, learning, and assessing. Definitions of critical thinking frequently include the concepts of analyzing information, applying strategies for deciding, readiness to consider ideas, using logical inquiry, making inferences, appraising evidence, testing conclusions, making accurate judgments, and analyzing assumptions.

Inherent in quality assessment of any skill or knowledge is an emphasis on accuracy, consistency, and objectivity. But in reality, the terms used to describe critical thinking contain judgmental elements, making assessment more of a challenge than in areas in which there is a single correct answer. As schools prepare for the 21st century, there is considerable debate on whether to focus on teaching discrete academic standards or to facilitate higher-level thinking, creativity, and problem-solving skills. Some believe these 21st century skills can't be measured; some believe that in this age of accountability, it is more important to test students on content knowledge. Others maintain that the United States cannot be competitive in a global economy unless our students have robust thinking skills.

Most teachers know that their students can move beyond facts into analysis, synthesis, and application of knowledge. First-grade teachers describe their students as critical thinkers when they predict what the characters in a story will do next. High school teachers cite vigorous discussions of current events in the classroom. A greater understanding of what critical thinking is will lead to enhanced ability to assess these skills.

There are strategies that can be utilized by schools and districts that want to structure their learning progressions around critical thinking. Developing a K–12 map that pinpoints grades and subjects where targeted skills will be taught is one such strategy. For example, all first graders work on compare-and-contrast exercises. Third graders create graphic organizers, fifth graders analyze the symbolic meaning of texts, eighth graders analyze arguments, and high school students synthesize information into original products. Alternatively, specific skills can be incorporated into selected content areas. For example, in language arts, students can discuss hidden meanings, innuendos, and drawing inferences from texts; in social studies, students can consider multiple points of view; and in science, students can seek additional information and analyze conclusions.

It has become the norm for standardized tests to drive the curriculum. Early in the era of standardized testing, some states developed tests of applied critical thinking. Newer tests are being planned that include performance assessments, and emerging testing technologies make it possible to create tests that measure critical thinking and problem solving.

Defining Critical Thinking

It can be difficult to describe a vacation experience in an exotic location to friends because the descriptions, settings, foods, and activities may be unfamiliar to them. Explaining the taste of poi or the sound of a cassowary can be challenging. Likewise, it can be difficult to define critical thinking because the terrain is unique and may also be unfamiliar to teachers and students. Experts describe it with different terminology. Edward Glaser (1941, p. 5) say it involves "knowledge of the methods of logical inquiry and reasoning and a predisposition to consider and resolve in a thoughtful way the problems and subjects within one's experience." Linda Elder's more recent definition (2007) is somewhat similar:

> Critical thinking is that mode of thinking about any subject, content, or problem in which the thinker improves the quality of his or her thinking by skillfully taking charge of the structures inherent in thinking and imposing intellectual standards upon them.

In Chapter 3, the main ideas of many voices on critical thinking were combined into the broad categories of applying, evaluating, analyzing, and synthesizing. Specific applications of those high-level skills include interpreting information, analyzing parts and wholes, evaluating evidence, comparing multiple perspectives, discerning patterns, and grasping abstract ideas.

The CCSS include these targeted outcomes as examples of critical thinking:

- Use various types of reasoning (inductive, deductive, etc.) as appropriate to the situation.
- Respond to the varying demands of audience, task, purpose, and discipline.
- Construct viable arguments and critique the reasoning of others.
- Draw evidence from literacy or informational texts to support analysis, reflection, and research.
- Analyze the purpose of information presented in diverse formats, and evaluate the motives behind its presentation.
- Reason abstractly and quantitatively.
- Use arguments to establish facts about the angles in triangles.
- Use data from randomized experiments to compare two treatments.

In Practice

These skills can be sorted, organized, and implemented in the classroom in various ways. Teachers may select the essential knowledge and core skills and then infuse critical thinking into the curriculum, a unit, or lesson plan. In some classrooms, teachers will explicitly teach critical thinking. In a third-grade science class, a teacher may teach how to compare and contrast, or how to classify ocean life, and ask students to make informed judgments about the future of our oceans. In a middle school health class, a teacher may teach the problem-solving process during a unit on teen relationships and use it to analyze and synthesize the research on best practices in reducing school bullying. In a social studies class, students may learn decision-making skills as part of a study on politics and then use facts to create arguments for election debates. In other classes, students may learn to write guiding questions or challenge existing beliefs.

One topic can lend itself to a variety of critical strategies. Asking students in the early grades to name the first three presidents requires simple recall. Asking them to identify the legacy that each has left for today's world raises their level of thinking. Predicting the outcomes of today's political decisions on our future requires analysis and reasoning. The challenge lies in assessing the student's constructed responses and products of learning.

Since food is of interest to most students and can provide opportunities for critical thinking in multiple content areas, let's begin there. Younger children can analyze their diet in relation to the U.S. Department of Agriculture Food Plate (formerly the Food Pyramid) and make recommendations on how they can improve their nutritional intake. In math, older elementary students can compare and contrast the daily values on food labels. Middle schoolers can evaluate the science of cooking, and make and test predictions of the effects of manipulating various leavening agents. High school students can grapple with the government's role in our food supply.

In Mrs. Greenly's classroom, an interdisciplinary unit on genetically modified foods begins with an introductory KWL (Know, Want to know, Learn) activity with the whole class. Student put their names on the back of their sticky notes. On the front of each one they write something they know about the topic and something that confuses them or that they want to learn. Then they post them in the matching column on the KWL chart. After she determines their baseline knowledge, she presents core vocabulary and information needed to proceed with the unit along with an empty outline on which students record the main ideas and facts and can track their progress. After a quick formative assessment such as a grab bag match or A-B-C summary and a review of the filled-in outlines, she decides what resources the students need and which instructional strategies to employ. Much of the unit is designed for collaborative learning. She believes this gives students with more knowledge an opportunity to take a leadership role, and other students the opportunity to have the benefits of the zone of proximal development.

Based on the formative assessments, she puts students in groups to read two articles with opposing views on genetically modified foods. The students then create a comparison chart of the arguments used by each side. This attends to the Common Core reading anchor standard of integrating knowledge and ideas. The groups are then reformulated by student choice. Students can decide to be a scientist, a farmer, a politician, or a nutritionist. Using previously learned digital literacy skills, they complete a web quest for in-depth information on the position of each of these groups on modified foods.

A world forum is then set up in the classroom with representatives from each of the interest groups. Some students are selected to present the group's findings, while others become part of the evaluation panel. The presenters decide how to impart their information and present their arguments. The evaluators ask questions at the conclusion of the presentations. All students participate in a peer review where they probe for understanding, evaluate the synthesis of information, question any gaps in information, and consider the depth and complexity of arguments. The evaluators use a rubric to complete a summative assessment of the content and to evaluate evidence of critical thinking. Rubrics measure standards and targets such as the objective use of data, quality of presentation, and the clarity and cohesiveness of conclusions. A written narrative that supports the student's ratings accompanies the rubric.

The final individually assessed activity for this unit is the preparation of a "product" that will be used to inform and enlighten others. This can be a brochure, PowerPoint presentation, Prezi, video, website, blog, handout, poster, or other platform. Class members are required to take a position on genetically modified foods and include five important facts for others to know. They are expected to include a persuasive argument for their beliefs. The project can be assessed using a rubric, peer review, or a self-assessment. What is important is that the desired critical thinking skills are carefully woven into the assessment and are clear to the students. Questions for peer and self-review must be carefully constructed so that they elicit the specific skills that the teacher is seeking. Asking "Why do you think that way?" is less effective than asking "What are two arguments used to defend your beliefs?" By the end of this unit, Mrs. Greenly has made visible a variety of 21st century skills through several pieces of evidence using multiple assessment strategies.

Figure 5.1 shows selected components of a teacher rubric for this assignment. The last two sections are written in student-friendly words to give you an idea of how the rubric can be personalized. You can use the more complete rubric in the Appendix to customize the outcomes. No single rubric is suited for all applications; it must be adapted for specific purposes. Other components of this project include collaboration, technology, and presentation skills; these can be added to the rubric at the teacher's discretion. Additionally, ideas in some of the standards can be divided into subsets. The rubric is designed to be flexible.

All content areas can incorporate critical thinking. Figure 5.2 shows examples of assessment of critical thinking in other content areas.

In summary, there is broad support and clearly stated justification for teaching critical thinking to students. Richard Paul and Gerald Nosich (2009) propose that there be a national assessment of higher-order thinking; such a test may be on the horizon. For now, in classrooms teachers may include critical thinking in teaching and learning but then grapple with developing strategies for assessing it. For now, here are a few ideas to get started with critical thinking at the classroom level.

Figure 5.1   Critical Thinking Rubric

Standard	Exceeds	Meets	Working Toward	Just Beginning	Score/ Weight
Critical thinking	Consistently demonstrates multiple skills in evaluation, analysis, and synthesis	Routinely applies two components of critical thinking	Developing multiple types of critical thinking skills	Able to understand basic content but struggles to evaluate and analyze information	
Analyzing information	Identifies main issues, establishes priorities among details, and sees unstated implications	Identifies and understands the main issue and a few stated differences	Needs help to move beyond the main issue With support, can identify a few distinct details	Describes the main issue inaccurately Unable to focus on key question or problem	
Uses data to develop critical insights	I could explain the data to others and understood what it meant well enough to make connections to my work	I was able to figure out what the data meant and could use the main idea to draw a conclusion	I was able to pick out some data that made sense to me	It was really hard to understand the data without some help	
Synthesizes multiple viewpoints	It was easy to find at least three main viewpoints and organize them in a way that is clear and makes sense to others	I was able to find two different viewpoints and could put them together into a logical summary statement	I was able to find two different viewpoints and restate the ideas in my own words	I was able to pick out one person's viewpoint from the information and tell it to my teacher	

Figure 5.2   Critical Thinking in Content Areas

Content Area/Standard	Instruction/Learning Target	Assessment
Arts: the evaluation of design elements in selected works of art	Viewing and recording learning about the work of multiple artists in comparison to selected design elements	Thoroughness and specificity of a mind map that sorts the elements of design evident in each work
Social studies: investigation of accuracy of newspaper articles	Comparative analysis of various news sources during an election campaign	Depth and detail in a compare/contrast of sources using a Venn diagram Technology skills: accuracy of Webquest and sources cited to support or refute data stated in articles
Language arts: analysis of character motives	Vocabulary building applied to character analysis	Correct use of vocabulary and accuracy of graphic display of characters and their motives

- Establish classroom seating arrangements (clusters, small groups, flexible seating) and routines (student presentations, group activities, use of questioning) that support critical thinking.
- Build content knowledge first, routinely following it with an application of knowledge.
- Assess both content and higher-level applications.
- Use a variety of open-ended questions that ask students to identify the problem, evaluate evidence, and make inferences.
- Include all the domains and levels of Bloom's taxonomy in teaching and learning.
- Assess critical thinking with student-friendly rubrics and checklists, self- and peer reflection and feedback, journaling, and learning logs.

Reflection

How would you compare the importance of content knowledge to the importance of critical thinking about content knowledge? Use the bar below to consider how you weigh the value of each.

How would you compare the importance of content knowledge to the importance of critical thinking about content knowledge? Use the bar below to consider how you weigh the value of each.		
100% Content Knowledge	*Half & Half*	*100% Critical Thinking*
Which 3 critical thinking skills are most important to you? Why? (Consider these and others: inquiry, considering ideas, inferences, analyzing, appraising evidence, applying, testing conclusions, synthesizing)		
How will you help students learn and apply them in your classroom?		
What strategies will you use to assess them?		

PROBLEM SOLVING

If I had one hour to save the world I would spend fifty-five minutes defining the problem and only five minutes finding the solution.

— Einstein

In some schools, the formal assessment of problem solving takes place only in math classes, but this practice ignores the importance of embracing problem solving in all content areas. Literary characters face problems, problems arise both in the science lab and in society as a whole, and people face problems every day of their lives. All of these types of problems are ones that students can address using a sequenced multistep process. The one described here can be applied in multiple content areas and multiple grade levels. It can be explicitly taught to students of all ages.

Defining Problem Solving

Problem solving is the basic process for identifying problems, considering options, and making informed choices. It is used when an easy answer or routine solution doesn't exist. The process begins with a clear description of the problem. It's not uncommon for students to explain a problem such as "My parents won't let me stay out after dark" or "My friends won't let me borrow their homework." The challenge lies in helping students see the complexity of the problem and defining it carefully. Typically, students will seek an easy solution such as wearing down their parents or finding another friend who will give them the homework. The problem-solving process kicks in when current strategies don't work to reach the desired goal.

It involves the following knowledge and skills:

- Describing the problem with depth and clarity; recognizing its complexity
- Looking at the problem with an open mind, evaluating alternatives, and considering multiple perspectives
- Gathering information to make an informed choice and develop a plan
- Implementing and monitoring with integrity
- Evaluating the outcomes and being willing to revisit the problem

The Steps in Problem Solving

1. Understand the Problem

   o Can you state the problem in your own words and define it clearly? Include elements such as the setting and situation and any pertinent supporting evidence.
   o What are you trying to find or do? (Be sure it is a problem rather than a symptom or a solution.)
   o What are the knowns, the unknowns, and the variables?
   o What information is included in the description of the problem as presented?
   o What information, if any, is missing or not relevant?

2. Brainstorm All Possible Solutions

   o Think broadly and creatively.
   o Any and all ideas are acceptable at this step in the process.
   o Don't prejudge any of the ideas.
   o Post all the ideas before moving to Step 3

3. Devise a Plan

   o Analyze, synthesize, and organize the ideas: Make a table, diagram, chart, etc.
   o What appears to be a logical starting point?
   o Select a starting point and develop a process to follow.
   o Consider resources, values, and goals in your decision.

4. Carry Out the Plan

   o Implement the strategy or strategies in Step 3.
   o Check each step of the plan as you proceed. This may be intuitive checking or a more formal proof of each step.
   o Keep an accurate record of your work.
   o Be flexible and reflective as you implement it.

5. Evaluate the Results

   o Analyze the solution in terms of the original problem. Does it make sense? Is it logical? Is it reasonable? What are the long-term ramifications?
   o Check the results in relation to the original problem: Did it resolve the problem or change anything?
   o If it wasn't successful, determine whether there is another method of solving the problem and cycle back to an earlier step in the process

In Practice

Mr. Eton's third-grade class has been reading many books this year. Each student has a list of favorites. They are all asked to pick one book that has a character with a problem. It doesn't matter whether they pick *George and Martha*, *Hedgie's Surprise*, *Stella Luna*, or one by Ezra Jack Keats. For this assignment, students will develop their perspective-taking skills by taking on the role of one of the characters. They will also take on the role of advice columnists who will help the characters solve their problems. Through this assignment, they will learn how conflict and problem solving are used as literary devices. They will develop skills in reading for understanding, describing characters, and writing for a particular task and purpose.

In a whole-class round-robin, students describe their characters and the problems each faces. To make the activity more fun and engaging, they can dress up and perform the roles of their characters. Mr. Eton keeps an anecdotal record during this activity so that he can later meet with individual students who need support in making a clear and accurate connection between the character and their problems. Mr. Eton then distributes exemplars of letters that contain examples of applied problem solving in an accurate letter format. In small groups, students discuss their characters, the problems, and the steps the characters could use to solve their problems. Students record these shared ideas in their notebooks. They then use this information to help write a letter to the character that aligns with the problem-solving process. They help the character define the problem he or she confronts, offer multiple solutions, then guide the character toward selecting the best one. They describe strategies for carrying out this plan and a way for the character to later evaluate how it worked.

After each student uses a rubric to assess her own performance, the letters are copied without the author's name, and the same rubric is used in a peer-review process. The summative assessment is done by Mr. Eton using the same rubric. Selected components of the rubric are shown in Figure 5.3.

Figure 5.3 Problem-Solving Rubric

	4. Expert	3. Competent	2. Apprentice	1. Novice	Score
Identifies the problem	I clearly described the problem in relation to the situation and included several supporting details.	I described the basics of the problem with some details and supporting information.	I explained some of the problem but had trouble understanding all the parts of the problem.	I had difficulty recognizing and defining the parts of the problem.	
Identifies multiple solutions	I came up with at least four feasible and clearly described solutions.	I offered two or three plausible solutions.	I described one or two possible solutions.	I had one solution, but I'm not sure it was right.	
Defends solution	I analyzed all the solutions and picked one that shows my understanding of the problem and the outcomes.	I evaluated the solutions and picked one that seems feasible.	I gave a simple explanation for the one choice that I thought made sense.	I wasn't able to explain a solution.	

The CCSS include the following standards related to problem solving:

- Make sense of word problems and persevere in solving them.
- Explain how an author uses reasons and evidence to support a point.

- Write arguments to support claims using valid reasoning and relevant and sufficient evidence.
- Conduct research projects based on focused questions.

There are demonstrable connections between problem solving, the CCSS, and content area standards. Figure 5.4 shows some of these. The final row has been left blank so that you can add your own.

Figure 5.4   Problem Solving in Content Areas

Content Area/Standard	Instruction	Assessment
Social studies: Cite evidence to support analysis.	Readings, viewings, and discussion of the decision-making process of Thomas Jefferson when purchasing the Louisiana Territory	A mind map of the facts and their influence on Jefferson's decision
Math: Solve word problems.	Calculate multiple ways to measure liquid volumes.	Illustrations and calculations with reflection on steps taken
Science: Evaluate the argument and claims in relation to the sufficiency of evidence.	Explain a line of reasoning and facts considered in drawing a forensic conclusion.	Empty outline of systematic problem solving after viewing a video on a problem that an investigator faced.

Beyond the classroom, problem solving has personal, local, and global applications. From disagreements with friends to world conflicts, those who developed problem-solving skills will be better able to resolve them.

Reflection

- Review the CCSS and find examples of where problem solving fits into learning outcomes.
- Add a problem-solving activity to an existing lesson. Explain how you would incorporate it and assess it.
- Identify a problem that you anticipate arising when incorporating 21st century skills and assessment in teaching and learning. Consider whether this is more teacher-based, student-focused, or systemic. Use the five-step model to work through it.

CREATIVITY

> *A rock pile ceases to be a rock pile the moment a single man contemplates it, bearing within him the image of a cathedral.*
>
> — Antoine de Saint-Exupéry

Po Bronson and Ashley Merryman (2010) report that in a recent poll of 1,500 CEOs, creativity was identified as the number one leadership competency of the future. Daniel Pink (2009) asserts that the Master of Fine Arts (MFA) is the new Master of Business Administration (MBA). Like a sport such as golf or a skill such as sewing, creativity can be strengthened, even learned. Consider the National Inventors Hall of Fame School in Akron, Ohio (www.akronschools.com/scienceschool/), where students are regularly challenged to creatively solve real-world dilemmas. Project-based learning and creative problem solving are at the heart of this school's curriculum, where despite 42% of its students living in poverty, learning outcomes improved last year, and students are actively engaged in planning, learning, and assessing. And who hasn't seen Sir Ken Robinson's TED lecture? This leader in creativity and innovation fervently urges schools to value and encourage creative and artistic expression (Robinson, 2006).

Corporations are learning about the value of creativity through their free-form Fridays where brainstorming and ingenuity are encouraged and shared. In contrast, American teachers feel that most of their time is spent in standards-based instruction and that there is little time left over for creativity. The arts are often one of the first cuts from a curriculum when test scores are low and budgets are tight. But creativity and standards are not diametrical opposites. In fact, it is not possible to be creative without a strong foundation in fact-finding and fundamental research.

In the 21st century, there must to be a balance between standards and creativity as each one supports the other. In a response to the CCSS, the Partnership for 21st Century Skills (2010a, p. 3) observed,

> Creativity as an outcome within the English Language Arts standards is nonexistent. This is particularly concerning, given the natural affinity between English Language Arts and creative expression. The ability for students to understand and employ metaphor, simile and allusion—not to mention creative forms of media—in the production of original, creative work is an incredibly important competence in the 21st century. The current standards attend to the use of metaphor and simile, etc. only in the

context of analyzing and/or producing informational or expository texts. Some attention should be given to the creation of original works also.

Defining Creativity

The first step in measuring creativity is to describe it. The dictionary defines the term as follows: "Creativity is marked by the ability or power to create—to bring into existence, to invest with a new form, to produce through imaginative skill, to make or bring into existence something new." According to the psychologist Carl Rogers (1967, p. 350), creativity is "the emergence of a novel relational product, growing out of the uniqueness of the individual."

The common threads among all conceptions of creativity are originality, uniqueness, imagination, flexibility, fluency, making connections, forming new patterns, and personal expression. Inquisitiveness and curiosity are at the core of emerging creative thought. The techniques of brainstorming and problem solving are recognized as foundational skills of creativity.

In physics class, Morgan and Sam are given an assortment of bicycle parts and asked to design a new mode of transportation. Inherent in this assignment is the ability to recognize alternative possibilities and turn them into realities. They are curious as to how gear ratios affect speed. After some trial and effort, and reading about gears, cranks, and radius ratios, they design a new gear ratio and ergonomically shaped handlebars. This generation of unique ideas is the application of content knowledge to creativity and innovation. Certainly, Morgan and Sam can be creative when given this assortment of parts, but their ability to build a unique bicycle is dependent on their core understanding of how gears, ratios, and wheels work, and also the ability to look at them in unique ways to create original designs.

To assess creativity, measurable indicators need to be identified and defined. Here are some characteristics of creativity that can be woven into classroom instruction:

- Curiosity: probing, asking questions, seeking deeper meaning
  - What do you want to know about this object?
- Fluency: production of a number of ideas
  - How many ways can shelter be constructed?
- Originality: ideas that are novel, fresh, unique, or unusual
  - What's next after Facebook?
- Elaboration: ideas that display intensive detail or add to existing detail
  - How can you turn this striped rug pattern into a tessellation?

- Imagination: dream up, invent new ideas or products, ingenuity
  ○ What will school be like in 2070?
- Flexibility: ideas that show a variety of possibilities
  ○ If your plan doesn't work, what will you do?

This multitude of ideas on creativity leaves a lot of room for classroom application and assessment. Denise Shekerjian (1991) in her book *Uncommon Genius* describes the creative talents of people who received MacArthur awards. She explains that these creative geniuses are people who are smarter in their art than in their lives. They can look at the same things as everyone else but see them differently. This could apply to highly talented people in fluid dynamics, geopolitics, technology, music, or the arts.

Many people equate artistry with creativity, and there are certainly strong connections between them. But in addition to creativity, most artists incorporate specific design elements in their work such as color, space, line, texture, balance, shape, proportion, form, and unity. Students can apply elements of creativity separately from elements of art or incorporate both. Designing a map for a utopian colony can incorporate social studies content, creative elements, or design elements, depending on the learning targets. Assessments can be tailored to fit those targets.

Assessment strategies for creativity include rubrics, checklists, peer/self-assessment, and reflection. It is also possible to use progress logs, observations, and anecdotal records as a way of noting progress. Whatever the assessment strategy used, it should be aligned with instructional targets, goals, and outcomes.

In Practice: Developing Understanding

In his eighth-grade world history class, Mr. Ferria introduces the topic of human creativity in relation to the survival of societies. He builds his lesson on the idea that creativity is an essential core element of the success of civilizations. He uses an heirloom potato to introduce the core components of creativity. Each student is given a potato along with a series of questions to answer and activities to do:

- Curiosity: What do you want to ask of this potato's history?
- Fluency: Turn these outlines of a potato shape into as many uses as you can think of.
- Originality: Think of ways this potato can be altered and still be a potato.
- Imagination: Close your eyes and follow this potato down a dark tunnel back to its origins. What's there?
- Flexibility and complexity: If you didn't have a knife to cut it, what could you use?
- Elaboration: What other purpose can this potato serve?

As he explains these ideas, he incorporates formative assessment by asking pairs of students to come up with another example of each component of creativity. Students in the class signal agreement or disagreement as the ideas are reviewed and the complexities and nuances of creativity discussed. Then, in small groups, students participate in a creativity challenge. Each group is asked to assemble ordinary objects into a new and useful product. Objects include clay, cardboard, cans, plastic containers, string, popsicle sticks, old floppy disks, cotton balls, and so on. Through a peer review, students check off and describe the elements of creativity that are evident in each product.

In groups, students then select an early culture and research how their use of elements of creativity supported their survival. Students can select from places and civilizations such as Phoenicia, Babylonia, Mesopotamia, Greece, Rome, and India. Using previously learned research strategies, they create a presentation for the class using a technology-based format such as a wiki, Glogster, Prezi, Second Life, or PowerPoint. These presentations include cultural elements and influences: geography, politics, economics, religion, science, the arts, and so on. They also incorporate the CCSS in social studies literacy: reading complex texts, summarizing details in a text, and analyzing and interpreting texts. This traditional assignment then takes on a 21st century twist when students are asked to consider each of the elements of creativity and show connections to the culture.

Mr. Ferria's hybrid rubric/checklist/reflection, shown in Figure 5.5, contains a range of standards and learning targets. Students check them off, then add their own reflections on how well they met each standard Then, Mr. Ferria completes the assessment with his rating and feedback.

There are many opportunities for teachers to customize this type of assignment for their content area learning targets. For example, to reinforce content knowledge, groups could also create a fact sheet on the culture being studied or develop a Venn diagram comparing that culture to today's U.S. culture. Standards, content, instruction, and assessment can be adjusted for grade level, allowing for flexibility and at the same time accountability and relevance.

In Practice: Elements of Design

The next example shows a more specific application of creativity to artistic production of student work. In her high school art class, Ms. Olynciw combines a lesson on culture, creativity, and artistry during a unit on Mexican wedding vases. She begins by explaining the goals of the unit and the processes and assessment methods to be used. She establishes baseline knowledge and learning readiness by asking students to brainstorm on what they know about wedding traditions, by providing

Figure 5.5   Hybrid Rubric/Checklist/Reflection for Creativity

Standard/Target/Checklist If desired, rate each on a 1 to 4 scale (Note: point values can be adjusted for each teacher's grading practices)	Student Rating: Exemplary, Proficient, Developing, or Missing (with elaborated reflection)	Teacher Assessment: Exemplary, Proficient, Developing or Missing (with elaborated feedback)
Content: Main points are clearly explained _____ Information is fully accurate _____ All core components of society are included _____		
Creative elements: Which ones are _____ Identified:_____ Accurately described _____ Supported using evidence and examples _____		
Reliable research: Multiple sources are used _____ Sources are accurately cited _____ Information is synthesized into a cohesive summary _____		
Presentation: Logical sequence _____ Stays focused on topic _____ Meets required length _____ All members participate _____		
Total Points Earned _____	Comments:	

some readings and visual materials, and then by asking them to compare and contrast wedding practices in different countries and cultures. She then shows students a variety of ceramic projects, and in small groups, they identify the components of creativity and design elements that have been previously taught and used. A generic outline for an artistic creativity lesson plan is shown in Figure 5.6. The rubric for the wedding vase assignment is shown in Figure 5.7.

Figure 5.6 Lesson Plan for Artistic Creativity

Unit:
Lesson:
Standards: • Common Core • Content Area • 21st Century
Goals and Learning Targets
Materials Needed:
Initiation/Preassessment/Instruction: Formative Assessments • Closure
Differentiation:
Assessment of • Content • Process • Products

As with the other examples, this can be customized for grade level and content area. CCSS can be included in reading, listening, literacy, and integration of knowledge. Assessment strategies of creativity lend themselves to multiple 21st century strategies, and readers are encouraged to make their own connections. What's important is that the assessment measures essential learning outcomes.

In Practice: Applied Creativity

All grades and students at Friendship School, a Grades 3–5 elementary school, participate in the annual "Invention Convention." This is an opportunity to apply creativity to the production of new and innovative products and ideas. There are many ways to approach such an event.

Figure 5.7 Rubric for Multicultural Art

Ceramic Benchmark Rubric—Design Elements: Pueblo Wedding Vase

1. Surface is Smooth and/or textured appropriately.
2. Graceful Necks have mirror symmetry
3. Connecting Bridge has good form (not cracking or fallen)
4. Negative Space is even and symmetrical.
5. All surfaces cleaned up prior to first firing (no lumps or blemishes)
6. Glaze application has been used to give an even glassy surface. (3 coats)

4 Exceeds standard	3 Meets standard	2 Near standard	1 Below standard
Comments: This wedding vase uses the negative space effectively to create a well-proportioned and dynamic form. Even coverage of the glazing enhances the pot. Excellent attention to symmetry and craftsmanship makes this vase very successful.	Comments: This wedding vase uses the bridge effectively to create an original form. But the shape and symmetry could have been improved by better balance between the elements	Comments: This form almost worked. The glaze application was uneven causing dry spots on the surface. More attention to symmetry would have made this vase successful. The bridge is cracking due to uneven drying.	Comments: The form was never really fully realized in this wedding vase. The bridge was poorly constructed and is off center. More attention to symmetry and surface preparation before firing was needed in this piece.

Use this checklist of standards in your self-assessment.

Standard 1: Construction

☐ Vase has a body, 2 spouts, and a sturdy, connecting bridge.

☐ Vase has excellent craftsmanship in the joining of all the parts: coil is well blended into seams.

☐ Shape is carefully constructed and exhibits bilateral symmetry.

☐ Negative space in center of bridge is precise and even.

☐ The bridge and/or spouts did not crack during drying.

Standard 2: Glazing

☐ Glazing is accurate, even, and covers completely (no bare spots).

☐ The choice of glaze compliments the style and form of the pot.

Standard 3: Design elements

• Describe the ones you used: color, space, line, texture, balance, shape, proportion, form, unity.

Standard 4: Creative elements

• Describe the ones you used: originality, flexibility, elaboration, unique idea, new patterns.

Narrative Reflection

• Evaluate the process you followed as you complete this product.

• Evaluate your final project in relation to the standards and requirements.

• What worked well and what would you change if you did it again?

• What are your conclusions about your project?

Conclusion: What score would you give yourself?

Source: Reprinted with permission from Carolyn Olczak, Art Teacher, Montville High School, Oakdale, CT.

In some schools, it is designated as a science fair; in others, it is based on solving a problem such as dropping an egg off the roof of the school without it breaking; and others use it across content areas. Friendship School decided to be very open-ended with the products and specific with the strategy.

The convention starts at the classroom level, where teachers and students work together to brainstorm needs in their own lives, their communities, and the world. They then look at famous inventors and their inventions. They discuss how the invention aligned with the inventor's knowledge and skills and responded to a need at the time. If the teacher wants to add a research standard, then students can each select an inventor and complete a standards-based research project. Alternatively, teachers could include a Webquest for students to select the invention of the century and then defend their choices. Teachers can also narrow the category of invention to be considered—for example, to technology, or improvements in the quality of life. Basically, the strategy that each teacher uses should meet both the needs of the students and appropriate standards for both grade level and content areas.

All teachers at Friendship School agree to explicitly teach creativity, including definitions and components, and then follow an instructional sequence that builds on creativity and incorporates problem solving and innovation. Teachers can choose from among several ways to begin the unit. Possibilities include Think, Pair, Share activities on best inventions, directed instruction using videos and PowerPoint slides, and applied activities such as reading response.

Teachers collaboratively develop the main objectives for the unit. Reasonable limits on cost and size are stipulated, and basic rules are reviewed. Inventions are judged against the following criteria:

- The inventor must demonstrate an authentic need for the invention.
- The inventor must show how the invention meets that need.
- The invention truly has some novelty, originality, complexity, and elaboration associated with it.
- The final product is solely the work of the inventor.
- Presentation displays must explain the process used to come up with the idea and develop the invention.
- Inventor must maintain a log with their schedule, progress, thought processes, challenges they faced, and their reflection on the final product.

Products that have been designed in the past include

- a dog leash/collar that carries a dog's water bottle,
- a "snandal" (combination sneaker and sandal),
- a twirling spaghetti fork and automatic coffee stirrer,
- a car seat for a pet,

- a sleeve sneeze catcher,
- an educational Twister game, and
- a new musical instrument with both percussion and wind.

Assessment of this process includes the following:

- Identification of a problem or a need
- Depth and accuracy of research on the problem
- Solves the problem; responds or is relevant to the need
- Prototype or model clearly represents the solution
- Creative elements are evident

As with other creative assignments, multiple assessment strategies can be used. The preceding list can be adapted into a rubric or checklist. Metacognition and self-reflection are important elements of creative assessment. Teacher observation and annotation of the process help keep track of and record progress. Student journals and learning logs also keep the task on course.

The invention convention format and assessment may seem more loosely structured than other lesson plans, but that's what creativity is about. Allowing students to use both convergent thinking and divergent thinking results in new ways of looking at everyday things, yet the structure ensures some consistency and the assessment reinforces the outcomes.

Rubrics and assessments earlier in this section assessed creative products, the one in figure 5.8 assesses the creative process. An expanded version is in Appendix A.

Figure 5.8   Rubric for Creativity

Standard	4. Advanced	3. Proficient	2. Basic	1. Beginner
Curiosity	I am intrigued by novel elements and ideas and actively seek them out.	I am curious about some things and usually am willing to explore new ideas and things.	With some help, I will explore new ways of thinking and doing.	I feel nervous and try to avoid new ideas and things.
Flexibility	I adapt well to new situations and can see many possibilities in my everyday learning.	I can work effectively even when things change and notice the potential of some things as I learn.	Sometimes it's hard for me to adjust to change. When someone reminds me to think differently, I usually can.	I am unable to be productive when things change. It's hard for me to "think outside the box."
Originality	I can come up with many new ideas on most topics.	I can come up with some new ideas on my own.	If I have some guidelines, I can usually come up with new ideas.	I need help thinking of new things.

A reflective analysis on the process of creating is shown in Figure 5.9. This can be used by students as well as teachers.

Figure 5.9   Reflection and Analysis of Creativity

Reflection on the creative process:
What were your first questions and thoughts?
What need is your creation meeting?
How did you decide your first step?
What motivated each step that you took?

How did you use/demonstrate each of these elements of creativity?
 	
    Curiosity
    Fluency
    Originality
    Imagination
    Flexibility and Complexity
    Elaboration

Keep a log of your work. Include the steps you took, an analysis of their outcomes, changes you made, and progress toward your final product.
What would you do differently next time? Are there different elements of creativity you would use, different resources, etc?

The Torrance Test for creativity has been used for over 50 years to assess children's creative abilities, and has proven to be remarkably accurate. For over 50 years, this test has tracked children's creativity. The correlation between childhood creativity and lifetime creative success is been strong. For the first time, the scores are going down (Zagursky, 2011). Whether it's due to more time in front of electronic devices or less room in the curriculum for creative expression, the concern is widespread. At the same time, there is evidence that creativity can be taught, learned, and assessed.

Reflection

- What does creativity mean to you?
- Do you agree or disagree with Dan Pink and others that creativity is an essential skill that children today have less opportunity for expressing?
- How can it be included in schools and classrooms?
- How do we really know when someone is creative?

METACOGNITION

Invest a few moments in thinking. It will pay good interest.

— Author Unknown

This is really hard.

— Sophia, age 9

Ask landscapers why they planted certain plants in selected areas of the garden and they will tell you that they considered sunlight, soil, water, seasonal changes, color, care, and other planting essentials. Ask new home gardeners why they planted what they did, and the answer is more likely to be because they liked the appearance or color of the plants, or perhaps because it was what the nursery had that day. As the novice gardener develops her skills and knowledge, she will begin to choose the best plants for the setting, seasons, the amount of time she has available, and her skill level. Over time, the thinking of the novice will more closely align with that of the expert.

Defining Metacognition

Metacognition is an expansive way of saying "thinking about one's thinking." Yet, it remains an elusive idea. As with the other elements of 21st century thinking, it's best to start with an understanding of its meaning and complexity. John Flavell (1979) of Stanford University was one of the early authorities on the subject. He described the essence of metacognition as the ability to manage and monitor one's thinking. This means being aware of, monitoring, and regulating one's thinking in relation to self, others, learning, and actions. It requires taking active control over thinking and learning and using strategies for enhancing learning and performance. Additionally, it considers how learners take in, store, and retrieve information.

Aligning with Piaget's theory of intellectual development, Flavell proposed that children acquire metacognitive abilities in stages. In the first stage, children identify information that they choose to store for later use. They then learn to keep selected knowledge available to use in problem solving and critical thinking. Last, they purposefully select information to use in a particular situation. As the brain matures and the frontal cortex develops, the ability to think about thinking improves.

In the classroom, metacognition has the following aspects:

- Purposeful, targeted, and goal oriented: Learning takes effort and focus
- Foresighted: focused on learning outcomes and future thinking

- Conscious: selective use of thoughts, ideas, and styles; aware of effects on others
- Self-regulated: Learning is continuously monitored and adjusted.
- Flexible/Plastic: Learning and thinking are mutable.

In the CCSS, the K–12 Anchor Standards in Research include drawing evidence from literacy or informational texts to support analysis, reflection, and research. This can lead teaching and learning toward introspection, but in general, the CCSS are more focused on the review and analysis of the work of others. In their review of language arts standards, the Partnership for 21st Century Skills (2010a, p. 1) points out, "There is virtually no mention of metacognition or learning how to learn. This is a significant oversight."

Students routinely need to be asked to think about their emerging knowledge and skills, write about what they know and want to know, appreciate how they think, and consider how they can monitor and manage their thoughts and actions. The following questions can guide them toward these outcomes:

- What did I think and do during my learning?
- What did I want to learn, and what purposeful strategies did I use?
- Why did I select them?
- How did those strategies work?
- What problems did I encounter, and how did I address them?
- Which strategies were more and less effective?
- What's my next step?
- How can I strengthen my use of the effective strategies?
- What questions do I have now?
- How will I know it worked?

Metacognitive Wrappers

Time is limited in today's classrooms, and content is a priority, so teaching and assessing metacognition can be incorporated in traditional lesson plans with the addition of a *metacognitive wrapper*. Originating with Marsha Lovett (2008) at Carnegie Mellon, it is "an activity that surrounds a pre-existing learning or assessment task and fosters student metacognition." She recommends using metacognitive wrappers before teaching to establish a baseline or mind-set, during instruction to track and record learning, and after instruction to reflect and summarize. Figure 5.10 shows how each level envelops and incorporates the previous level.

In a science lesson with a metacognitive wrapper, Common Core and content standards are made transparent, and students are asked to use their lab journals to recall vocabulary from a prior lesson, plan the steps to complete this lab, record their learning in a purposeful way, and evaluate their skills and knowledge. At the end, they reflect and describe what

Figure 5.10   Layers of Metacognition

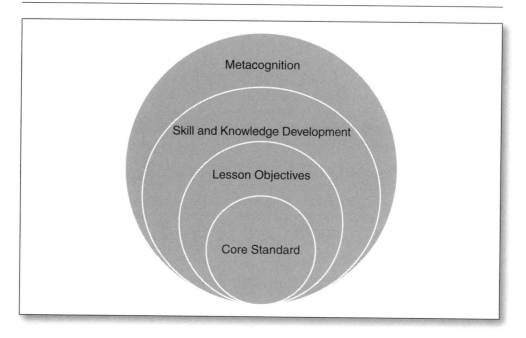

worked or didn't work, what types of thinking helped them be successful, and what they might do differently next time.

In a second-grade class, students read their creative stories, then pause at the end and add a reflective "wrapper." They conclude their presentation by explaining what they would do differently next time. One student says he would describe the setting with more detail, "maybe, describe the snowy forest better," and another says, "I'd make the ogre meaner."

This wrapper (Figure 5.11) can work in all classes where students are thinkers and researchers. As they work on their assignment, they take a few moments at each stage to record their thinking. Some teachers have found that the first time they do this, the responses are scant, but over time, students develop a better understanding of the process. With support, scaffolding, and feedback, they are able to add more detail. The dual purposes of this exercise—helping students to improve their thinking strategies and to develop good research skills—provide transparency for the teacher and serve to build and develop metacognitive abilities.

In Practice

When Wylie says he doesn't understand fractions, there are many possible ways to interpret his statement. Does he not understand the language of numerator and denominator, or is he having difficulty with number sequences, or recalling strategies for basic division? Through a metacognitive process, the teacher can identify and resolve problems early on. In a conversation with Wylie, he says that he can't write the fraction that shows

Figure 5.11   Metacognitive Reflection

Respond to the following prompts as you complete your research project.

1. *Planning*

   a. What do you know about this topic now?
   b. What do you want/need to know about this topic?
   c. What resources are you considering exploring?
   d. How did you decide where and how to begin?
   e. Where did you start? What did you do first? Why?

2. *Acting*

   a. How did you proceed? Describe your steps.
   b. What resources seem worthwhile? Why? How did you evaluate them?
   c. List the resources you explored; mark those that were most useful with an asterisk (*).
   d. How did you decide which ones to mark?
   e. How did you know how you were doing? What did you ask yourself?
   f. What problems did you run into? How did you change or adjust your process in response?
   g. How did you know when you reached your goal?

3. *Evaluating*

   a. What worked to produce a high-quality product?
   b. Describe any new strategies you used.
   c. What could you do differently if you were starting over?
   d. How well did you do in relation to the requirements of the assignment?

What other thoughts do you have about your research or your metacognition?

how he divides his bag of 12 apples equally among his three friends. The teacher can ask him to use words to explain his thinking and to describe what he has done so far to understand it. This helps uncover misunderstandings and guide appropriate responses that include additional resources, peer support, or teacher intervention.

After explicit teaching on the components of metacognition, Mr. Cassidy's students research, produce, and present biographies of famous people who have demonstrated metacognition. Students can use their choice of technology to present their work. Requirements include summary of the person's history and highlights of the individual's contributions. They are also required to incorporate a graphic organizer that shows the connection between the individual and their use of metacognitive strategies. In their presentations, students demonstrate their understanding of metacognition, how individuals control it, and its connection to personal productivity. Checklists and rubrics can be designed to incorporate metacognition.

Writing is a very complex process that incorporates both cognitive thinking and metacognitive skills. Students in Ms. Perla's class start with brainstorming, planning, outlining, and drafting. Using a metacognitive wrapper, they evaluate the difficulty they had with each step by ranking each step on a scale from easy to hard. Figure 5.12 is an example.

Figure 5.12   Monitoring Thinking

	EASY_____explain each_____HARD
Coming up with an idea	_____
Writing an outline	_____
Search for more information	_____
Reading more about it	_____
Taking notes	_____
Synthesizing my ideas	_____
Writing a draft	_____
Asking another to read it	_____
Revising content	_____
Revising mechanics	_____
Preparing final work	_____

As Ms. Perla reviews this reflection along with the students' writing, she can see where they are most challenged in the process. She asks students to summarize and synthesize their conclusions also, and together they decide on appropriate interventions and next steps.

In the following example from a capstone project, students are explicitly taught about metacognition and then required to analyze and make connections to their own lives.

Capstone Project: Metacognition Unit

Know Thyself

Activity 1   Read pages 1 through 4 of Daniel Goleman's article "Know Thyself" (in Goleman, 1995) and respond to the following:

A. Reflect on the following question: What is the value of knowing your thoughts, feelings, reactions, tendencies, and predispositions? Explain three benefits of this understanding. Be as specific as you can.

B. How can you learn about yourself: your thought processes, personal strengths and skills, learning styles, etc.? Describe three ways to learn more about who you are.

Activity 2   Complete at least three self-assessment instruments on your thinking, information processing, and dispositions. There are no right or wrong answers and no better or worse outcomes. These instruments are simply a measure of who you are at one place in time and space.

Activity 3   For each instrument, reflect on the following statements. Submit your instruments *and* reflections.

A. What did you learn about yourself from this inventory? Did you know this already? If so, how? If you learned something new, describe your reaction.

B. Describe your strengths and their benefits to you, friends, family, workplace, and others.

C. How can you apply this knowledge to this class, to your capstone project, and in your future?

In these examples, students are engaged in their learning and thinking about their learning at the same time. They are asked to analyze the processes they use, draw conclusions, and learn from and put their ideas into practice.

Self-assessment can help students uncover their thinking process, understand whether they learn best through concrete examples or more verbal cues, or recognize whether their thinking flows more sequentially than randomly. When they can explain these thought processes, learning becomes more transparent and response can be personalized. It doesn't mean that teachers will teach solely to each individual student's strongest modality, but rather that together, teachers and students will find ways to learn as vigorously and meaningfully as possible.

Metacognition is also related to other 21st century skills. Critical thinking becomes metacognitive when students are asked what thinking skills they used. In relation to problem solving, students can analyze how the transfer of knowledge from previous experience relates to this new problem. For presentations, students can consider what strategies are most and least effective in different settings and for different audiences.

Assessment strategies useful for metacognition that can be wrapped into other assessments include

- "think-alouds," where students talk, think, and record thought processes;
- written responses to and reflections on writing prompts;
- graphic organizers of work that can be completed while the work is in progress or retrospectively as students consider the process or outcomes;
- anecdotal records;
- student conferences;

- learning wrappers used to record thinking as students work; and
- questionnaires and self-reporting instruments that give students insight into their work.

Metacognition extends beyond the classroom too. There are lessons we can take away from thought leaders, both past and present. Charles Darwin observed that "Ignorance more frequently begets confidence than does knowledge." Harold Stevenson (1990) at the University of Michigan discovered that students in the United States outrank those in other countries in their self-confidence about their abilities, yet in actual performance, American students were behind those in other countries. In classrooms, ignorance cannot be bliss. When an athletic team loses a game, they go back and review the tapes. They analyze errors and devise strategies to improve their success in the next game. This is an idea that can be embraced throughout education. Rather than strict adherence to pacing guides, perhaps engaging students in planning to learn, reflecting on learning, and identifying next steps in learning will serve everyone better.

Reflection
Do you think all students at all grades can be metacognitive? How important is this?
How might this look at different ages and stages?
What do you think the impact of our fast paced digital age is on metacognition?

Think of a way to incorporate a metacognitive wrapper in your teaching and learning.
    Follow the this lesson design:
    • Standard
    • Goal/Objective
    • Content Skills and Knowledge Success Criteria
    • Metacogntion

How will you know when your students have grown in their metacognitive abilities?

FINAL CONSIDERATIONS

Throughout this book, the emphasis has been on moderation and balance between traditional and 21st century learning outcomes. Schools must be places where the rigor of content melds with the relevance of application. A complete change of direction in assessment isn't required, but rather an incorporation of critical thinking skills into assessment practices, from the individual classroom to the international level. Our students must be prepared for the global world and workplace. While the U.S. tests have traditionally measured content, international measures such as the Programme for International Student Assessment assess the ability to think critically, analyze information, and apply it in real-world situations. The imperative is in place to not just keep up with the world but to forge ahead.

Reflection

For each skill, describe a way you would apply it in your school or classroom:

- Critical Thinking

- Problem Solving

- Creativity

- Metacognition

6

Assessing Actions

The thinking skills in Chapter 5 are translated into actions through communication and collaboration, and are enhanced by the use of learning tools. These are essential elements in that they ultimately lead to the processes and products of learning.

COMMUNICATION

Most life forms communicate in some manner. Even viruses communicate with cell receptors. Someday, one of your students may discover how that works and put an end to the common cold, HIV, or some other disease. Humans communicate in the most complex ways: in writing, orally, visually, and through multiple sensory modalities. Communication involves create meaning, imparting knowledge, skills, and beliefs to others, and receiving input from multiple sources.

People have communicated since the beginning of humankind. Oral traditions such as bedtime stories continue even today. Early alphabets made written as well as oral communication possible. In the 1400s, Gutenberg's printing press brought the written word to the masses. Univac, the first commercially available computer introduced in the 1950s, led the way to personal computers, laptops, tablets, and smartphones. The result is that in today's world, good communication is more complex than ever, yet is more essential than ever.

In schools and classrooms, homes and workplaces, learning is based on effective communication. Traditionally, teachers have communicated by verbally conveying information through lectures. Today, they have a vast array of other resources available to deliver information: video, digital images, audio, and technologies that connect students, in real time, to speakers in remote locations.

Students receive and produce vast amounts of communication. They can record their learning and explain their thinking, inform and share with others through written and oral communication, and display their work graphically and digitally. When students use all this to construct knowledge, its relevance and meaning is strengthened.

Mr. Walters' fifth grade class is studying early American history. CCSS expect students to "read and comprehend information texts and determine the main ideas of a text." The local curriculum is built on a standard that says: *Students will use a variety of intellectual skills to demonstrate their understanding of the major ideas, eras, themes, and turning points in the early history of the United States.* During this unit, students read source material from early settlers and historical fiction, view a movie, and listen to a speaker whose family was one of the first in their choice of area such Norfolk, Virginia, or Boston, Massachusetts. They produce journals as if they were residents of that place and time, create artifacts from the period from eating utensils to weapons, work in groups to solve problems of daily life, and complete the unit with a summative test that uses a graphic organizer to guide the composition of an essay describing life in early America.

The amount of information available to today's students, multiplied by the channels available for sending and receiving it, can add to the complexity of decoding and using it. Because of the breadth of content, much time is spent conveying information without slowing down to check how it is being received. It may seem unnecessary to explicitly teach communication skills, but remember the adage "I know you think you heard what I tried to say but I'm not sure that what you heard is what I really meant." And some readers may remember the Abbott and Costello routine "Who's on First?"

Defining Communication

Communication requires a multitude of 21st century skills: analysis, evaluation, problem solving, metacognition, collaboration, and technology. Many content area standards are built on the foundations of the CCSS, which target the following writing, speaking, and listening skills:

- Write informative texts to examine and convey complex ideas and information.
- Produce clear and coherent writings in which the development, organization, and style are appropriate to the task, purpose, and audience.
- Present information and findings such that listeners can follow, and in an organized manner and appropriate style.
- Adapt speech to a variety of contexts and communicative tasks.
- Participate in a range of conversations with diverse partners.
- Integrate and evaluate information presented in diverse media formats.

Advanced competence in communication takes much practice over many years. Communication skills can be taught explicitly or embedded in the teaching and learning of other subjects. At all grade levels, reading, listening and observing are essential. Conveying information and solving problems through language are central skills. As students progress through the grades, analysis and synthesis of communication becomes vital.

These are essential core elements in education, but in the 21st century the skill set required to realize these broad goals is changing. Digital age literacy requires communication using technologies, as well as interpreting and using digital and visual information. Consider this list of interactive communication formats: written, verbal, visual, synchronous, asynchronous, electronic, virtual, and more. In addition to the CCSS, the following communication skills have been identified by organizations advocating 21st century practices in education:

- Identifying and using a variety of types of verbal communication such as conversation, debate, and persuasion.
- Engaging in constructive dialog with others.
- Demonstrating receptive communication skills: paying attention, listening reflectively, and comprehending.
- Identifying, using, and understanding a variety of types of written communication: formal, informal, and scientific.
- Reading, viewing, and listening to multiple types of media for multiple purposes.
- Producing effective communication through multiple media: oral, written, visual, nonverbal, and technological.
- Using communication persuasively: expressing views and preferences in a neutral manner.

In Practice

As a new teacher, Mr. Espinoza has many goals for himself and for his students. As he works on his new teacher induction requirements, he also sets a goal of engaging students in learning by having them take an active role in knowledge creation. He challenges himself and his students to make learning as real as possible and starts with a unit on understanding communities and neighborhoods. This can be adapted to a few blocks of an urban area, a walking tour of a small town's downtown, or an exploration of a more rural area. Mr. Espinoza wants to extend this project over time and incorporate into it multiple subjects such as reading, writing, math, science, physical education, technology, and the arts. But an important emphasis for him is the development of communication skills in his students. Here are some of the activities he plans:

- Read grade-level stories about living in a community, then hold a book chat. Have students write a summary of the story and their chat.
- Take a neighborhood or community tour. Take notes on what you see and hear.
- Create a labeled map or diagram of your neighborhood or community.
- Take photos and use them to annotate your map.
- Interview members of the community about their lives, experiences, and history.
- Create and publish a classroom chronicle of the people who live in the community being studied.

Extensions of learning:

- Plan for a natural disaster that could happen in your neighborhood. Learn about disasters caused by hurricanes, earthquakes, tornadoes, and nuclear power. Design a way to inform your neighbors about what to do in case of a disaster.
- Develop a community service project such as a neighborhood beautification, planting a community garden, or starting a food pantry.
- Incorporate technology skills through the use of GPS, Google Earth, and presentation tools.

Students can be grouped in various ways for these activities, the content can be differentiated for student level, and different kinds of assessments can be used. But Mr. Espinosa makes sure that he includes elements from the CCSS in each activity.

Assessment of this unit takes many forms. Literacy is graded on traditional reading and writing skills. Mapping is graded on the math curriculum's standards. Similarly, science and technology are graded using the standards from those disciplines. But Mr. Espinoza is not sure how to assess communication skills until his mentor teacher shares some strategies. The rubric in Figures 6.4 and the checklists in Figures 6.5 and 6.6 gave him some ideas to get started. He then created a blended assessment for this project as shown in Figure 6.1.

Figure 6.1 Blended Assessment of Communication

Tracking my learning: New learning in these subjects score _____

Reading and writing _____ Score _____

Math _____ Score _____

Science _____ Score _____

How many ways did I listen and communicate in this unit? How did I demonstrate each one? What worked well and what would I change if I were doing it over again?

- Listening
- Looking
- Speaking
- Writing
- Presenting and persuading
- Using technology

How do I rate my communication skills on each scale?

(Support where you placed your X on each scale by explaining your strengths and/or making suggestions for improvement.)

Listening

I'm all ears ←——————→ Need to open my ears

Speaking

Clear as a bell ←——————→ Reluctant

Writing

Accurate and organized ←——————→ Not easy for me

Use of Resources

Skilled: I produce credible work ←——————→ Need more practice and time

Reading reflection: How can I apply what I learned about communities and neighborhoods to my own life and school?

Most frequently, the teaching of communication skills is incorporated into content areas and the standards for those areas, rather than being treated as a stand-alone lesson. In this section, rather than one communication lesson, many examples are offered: for elementary school (Figure 6.2), middle school, (Figure 6.3) and high school (Figure 6.4). They can be used alone or incorporated into other learning; they can be adjusted for your grade and subject. As you read through them, picture each of the activities as part of a larger continuum of planning and learning that looks like the one below. You'll find this format again at the end of the chapter, where you can personalize and customize the ideas. Also note that this is only part of a comprehensive lesson design for 21st century learning that can be found in the Appendix B.

Common Core Standard	21st Century Skill/ Knowledge	Teaching and Learning Strategies	Assessment

Figure 6.2 Communication in the Elementary Classroom

Applied/Authentic Learning	Assessment Strategy
Read a story about someone who didn't pay attention and gets into a difficult situation. Use these ideas and your own experiences to write a story about a time you ran into a problem because you didn't pay attention.	Assessment: Students create a mind map of ways to take in information: ears (words and tone), eyes (body and artifacts), other senses (touch, smell). They explain how they use each. (Rated with a rubric for elaboration and clarity). Students compare and contrast the differences when they listen with just their ears versus listening with their eyes and other senses too. (Rated on a checklist for details, depth, and accuracy)
Play a game in which students listen to a list of five or more facts, vocabulary words, or items from a lesson. See how many they can remember. Then do the same activity with a different list of items, this time presenting the list both orally and in written form simultaneously.	Create a graphic organizer comparing how many they remembered with each communication strategy. Reflect on why recall was better or worse with each type of communication.
Visual interpretation: Look at a picture of two people who seem to be disagreeing about something. Generate a story about what is happening based on what you see. Support your story by using visual information from the picture.	Assess the clarity, depth, and sequence of explanation on a scale. Students can reflect on their ability to make connections to information in the image.
(Add your own application.)	

Figure 6.3 Communication in the Middle School Classroom

Applied Learning	Assessment
Writing for a purpose: Science: Write a letter to a corporate CEO, urging that the corporation's processing plant should stop discharging pollutants into the local water supply Math: Convince others why math is important Include examples of how it is used everyday	Peer evaluation by a panel of editors. Evaluated for content, staying on point, clarity, accuracy of information, persuasiveness
Pass it along: In sequence, Student 1 expresses one idea, fact-backed opinion, or solution to a schoolwide problem (or a content area problem). Student 2 listens to what Student 1 says and reflects back the main ideas without judging, interpreting, or adding to it. When Student 1 agrees that the reflection was accurate, the student turns to the next person in sequence and states his idea, opinion, or solution. Student 3 then reflects back the main ideas, and the process continues.	Checklist (Figure 6.5) measuring student's ability to make a convincing, fact-based assertion and listen reflectively to another. Self-, peer, and teacher assessment using checklist of listening and speaking skills
Dear Abby: Respond to a letter or watch a video about someone being bullied.	Assessed using writing rubric combined with communication rubric: clarity, depth of content, feasibility of response
Add your own application.	

Figure 6.4 Communication in the High School Classroom

English: While reading poetry, short stories, or novels, work in small groups to identify barriers to effective communication between characters in the written works.	Teacher observation/checklist of student participation in discussion. Relevance and accuracy of contribution and attentiveness to others
Communication in a group on an assigned topic, with no time allowed for preparation. Compare to communication on a self-selected topic with time to gather information and plan a presentation.	Evaluate both approaches using a checklist. Compare, contrast, and analyze the differences. Checklist of communication in a group (Figure 6.6)
Tell a story about someone on a job interview who hadn't read the job description, yawns during the interview, uses an inappropriate strategy for conflict resolution, and explains why it was the boss's fault he was fired from his last two jobs because he didn't think it was important to follow protocols.	Assessment of content knowledge: Students list four things the person did wrong. Assessment of application: Students create skits (can be videotaped) that show good interviewing skills. Scored for accuracy of content and use of technology

(Continued)

Figure 6.4   (Continued)

Watch the film *12 Angry Men*. Analyze and sort the types of communications: persuasion, using support for a viewpoint, listening, clarifying information, problem solving, decision making.	Assessment: mind map with accurate analysis showing type of communication and a quote or example from the movie to support it
Add your own application.	

Figure 6.5   Rubric for Communication (expanded version in Appendix A)

Skill/Knowledge	Exemplary	Proficient	Basic	Novice	Score/ Weight
• Conveys message for selected target	• Recognizes the purpose and can organize and present information to meet it	• Aware of the purpose • The information and presentation serves the intended purpose	• Somewhat unclear on the purpose, thus compromising the quality of information and presentation	• Confused about the purpose of communication and has difficulty focusing on content and process	
• Receptive communication: Listens, reads, views purposefully	• Distinguishes statements of fact from opinions, recognizes intent of messages, identifies support for viewpoint	• Identifies facts and recognizes attempts to persuade • Identifies and summarizes the main ideas	• Can identify some statements of fact in a message • Developing skills in interpreting messages	• Restates facts • Partially understands the purpose of a message	
• Uses a full range of resources to express ideas	• Selects and uses a combination of communication resources appropriate to the topic and purpose	• Regularly selects a few resources that are a good match for the assignment	• May be able to pick one or two independently, but generally requires support to communicates through additional resources	• Familiar with few modalities for expressing ideas resulting in work that is compromised	

Figure 6.6   Checklist for Communication

Standard/Target	Student Rating: Exemplary, Proficient, Basic, Novice with explanation	Teacher Assessment: Exemplary, Proficient, Basic, Novice with explanation	Strategy for Improvement
Receives information: ___ Pays attention ___ Listens reflectively ___ Uses information			
Uses multiple channels to communicate: ___ Verbal ___ Nonverbal ___ Visual			
Convinces others ___ Organized/sequenced ___ Accurate/fact-based ___ Persuasive ___ Easy to Follow			

Figure 6.7   Checklist for Communication in a Group

Group Communication	Comments
✓ if satisfactory performance according to standard X if not satisfactory based on standard or guideline	
Introduction captures the attention of the audience.	
Purpose is evident throughout.	
Content is understandable and logically sequenced.	
Speech: Language is appropriate to the purpose. Volume, rate, and articulation are effective.	
Engages with audience through body language, eye contact, and gestures	
Used technology to support message	
Summary synthesizes main ideas in presentation.	

The following are other teaching and learning activities that directly incorporate communication skills. These can be integrated into other instructional goals and standards or used as stand-alone activities to support the development of communication skills.

- READING: Read a book about someone who uses idioms and misunderstands them, for example, *Amelia Bedelia* (Parish, 1963) or *Butterflies in My Stomach.* (Bloch, 2008) Discuss literal versus inferred meaning of statements. Brainstorm more idioms and compare literal to colloquial use. Assess with a diagram or mind map that includes examples of literal meanings, idioms, euphemisms, and innuendo.

- MULTICULTURAL UNDERSTANDING: Students complete a task such as following directions, but they all speak a different language, and each student has been given just one word to use from the primary language. They can only use that one word to communicate with others to complete the task. Directions can be adjusted to the subject or content such as explaining how to use software or a website. Assess with a reflection of student's learning about communication: What worked, what were the challenges, and what does this mean in our classroom and for global communication?

- MATH: Students sit back to back in pairs. One has a diagram such as a drawing of interconnected shapes from a math lesson. The other has a blank sheet of paper. In the first round, the student giving directions is the only one allowed to talk. The person listening to the directions draws the diagram, following as best as possible without asking the pair to slow down or repeat or clarify the directions. In the second round, the pair can talk to each other, ask questions, and adjust pacing throughout the process. Assess with the ability to explain the difference between the two and how that applies to real-world situations. This can also be done in science—for example, one student is explaining to another how to create a DNA sequence.

- GAMES: Play adaptations of popular content-based games such as Jeopardy or Millionaire where students additionally have to explain and justify their answers and use persuasive arguments to convince others that they are correct. Assess by having students pretest individually, and then check their scores after a collaborative round.

- SUMMARIZING: A Mirror Game can be used as a review. One student makes a summarizing statement, and another has to rephrase it in his or her own words. For older students, one reads a paragraph from the text, and the other then paraphrases it. Additionally, an example can be added or a clarifying question can be asked also. Assess the alignment of the statement with the restated one for content and intent.

- POST ME: In teams or pairs, students are given readings on an idea or concept. They summarize the readings and select key facts and main ideas to communicate to other students. In turn, the other students record three to five facts from the reading on sticky notes. After the readings, they can sort the information by writing it on a sticky note and placing it in a column or box that it best fits. For example, with readings on the government, the sticky notes could go into executive, judicial, or legislative branch columns. Assess for accuracy of content and ability to defend placement.

- TEACH ANOTHER: Each student takes on the role of teacher. This could involve teaching a computer skill, a cooking technique, a math solution, punctuation, or lab procedures, which is then assessed with a rubric that includes accuracy of content, instructional strategy used, and learning outcomes.
- FISH BOWL: Students are seated in two concentric circles. Those in the inner circle are assigned a topic to discuss. They prepare by reading reference material, either provided by the teacher or located themselves. Those in the outer circle observe the discussion and assess for content, presentation skills, and respectful listening.
- DEBATES: Debates are a complex yet versatile way to embed content with communication. They can be used with many topics in most subjects in the curriculum. Here are a few examples:

  o Social studies: U.S. foreign policy (isolationist versus expansionist); immigration laws
  o Math: metric versus English system
  o Science: stem cell research
  o Language arts: TV and movie ratings; freedom of speech; blocked websites at school

Before the debate begins, students can establish and agree to basic rules concerning respectful participation, attentiveness to the presentations, and adherence to time requirements. Guidelines for the debate also need to be predetermined and clear to all. This includes the process for selecting teams and the time allowed for each step: planning, presentation, conferring, and rebuttal. The debate can be assessed on content knowledge displayed as well as communication and debate skills.

The debate rubric shown in Figure 6.8 can be used to for self, peer, or teacher assessment. A longer version is in Appendix A.

Assessment of communication skills depends on the content and purpose of the assignment. The means a teacher uses to assess depth of information may be different from those used in a peer assessment of audience engagement. A formative assessment will include room for improvement and may differ from a summative assessment in format and purpose. Different communication skills will also require different assessment methods. Writing for a target audience will be evaluated differently from interpreting a verbal message. This will also hold true for communication that uses technology or is embedded in other content

Figure 6.8   Debate Rubric

Standard	4 Exceeds Expectations	3 Meets Expectations	2 Working Toward	1 Below Standard	Score
Content: Opening remarks, rebuttal	Strong argument with clear views. Logical, specific and on target.	Perspective is clear. Arguments are mostly convincing and focused.	Viewpoint is a little nebulous. Remarks are neutral and somewhat vague in detail.	Focus is not established. Unconvincing statements.	
Support	Support is fact-based, detailed and compelling.	Support contains facts and data and is purposeful.	Support is incomplete in facts, purpose, and focus.	Support is not evident.	
Organization	Fluent, clear, and logical process. Effective use of time.	Sequential progression of topic that demonstrates good use of time.	Sequence is difficult to follow. May not meet time requirements.	Limited sequence and organization that doesn't meet time requirements.	
Presentation	Poised and professional resulting in high audience attention.	Effective style that engages the audience.	Needs further practice in presentation skills and audience engagement.	Disengaged from presentation and audience.	

areas. The advantage of this is that assessments don't have to be one-size-fits-all but can be customized for the standard, process, and product. Note that some of the activities, assessments, and rubrics in this section are very dense and can easily be divided to meet your specific learning targets.

Reflection

- What are your priorities and needs for teaching and assessing communication skills?
- Design a lesson to explicitly teach communication in your classroom. Use the lesson plan in Appendix B as a framework.
- Adapt an existing content area lesson to incorporate communication skills.
- How would you assess those lessons?

COLLABORATION

Alone we can do so little; together we can do so much.

—Helen Keller

Collaboration builds on the skills of effective communication by placing it in an interpersonal setting. But collaboration is more than cooperation. It is about learning to plan and work together, to consider diverse perspectives, and to participate in discourse by contributing, listening, and supporting others. It happens when members of the group go beyond what any member could do individually. It is about recognizing and valuing individual contributions toward the group's productivity and improvement. A study by Cakir, Zemel, and Stahl found that "group participants, in order to collaborate effectively in group discourse on a topic like mathematical patterns, must organize their activities in ways that share the significance of their utterances, inscriptions, and behaviors" (2009, p. 115). In other words, the ability to use 21st century skills is associated with the ability to process knowledge and information through spoken language, written communication, and actions.

Collaborative learning is based on the idea of synergy—that the whole equals more than the individual parts. This happens routinely in Mr. Williams's project-based class. After working together for several months to understand and assimilate Costa and Kallick's (2000) *Habits of Mind*, students begin working on their individual service projects. During the biweekly group check-ins, invariably, one student is stumped by a problem. And invariably, others come to their rescue. When Mike couldn't figure out how to mobilize his firefighting robot, a student suggested he use a remote control car chassis. After some trial and error and problem solving, Mike was able to make it operational. When Kathleen couldn't decide how to publicize her upcoming fundraiser to fight hunger, the entire class put the information on their Facebook pages and blogged and tweeted it, and instantly, the entire "village" beyond the walls of the school and the boundaries of the town was informed.

Many of today's best ideas have come from collaboration. Facebook was created from the ideas of several people. Pharmacists around the world collaborate on the development of next generation drugs, cars are assembled from parts produced globally, and whatever your thoughts about Wikileaks, it was definitively a global collaboration. In fact, most of the world's most significant problems can no longer be solved by one person.

Defining Collaboration

Collaboration is more than simply working with others. It also includes active listening skills, responding with respect, expressing ideas clearly through multiple channels of communication, and using these skills to reach consensus and compromise. In a collaborative classroom, students work on shared goals, learn together, engage in meaningful tasks, and build on prior learning to generate ideas and products.

The CCSS include the following collaboration standards that start with broad ideas and then build by grade level:

- (K–12) Participate effectively in a range of conversations and collaborations with diverse partners, building on other's ideas and expressing their own clearly and persuasively
- (K–2) Follow agreed-upon rules for discussions
- (3–5) Come to discussions prepared, having read required material
- (5–8) Pose and respond to specific questions; make comments that contribute to the topic; acknowledge new information expressed by others

Specifically for Grades 9–12 are the following:

- Work with peers to promote civil, democratic discussions and decision making, set goals, and establish roles
- Propel conversations by posing and responding to questions that probe reasoning and evidence and promote divergent perspectives
- Respond thoughtfully to diverse perspectives, synthesize comments, resolve contradictions, and seek additional information

Essential 21st century collaboration skills also include the following:

- Balance listening and speaking, leading and following, in a group.
- Demonstrate flexibility, compromise, and empathy-taking skills.
- Consider, prioritize, and advance the interests and needs of the larger group.
- Value, recognize, and use the contributions and strengths of group members.
- Work together to create new ideas and products.
- Actively participate, contribute, and assume shared responsibility for completing the work.
- Work respectfully with others to make decisions that include the views of multiple individuals.

- Identify areas of agreement and disagreement and seek to resolve conflicts.
- Participate respectfully in frank discussion, debates, and disagreements.

In Practice

When an observer enters a collaborative classroom, one of the first differences he notes is that the teacher is not the sole authority. Knowledge and learning flows between all members of the class; the teacher serves as a coach and facilitator. This doesn't mean the teacher is tolerant of haphazard learning, but rather that the teacher has established the framework that supports students as they fill it in. Grouping is flexible and based on the topic, purpose, and goals. A heterogeneous group may work together on a science assignment and be regrouped homogeneously for language arts.

Within a group, students can take on the role of facilitator, restater, monitor, or recorder. The sequence of work starts with defining a purpose and setting goals. Goals can be predetermined based on standards, or they can be set by students. As students share and develop knowledge, ideas and questions can be sorted and sequenced to guide learning.

In a science class, the goal may be analyzing magnetic forces, but students can decide whether to measure the strength of magnets, explore polarity, or show the connection between magnets and electricity. In social studies, each collaborative group might look at the causes of specific wars: the Civil War, World War I, World War II, Vietnam, and Desert Storm. Groups then reassemble to compare, contrast, and analyze their findings. English student groups might revise a classic Hans Christian Anderson story as a Disney-like adaptation using Second Life software. This work can be self-, peer, and teacher assessed using rubrics, checklists, logs, and mind maps.

New and emerging technologies allow students to create and design collaboratively. Computer-supported collaborative learning (CSCL) facilitates learning through a server and allows participants to share and construct knowledge together. Learners can engage in conversation and discussion, produce original materials, or solve problems. With all these ways to produce and share, the three-page paper may be a thing of the past, due to wikis, Google Docs, Skype, and interactive whiteboards.

Students can use these tools for global collaboration to share ideas on world hunger or comparatively analyze the nutritional value of their school lunch menus. Teachers from different countries can connect their two classrooms using wikis and Skype. In one collaborative project, students shared and compared ideas for protecting endangered species in their respective communities, and then shared their information with the world.

Collaboration can also incorporate and build on other 21st century skills such as problem solving; digital literacy; and oral, written, and visual communication skills. Figure 6.9 shows some examples of this.

Collaboration can also be accomplished using wrappers coordinated with existing curricula and standards. Prior to instruction, a formative Corners activity can generate like-minded teams that then defend their ideas and positions. Students begin by collectively identifying what they know using a list or graphic organizer. During the learning process, the team works together to summarize the main ideas or most important outcome. They then post these in a Gallery Walk and review each other's work

Collaborations can also be done across classrooms and content areas. Here are a few ideas:

- Digital illustration and literacy: create a graphic heroes story
- Science and cooking: learn about and demonstrate the characteristics of starch, yeast, or gluten.
- Science and life skills: recycling strategies and benefits

Assessment strategies can include a wide range of those described in Chapter 4. They range from standardized measures of content learning to student-managed contracts. A rubric for collaboration is shown in Figure 6.10 with an expanded example in Appendix A.

Other assessments of collaboration include the following:

- *Contracts* are entered into before starting an extensive group project. Team members agree to comply with the rules of collaboration. They also agree to be accountable for research, learning, time management, etc.
- *Narratives* provide an opportunity for the group to describe their learning process and outcomes. The group submits a description of their work as it aligns with the rubric being used for evaluation. The teacher compares this to his or her observations and running records.
- *Portfolios* of ongoing work serve to maintain a record of steps taken, resources used, and individual contributions. Electronic storage of these records makes it easy to monitor ongoing progress and can help students plan next steps.
- *Graphic organizers* can be used to show the roles of group members how well they fulfilled them. This provides a visual record of individual contributions.

Figure 6.9   Collaborative Learning and Assessment

Subject	Collaboration	Assessment
Language arts: Sell the Poet	Each group reads the work(s) of a different poet. Assigned jobs: recorder, questioner, reflector. Groups analyze the poet's style, theme, view, purpose, etc., synthesize their findings, and then market their work to others, applying standards of good poetry.	Individual • Annotate and analyze a poem or poet. • Use a rubric to assess content, accuracy, and detail of the analysis. • Learning log of new learning and processes of learning Group • Collaboration rubric • Peer assessment of assigned jobs
Science: Solve the Drought	Each person on the team is assigned a profession: politician, meteorologist, environmentalist, journalist, etc. Each person researches and reports from his or her unique perspective. Group must identify the problems and build consensus on a solution.	Individual: rubric on research Group: rubric on collaboration and consensus building Shared: Write test questions for other groups to answer.
Geography: Latitudes and Attitudes	Every day begins with a posting of coordinates. Students work in small groups to determine the weather, geography, water system, animals, and plant life at that location	Log of daily latitude and longitude with geographical descriptors Ability to use data to defend their reasoning
Social studies: Renaissance Rebirth	Renaissance project: Students research and present changes brought about by the Renaissance. In groups, students decide how to proceed with their research and presentation. Final outcome must include architecture, clothing, science, art, food, and families. Significant individuals of the time must be included.	Teacher and group self-assessment with opportunities for individuals to report on their personal contribution to the project. Rubric includes collaboration, content, process, and presentation.

Figure 6.10   Rubric for Collaborating

Skill/ Knowledge	Exemplary	Proficient	Basic	Novice	Score/ Weight
Works productively	We used all our time efficiently to stay focused on the task and produce the required work. Everyone did his or her assigned duties and sometimes more.	We worked together well and for the most part stayed on task until we completed our work. Each person performed nearly all assigned duties.	We worked together sometimes, but not everyone contributed or did his or her job, making it hard finish our work.	We really didn't work together very well. Everyone wanted to do his or her own thing and tell others what to do rather than focus on the task.	
Demonstrates respect	Everyone respectfully listened and discussed ideas that were shared.	Members listened and interacted respectfully most of the time.	Some people had difficulty being respectful of others' ideas.	Members were unwilling to listen to others and were argumentative with teammates.	
Compromises	Everyone was flexible in working together to achieve a common goal.	We usually were able to compromise to move our work forward.	If more people compromised we would have moved forward faster.	There was a lot of disagreeing, and some individuals wanted it only their way.	
Shared responsibility; everyone contributes	Everyone did their best work and followed through on assigned tasks.	Most people followed through on their parts.	It was hard to get everyone to do his or her part.	We really couldn't depend on everyone to do his or her part.	

- *A checklist or rating scale* with the following list offers a quick way for both teachers and students to stay on track.

---

1. Each person completed the assigned role.

   With precision   This seldom happened

   5   4   3   2   1
   Comments:

2. Everyone worked equally hard on the assignment.

   Complete equality   Some didn't contribute

   5   4   3   2   1
   Comments:

3. We did better together than we could have individually.

   Much more productive   Not much difference

   5   4   3   2   1
   Comments:

- *Self- and peer evaluation and reflection* can be done of the group process and a group presentation. It can include open-ended and general questions such as what worked best or what would you do differently next time. Other questions can be specific to the assignment. Learners can be asked to identify the most helpful resource they used or three things they know now that they didn't know before.
- *Teacher observation* is an important tool for assessing collaboration. Supporting learners through the process, suggesting strategies, and resolving disagreements will all serve to move the process forward. The validity of assessments based on teacher observation can be strengthened by looking for evidence of such factors as student use of research strategies, communication skills, and problem-solving skills.

- *Student logs and journals* note specific goals that were achieved and ongoing assessment of progress. Daily check-ins using a checklist or brief narrative can incorporate perspectives on an individual's contribution for the day and plans for next steps.

There are challenges involved in teaching, learning, and assessing collaboratively. Time constraints and a concern for student safety, both electronic and personal, can pose obstacles. It's easy for the teaching of content to get overlooked in an overemphasis on the collaborative process. Yet, since our students use the newest forms of social networking outside of the classroom, we disconnect them if we cut them off from those resources when they enter the schoolhouse. To encourage classroom use, some websites, such as ePals, Glogster EDU, and Prezi, are setting up school-safe zones.

Assessment becomes complicated when trying to find a fair and equitable balance between individual learning and group productivity. It's not simply about assigning a grade, but rather looking at the complexity of the process and the outcomes of the collaborative work. It's about growth in learning (not just a final score), the process (strategies, resources, decisions, cooperation), and the outcomes (products, relevance, usefulness, completion, and connection to goals). An uncomplicated in-class collaboration such as solving a math problem together is different than a long-term complex project such as developing an antibullying campaign.

Whether to grade the group as a whole or grade individually depends on the type of assignment and how collaboration serves the twin goals of knowledge and skill building. The weight assigned to each goal can be adjusted in relation to the assignment. Labeling cell structures may be an activity that should be assessed primarily as individual learning, whereas role plays based on classic and contemporary literature might be evaluated on group-based criteria. In addition, many aspects of collaboration must be taken into account in accessing collaborative work. These include individual contributions, positive teamwork, respectful problem solving, and productive strategies.

As a general rule, provide a combined grade that reflects a balance of both individual achievement and group process. A science lab experiment may have two grades: one that reflects the individual student's learning through a lab journal, and another that reflects that student's contribution to the group and the group process. A project, too, may have two grades: one that reflects learning outcomes for each individual student and one that reflects the collaborative process.

Collaboration can be time-consuming, noisy, and untidy. On the other hand, positive collaboration is dynamic, engaging, and constructive, and supports social learning foundations as described by Vygotsky and Bandura.

Architect Frank Lloyd Wright told how a walk with his uncle and cousins at the age of 9 contributed to his philosophy of learning. As they walked across a snow-covered field, they stopped to look back at their paths. His uncle's tracks went straight across the field, whereas his cousins' wove back and forth from the trees to the fence to the cows. It took more time for them to cross the field. Although his uncle urged him to always follow the leader along the path, Wright recognized the enthusiasm of his cousins for the things they discovered and learned together along the way. Vince Lombardi sums it up well: "People who work together will win, whether it be against complex football defenses, or in the problems of modern society."

Reflection
Complete this plan as it relates to your content area and grade level.
Collaboration plan content area/grade:
Standard:
Learning outcome/problem to solve:
Collaborative lesson plan (Initiation, assignment, resources):
Implementation in action (students' roles and steps):
Assessment of product/learning:
Assessment of process:

DIGITAL LITERACY

Digital literacy does not replace text. It broadens and deepens our understanding of texts.

— Philip M. Anderson

When today's students want to find an answer to a question, they have many options at their fingertips. In a recent language arts exercise on the rules of language, students were asked to list as many anomalies in the English language as they could. Here are a few they discovered:

If the plural of *mouse* is *mice*, why isn't the plural of *spouse spice*?

Why are *though* and *cough* pronounced differently?

How come the sewer (stitcher) fell into the sewer (septic hole)?

If writers write how come fingers don't fing?

It was relatively easy for them to find more of these conundrums online. But they were stumped when asked to pronounce the word *ghote* and were told it did not start with a *g* sound of any sort. Their teacher sent them off to find as many ways as they could of solving the challenge. After about 20 minutes, they reconvened and shared their ideas. One student called her mother, an English teacher in another school. Another texted a friend, and a third asked the assistant principal. Others "Googled" it, and one posted it as her Facebook status. But unlike on "Who Wants to be a Millionaire?" reaching out to these lifelines was to no avail. The teacher explained that she had learned of this challenge B.C. (Before Computers), and apparently this generation has not discovered that it spells "fish." The "gh" is pronounced as in the word *enough*, the "o" as in the word *women*, the "t" as in the word *nation*, and a silent "e" on the end.

In Chapter 1, evidence was presented that rapid change is the new norm. The world is changing, students are different, and the workplace is rapidly evolving. In relation to new digital and visual literacies, there are over 1 billion people reading information online (Nielsen Company, 2012). Social networking, music, and video are among the leading uses of the Internet by students. As Linda Ellerbee, host of Nick News, points out, "Media literacy is not just important, it's absolutely critical. It's going to make the difference between whether kids are a tool of the mass media or whether the mass media is a tool for kids to use."

The *Kids and Credibility* report from the MacArthur Foundation (Flanagin & Metzger, 2010), found that 89% of 11-to-18-year-olds believe that some to a lot of information on the Internet is credible. *The 2010 Horizon Report* (Johnson, Levine, Smith, & Stone, 2010) says that the overabundance of resources challenges educators to help students make sense of and assess the credibility of information.

Today's students are using all the tools at their fingertips, as just that: utensils to fix or serve up something else. Donald Leu (2010), at the New Literacies Research Lab at the University of Connecticut, suggests they need to go further: All these emerging technologies should interface seamlessly with teaching and learning. He believes that as reading changes from paper to screen, the nature of reading comprehension also changes.

Defining Digital Literacy

Leu (2010) describes the new literacies as "skills, strategies, and dispositions required for successful reading comprehension on the Internet." In addition to websites, emerging communication technologies are changing the way students acquire and use information. Blogs, tweets, and Facebook allow students to instantly share and compare new learning and analyze emerging events. Students are learning through gaming software, simulations, and video. With new ways to gather information come new ways to present it. PowerPoint is old school as compared to Prezi, Glogster, and Xtranormal. And new tools for animation, 3D, and virtual worlds are developing rapidly.

Emerging technologies require students to adapt and expand traditional literacy skills to include

- selecting core information and identifying the central problem from a large amount of data;
- effectively using key words and search strategies;
- managing the flow of information from multiple sources;
- critically evaluating and verifying online resources for accuracy and reliability;
- evaluating, comparing, and synthesizing information from various sources;
- appreciating the purpose and persuasiveness of media messages; and
- considering the effect of messages on beliefs, behaviors, and values.

Although the CCSS do not explicitly espouse digital literacy or distinguish it from more traditional literacy, they do include the following standards related to digital literacy:

- Make strategic use of digital media and visual displays of data to express information and enhance presentations.
- Gather relevant information from multiple sources and assess its credibility and accuracy.
- Evaluate the argument and claims in a text for validity and relevance.

Although most teachers are well aware of the limitations of Wikipedia, in this case the site's definition is rather clear and concise:

Digital literacy is the ability to locate, organize, understand, evaluate, and analyze information using digital technology. It involves a working knowledge of current technology and an understanding of how it can be used. Digitally literate people can communicate and work more efficiently, especially with those who possess the same knowledge and skills. ("Digital Literacy," n.d.)

Most homes today have Internet access, and the majority of jobs require computer use, yet analog teachers continue to assess digital students with paper-and-pencil tests. New literacies are reshaping the way today's learners assemble, view, and use language and images. Reading from electronic sources is unlike learning from traditional written materials. Locating, evaluating, compiling, and presenting information is also different. This shift is the equivalent of changing from oral traditions to the Gutenberg printing press.

In Practice

Digital Search Skills

There are steps that teachers and schools can take to be responsive to this changing environment. Explicit strategies can be taught to build digital literacy. Six digital skills are described in the following.

1. Identifying a central issue and narrowing a search through essential questions
   - Begin with a question that will guide learning
   - Focus on the essential learning targets
   - Good questions will lead to useful search words. Often, students flounder in their Internet searches because they don't understand how important it is to form the essential question.

Example	
Less Informative Question	*More Informative Question*
How do I make a video?	What video software is available without cost, and how can I learn to use it?
How do I raise money?	What fund-raising strategies can I use to help reduce hunger, and for which organizations?
Write your own questions:	
Assessment: Feedback on quality, depth, complexity of question	

2. Locating information through the use of high quality search strategies (Note that a Google search for "best search engines" does not bring up Google first.)

- Understand how information is organized: Boolean logic and search algorithms.
- Develop effective and efficient search strategies.
- Use keywords effectively, for example, "War of 1812" versus "War of 1812 economic causes."
- Understand the significance of domain names, and a recent decision to not limit domain names to .com, .edu, .net, .gov.
- Learn to skillfully interpret the information on a list of links.
- Distinguish advanced search strategies, for example, using Google Scholar rather than Google.

Example

Compare the information you get from each of these comparable searches using different words.		Number of sites found:
		How many are:
		.com
		.edu
		.org
		.gov
		Other
Monarch Butterfly	Monarch Butterflies and habitat	
Food	Healthy eating	
Headache	Headache causes	
Add your own search comparison.		
Assessment: Teacher feedback on completeness of chart and details of comparisons		

3. Evaluating and verifying information: important considerations in evaluating quality

- Who wrote the page? Is the domain/publisher appropriate to your search?
- What are the author's credentials? (Reliability)
- Is it consistent with other sources? (Validity)
- Can it be verified? Are sources documented?
- Does it include a date? Is it current?
- Can you recognize multiple viewpoints? It is important to be aware of possible bias in information.
- Consider information with a healthy amount of skepticism.
- Recognize the persuasive constructs of media messages.

Example

Pick a website and answer the following questions:

- Who wrote the page? What can you tell about this source?
- Describe how the page is organized. Does it seem to follow a logical sequence?
- What are the credentials of the author or the source? How did you verify this?
- Can you find similar information on another site? How alike or different are the sources?
- How can you tell if the information is current?
- Describe the links: Do they work? Are they useful?
- Assessment: self-evaluation and teacher feedback on completeness, depth, clarity, and accuracy of response

---

4. Synthesizing information: Students should be able to

- carefully collect relevant information from multiple sources;
- exclude information that is not related to the topic or purpose;
- combine information from multiple sources while avoiding redundancy;
- link together facts to create larger understandings;
- recognize and describe patterns in the information;
- determine when the question has been answered; and
- cite sources to give credit to authors and adhere to ethical use and copyright laws.

Example

Here are two websites for you to use about your sense of smell:

- http://library.thinkquest.org/3750/smell/smell.html
- http://faculty.washington.edu/chudler/chems .html
- Find your own third site to use.

Read each site and produce a summary of what you have learned about the sense of smell.

Assessment: incorporation of multiple sites in summary, selection process, accuracy of comparison, correctness of conclusions drawn

---

5. Sharing and communicating information
   - Creates a clear message constructed from the work of others
   - Uses multiple strategies and modalities for sharing information
   - Presents findings objectively or with knowledge of bias
   - Is receptive to the feedback and views of others

Assignment is a project similar to the one in Chapter 10 on multipurpose applications, and assessment is with the synthesized presentation rubric in Appendix A.

Example

Pick a current event that is in the news. Find and triangulate three sources of information on the event. Prepare you own blog entry or webpage. When others respond to it, view and summarize their feedback and make recommendations for adjusting your work in response.

Assessment: Quality of sources, Digital Literacy rubric (See Figure 6.12) writing/communication rubric for the blog or webpage and response to feedback.

---

6. Ethical Use

   - Practicing safe, legal, and responsible use of information
   - Giving credit to source

Example

- Students complete a copyright Webquest. Assessed for accuracy
- Students cite sources in APA or MLA format in projects. Assessed for correctness.

Hoax Sites

A good starting point for teaching and learning digital literacy is the use of hoax sites. Several are available on the Internet (subject to change). At first glance, these sites all appear to be real, with accurate information, images, and links.

- All About Explorers: http://www.allaboutexplorers.com
- Dihydrogen monoxide: http://www.dhmo.org/
- Pacific Northwest Tree Octopus: http://zapatopi.net/treeoctopus/
- Victorian robots: http://www.bigredhair.com/robots/

Before students in Mr. Finn's eighth-grade class look at hoax sites, they work in groups to come to consensus on the following questions:

- What do you expect to see on a homepage?
- How much of the homepage of a website do you have to you read to get an idea of what it is about? Support your response.
- How do you decide whether the site is useful to you?
- How do you decide what links to click on?

Then he provides his students with a digital literacy worksheet such as the one in Figure 6.11 and directs them to a hoax site to research their topic.

Figure 6.11 Digital Literacy Workout

STARTING OUT What do we want to learn about our topic?	
AT THE SITE What can you learn from the URL? How can you find out about the author and his or her credentials? What can you tell from the site design, contact information, recent updates, and links?	
ANALYSIS How can you tell if the information is accurate? Does the information seem up to date? How can you tell? What different viewpoints are presented? How would you verify the information at the site?	
CONCLUSIONS:	

After each group completes its work, Mr. Finn shows examples and videos and explains how to discern fact from fiction. Each student then completes a self-assessment similar to the one in Figure 6.12.

Figure 6.12 Rubric for Self-Assessing Digital Literacy Skills

Skill/ Knowledge	Exemplary	Proficient	Basic	Novice	Score/ Weight
Selects	I am very skilled at understanding the partiality of sources and able to thoughtfully select and evaluate them.	I have sufficient understanding of source bias and can usually select credible sources that match my goals.	I can pick out a few good sources but sometimes can't decide which are better for my topic.	With help from my teacher I can find sources and figure out whether they are good ones.	
Evaluates	I am very good at verifying the author and the source to make sure they are good ones.	I can usually check the author's credentials and make sure the information is consistent.	Most sites look pretty good to me, but it's helpful to have a checklist or guide.	I've been fooled by fake websites and need help to sort them out.	
Considers source, message, effect	I am aware of the persuasive nature of electronic sources and understand why they do have this effect.	I am aware that sources may have a bias that could influence my decisions.	I am generally accepting of digital information but can spot blatantly incredible information.	I think most websites provide information that is in my best interests.	
Self-reflection on hoax websites: What did you learn, and how can you use it in the future?					

Research Project

Mr. O combines a research project with a reflection on metacognition when he asked his students to learn more about their brains. He begins with an introduction to student's brains by asking a series of restricted-response questions. Students respond by going to a designated corner of the room.

- Which is bigger, the male or female brain?
- How many hemispheres and lobes are there?
- Who has more neurons, 10-year-olds or adults?
- What part of your brain is the last to develop?
- Your frontal cortex is for riding a bicycle or thinking about your future?

Based on this preassessment, he prepares a classroom presentation on the basic neurobiology of brain structure and function that includes a video, brief readings, and a vocabulary scorecard. Students are then given the choice of selected subtopics to research. Before they begin, he reviews Internet search strategies and information evaluation strategies. The students then carry out their research, making use of at least three accurately cited sources, and choose an appropriate format in which to present their findings to the class. They could do a blog, a website, a Prezi presentation, a poster, a simulation, a script/skit, a video, a song, or an other method of presentation.

Accompanying the research project assignment is a research metacognition work-along (Figure 6.13), in which students record their thoughts while carrying out their research. They are asked to note where they began

Figure 6.13   Self-Assessment of Digital Research Skills

Search strategies	My steps
Search engine used	Why?
Search words used	What was most successful?
Site selection	What factors did you consider in selecting sites?
List three sites used	Explain why you picked these.
Verification of information and author's credibility	How did you do this?
What did you learn from this project about digital information and your skills?	

their research and why and to record search words used and resources selected. What did they do when they ran into trouble? What thoughts went through their minds as they decided how to assemble their information into a high-quality product for presentation? Finally, they are asked to reflect on their project and presentation.

This combination of research and use of digital literacy was illuminating for Mr. O. He noted that almost all students used rote methods for their assignment: Go to Google, perform a one-word search, click on the first site, and accept information at face value. He also noted that students who were more successful in their projects were more reflective during the research process and were better able to critically analyze resources and systematically synthesize their findings into a focused product that met the assessment criteria: accurate content, feasible synthesis, intentional organization of information, quality presentation skills, and engagement of audience.

This mixing of content knowledge building with new literacies is exactly what Donald Leu is talking about, but unfortunately

> few, if any, of the new literacies have found their way into the American classroom. Indeed, many seem to be resisted overtly by deliberate educational policies or covertly by educators who sometimes are not nearly as literate with the Internet as the students they teach. (Leu, 2010)

Reflection

- Think of a time that you have been misled by information on the Internet. What did you learn from that experience?
- What are some strategies that you can use to help students sort through the overabundance of information?
- How would you compare digital reading to more traditional forms of reading? Think of a purpose for each type of source material.
- Should standardized tests be given in a digital format?

VISUAL LITERACY

As the world is becoming increasingly digital, more time is being spent in visual learning. With the notion that pictures and images can be read, the concept of literacy has expanded from the decoding of written texts to include a variety of complex, nonsequential experiences. Visual messages are everywhere in the digital world, but also in the nondigital world: on T-shirts, billboards, and elsewhere. New conceptions of visual literacy are emerging so rapidly and are changing so quickly that the complexity of the field cannot be completely captured in this chapter; a brief overview is presented.

Defining Visual Literacy

The definition of *visual literacy* is evolving as new forms of images are emerging. It has a dual meaning, referring both to the understanding and the production of digital images. In regard to understanding, visual literacy involves interpretation, analysis, and evaluation. In regard to production, visual literacy involves creativity and the synthesis of ideas. It can extend beyond seeing to include other sensory modes as well, such as hearing and tasting—the skills that musicians and chefs use every day. Perhaps in time it will be called *sensory literacy*.

The CCSS include nothing about visual literacy, but do make reference to the use of digital media to convey information. Such visual literacy skills include

- interpreting information presented in an image,
- expressing ideas and communicating through images,
- evaluating visual representations,
- selecting and using the appropriate tool for the expressed purpose, and
- creating visual conceptions and models.

Methods and modes of visual expressing include

- pictures,
- photographs,
- comics,
- symbols,
- maps,
- diagrams and graphic organizers,
- tables and charts,
- graphs,
- timelines,
- cross sections, and
- flow charts.

Ralph Lengler and Martin Eppler at Visual-Literacy.org have developed a Periodic Table of Visualization Methods shown in Figure 6.14. A click on each box provides an example of each.

In Practice

Early learning has always been based on storybooks with visual and auditory prompts. Young children start with the images, then learn the words. Written literacy is emphasized throughout most of the school years. Now some secondary schools are experimenting with visual books such as *American Born Chinese* (2006) by Gene Luen Yang, *The Number*

Figure 6.14 A Periodic Table of Visualization Methods

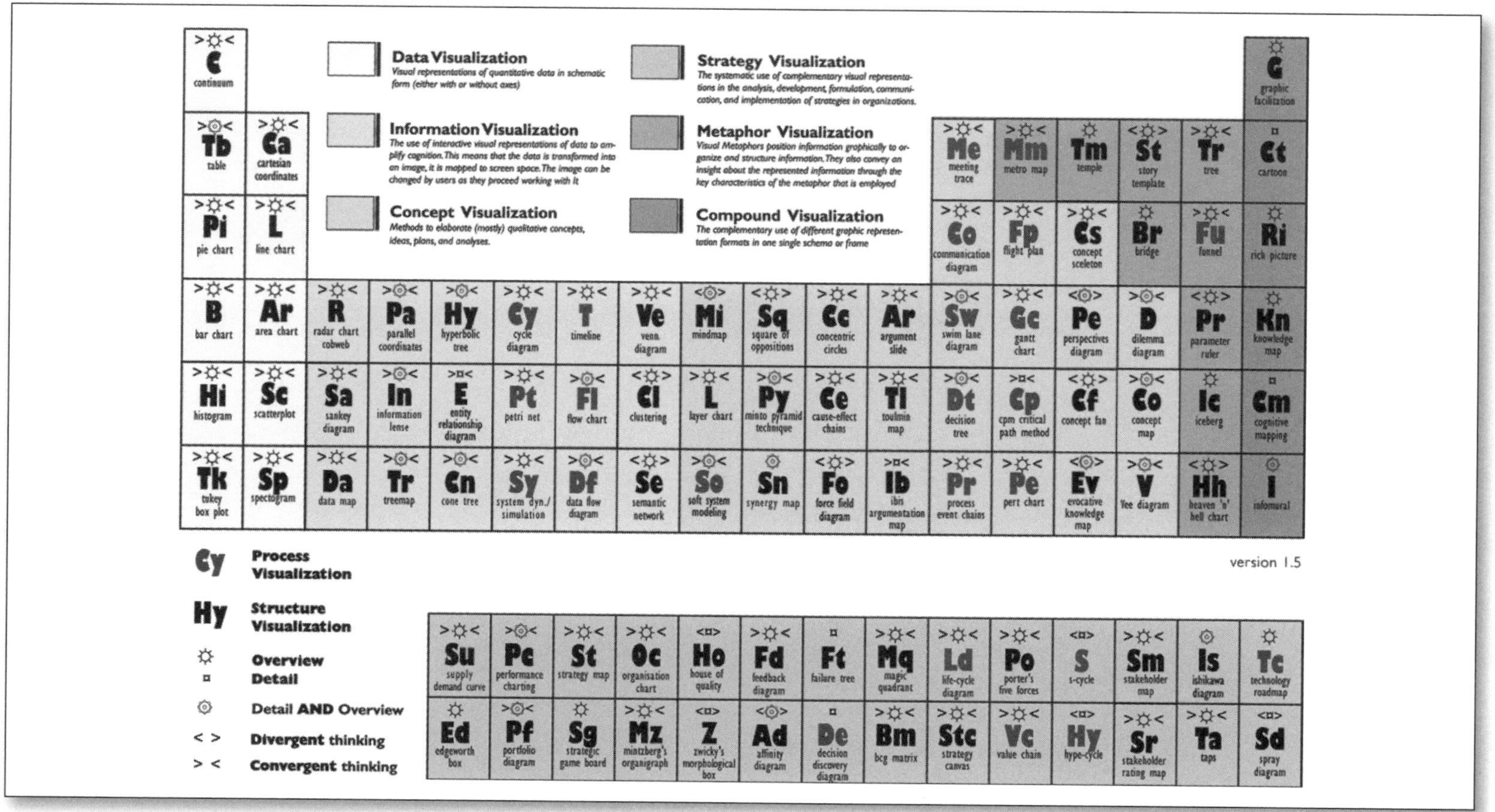

Note: Depending on your location and connection speed it can take some time to load a pop-up picture.

Source: © Lengler & Martin (2007).

Devil: A Mathematical Adventure (1998) by Hans Enzenberger, *The New Ways Things Work* (1998) by David Macaulay, and *The Arrival* (2007) by Shaun Tan.

Assessing visual literacy can be accomplished in a few different ways. When a student is drawing a diagram to illustrate what he has learned, a checklist or rubric that includes organization, labeling, and use of color will help him understand the grading criteria and also ensure consistency on the part of the teacher. Each specific subject area will have its own criteria and desired outcomes. For example, map reading requires content knowledge, comparison, interpretation, and analysis. Map drawing requires measurement, planning, and organization.

Written responses to visual images can be done using traditional criteria: opening sentence, organization of paragraphs, accuracy of content, and writing conventions. Students can also turn visual images into outlines and notes pages. This work can be done individually or collaboratively.

Many 21st century skills come into play in the interpretation of visual images. Methods of assessing each skill will vary depending on instructional standards, goals, objectives, and targets. Because these ideas are all rapidly emerging and changing, the suggestions made here for checklists and rubrics are very general and can be developed in more detail for specific visual assignments.

A checklist for students' use of visual texts may include the follow criteria:

- Considers the author's purpose in the use of visual techniques
- Interprets symbols used in the imagery
- Understands literal meaning and draws inferences
- Compares source to other resources on the same topic
- Draws on background knowledge to determine meaning
- Critically analyzes the work
- Translates images into written language in one's own words
- Creates a visual response to the work

For younger children, consider the following rubric criteria for a diagram:

- The diagram includes a clear heading that identifies the illustration.
- Parts of the diagram are clearly labeled.
- Connections between parts of the diagram are shown.
- Drawing is clearly done, making it easy to understand.
- Color is used appropriately to enhance the diagram.
- Additional brief and concise information to explain the diagram is available.

Assessment of a diagram of a cell or an engine could be done in a posted gallery of work that is peer reviewed with checklists and feedback. Visual messages are everywhere; incorporating them into teaching is an old idea that takes on a new importance in the contemporary world. It shouldn't be difficult for you to forge a path that makes use of them in your teaching.

Reflection

Predict how your students' lives will be different in the next decade as a result of increasing exposure to visual information and decreasing exposure to information conveyed in linear written form.

How do these predictions change your thinking about teaching?

In light of this, what will you do differently in your classroom and school?

TECHNOLOGY LITERACY

We shape our tools and afterwards our tools shape us.

— Marshall McLuhan

Many of the ideas surrounding the use of technology captivate digital immigrants, yet are taken for granted by digital natives. When the automobile was invented, visionaries saw it as a new way to get from here to there. Yet, others were unshakable in their belief that the horseless carriage was but another youthful folly. Technology and its applications are growing boundlessly. Futurists see a time when a thought can be directly translated from your brain into a written line of text or when people anywhere in the world can talk face to face, in person, in real time. Perhaps brain mining, molecular replicators, and time travel aren't that far away.

Given the multifaceted nature of contemporary technology, recent advances have resulted in research and publications on a vast array of educationally important subtopics. These come from groups such as the U.S. Department of Education's National Education Technology Plan, the International Society for Technology in Education (ISTE), and the Science, Technology, Engineering, and Math (STEM) Education Coalition. Emerging technologies support online learning, virtual worlds, social networking, and more. In this section, we will first consider how to use technology as a tool to support and extend learning in the classroom and then how to assess these practical applications.

But are our students the same as the students of a decade ago? Some question whether technology is changing our brains. According to the Kaiser Family Foundation Study (Rideout, Foehr, & Roberts, 2010), today's

8- to 18-year-olds are spending 8 to 10 hours a day interfacing with media in the form of TV programs, music, and computer and video games through the use of MP3 devices, cell phones, and computers. Nicholas Carr in *The Shallows* (2010) explains that deep reading of texts is being replaced by cursory, distracted thinking and superficial learning. In these mental shallows, we briefly interface and quickly multitask with information from a wide range of sources. He believes that this constant bombardment by stimuli is changing the way our brains interface with and process information. When we read a book, we control the pace. When we "read" the Internet, there are new stimuli constantly popping on the screen and many attractive images to draw our attention. He believes that this blast of information interferes with the brain's ability to process and transfer fine points from working memory to long-term memory. Gary Small (2009) at UCLA monitored the brains of learners as they performed a web search and again as they read a page of text. He found that digital natives (students born into a technology-based world) are better at multitasking and short-term decision making but less capable of complex reasoning and emotional aptitudes such as empathy.

When students are surveyed about their technology use, there is no denying that they are involved and adept. Social networking is the way they share and collaborate. By high school, nearly 70% report using social networking to communicate about school work. Twenty percent report using blogs and wikis, and about 10% videoconference. Outside of school, these numbers all increase by 10% to 20%. The use of technology is widespread, with 25% playing games, 70% downloading videos, and an equal number posting photos and videos. When asked about the value of technology for learning, the majority agreed that they would use and learn from online resources such as games and videos. Seventy-six percent said it would increase their engagement, and over 50% said it would help them develop critical thinking skills and creativity (Project Tomorrow, 2010).

At the same time that dramatic technological and social changes are occurring, research continues to illuminate what good teaching looks like: clear targets, effective and engaging instruction, higher-level questioning, applied learning, and embedded formative assessments. These techniques for effective teaching can and should be coordinated with new technologies so that each supports the other.

Defining Technology Literacy

Standards

The explosion in the creation and sharing of information and knowledge is changing the teacher's role from that of a deliverer of information to that of a conductor of learning who helps students reflect on and apply what they learn. If we consider learning as a space station rather than a train ride, then students need the fuel, safety nets, and docking stations to manage their learning using emerging technologies.

Therefore, assessment must also be flexible. Multiple methods using multiple modalities will give students opportunities to demonstrate their skills and knowledge in compound ways. Rather than a selected-choice test, students will use technology to apply their learning to the design of products, story building, creation of artifacts, and collaborative results.

Technology will both guide and track learning and support assessments that align with Common Core and technology standards. The ISTE has identified technology standards for students: NETS (National Education Technology Standards). A crosswalk in Figure 6.15 shows alignment between ISTE and the CCSS.

Figure 6.15   Alignment Between NETS and Common Core State Standards

Selected ISTE Student Standards	Related Common Core State Standards
1. *Creativity and Innovation* Generate new ideas and create original works.	*Writing* Use technology to produce and publish.
2. *Communication and Collaboration:* Interact, collaborate, and publish with peers employing a variety of digital environments and media. Communicate information and ideas effectively to multiple audiences using a variety of media and formats.	Speaking and Listening—Comprehension and Collaboration: Prepare for and participate effectively in a range of conversations and collaborations with diverse partners. *Writing–Production and Distribution:* Use technology, including the Internet, to produce and publish writing, and to interact and collaborate with others
3. *Research and Information Fluency:* Locate, organize, analyze, evaluate, synthesize, and ethically use information from a variety of sources and media. Process data and report results.	*Writing–Research to Build and Present Knowledge:* Gather relevant information from multiple print and digital sources, assess the credibility and accuracy of each source, and integrate information. *Speaking and Listening–Presentation of knowledge and ideas:* Use digital media and visual displays of data to express information and enhance understanding.
4. *Critical Thinking, Problem Solving, and Decision Making:* Collect and analyze data to identify solutions or make informed decisions.	*Speaking and Listening–Presentation of Knowledge and Ideas:* Make strategic use of digital media and visual displays to data to express information and enhance understanding of presentations. Math: Represent and interpret data.
5. *Digital Citizenship*	Slight connections
6. *Technology Operations and Concepts*	Slight connections

Skills

Each of the 21st century skills was defined in Chapter 2. A brief review of the technology skills is included here:

- Understands primary computer functions
- Utilizes multiple types of computer software, programs, and applications for selected purposes
- Enhances creativity by using appropriate and purposefully selected media and technologies
- Uses technology as tool to research, organize, evaluate, integrate, create, and communicate information
- Uses technology to produce, publish, write, and communicate and network with others
- Uses technology to identify and solve complex problems in real-world contexts
- Understands and considers legal and ethical issues in relation to the use of electronic technologies
- Continuously learns and critically evaluates emerging technologies

Tools

Technology is a tool to help learners reach specific goals. Such goals could include content knowledge, application of knowledge, synthesis of learning, collaboration with others, and creation and sharing of new ideas and products. So many technology tools are becoming available that an attempt to list them would be futile. The brief list in Figure 6.16 connects functions with selected technology tools.

In Practice

Classroom Ideas

Both teachers and students find technology-based learning relevant and engaging. Some examples at multiple grade and content levels are shown in Figure 6.17. Note that most of the technologies are generic descriptions (with a few exceptions, sites are noted) as the technologies and websites are changing more quickly than ever.

Consider the following also as you plan your use and assessment of technology:

- Participate in web collaborations.
- Produce interdisciplinary, real-world products.
- Promote an idea or product.
- Convey information using technology.
- Create a virtual tour.

Figure 6.16   Technology Tools

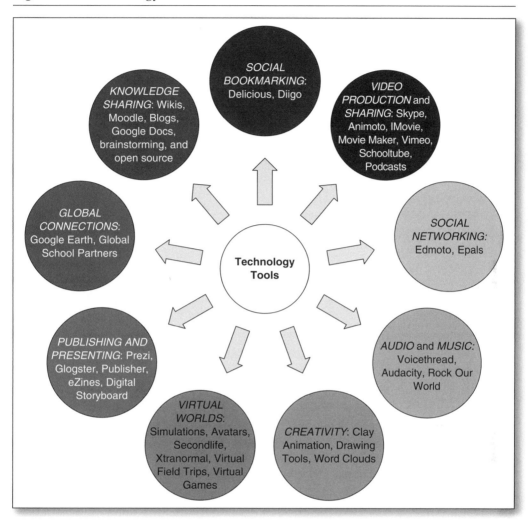

Figure 6.17   Multigrade Technology-Based Learning

Elementary	Technology-Based Learning	Technology
Kindergarten	Graph daily changes in weather.	Graph maker
1st-grade science	Sort toys and categorize their actions.	Interactive whiteboard
2nd-grade language arts	Post your story on the Internet.	Animoto, Zooburst
3rd-grade math	Calculate your profits from a lemonade stand.	Excel

(Continued)

Figure 6.17   (Continued)

Elementary	Technology-Based Learning	Technology
4th-grade science	Compare students' eating patterns.	Mypyramid.gov
5th-grade math	Create a shopping plan for best-priced school supplies.	Internet shopping
Upper Elementary	Map your neighborhood.	Design and drawing programs
Middle Elementary	Create a virtual tour of the planets.	Virtual sites
Middle Elementary	Add images and music to the "I Have a Dream" speech.	Movie maker/ slide show

Middle		
6th-grade language	Create a vocabulary-based crossword puzzle.	Puzzlemaker
7th-grade social studies	Create a digital story about immigrants.	Digital Tablet
8th grade math	Build bridges.	CAD
Middle School	Create an ad to promote healthy eating.	Publishing Tools
Middle School	Hold a videoconference on a global issue.	Global Connections
Middle School	Talk with an author.	Skype

Secondary		
9th-grade social studies	Plan and take a virtual trip to another country.	Google Earth
10th-grade math	Calculate your carbon footprint.	Carbon footprint website
11th-grade tech ed	Copyright scavenger hunt.	Internet webquest
12th-grade	Track college application process.	Naviance
High School	Write a digital story for an elementary reading buddy.	Storyboard

- Produce an e-zine.
- Re-create a period in history.
- Identify three ways to display the structure of DNA; use one to create a replica.
- Design a museum.
- Create an electronic game.
- Create a simulation of life on another planet.

Assess these products with

- rubrics (a generic technology literacy rubric is in Appendix A);
- checklists;
- student contracts;
- learning logs;
- thinking and acting logs and journals;
- peer and self-assessment;
- observations, anecdotal evidence, student conferences;
- portfolios of work; and
- storytelling.

It's the time of year for Mr. Roy's high school English class to participate in Read Across America. Every year, they select children's books and partner with a community elementary school. This year, they decided to write their own books and present them electronically. The day, sponsored by the National Education Association, is a celebration of the life work of Dr. Seuss, or Theodor Geisel. Mr. Roy's goal for the high school students is to analyze the way social issues are incorporated into Dr. Seuss stories. The students' goal for the younger children is to build vocabulary and rhyming skills. Students in the class first learn about children's literature and developmental reading skills. Then, they begin to plan their work. An example of a planner is presented in Figure 6.18.

Assessment of the plan includes teacher feedback on completeness, detail, and feasibility. Students then write their stories following guidelines that Mr. Roy gives them for writing children's books. They first draw a storyboard mockup that is displayed anonymously in a gallery format for peer review using the form in Figure 6.19.

Figure 6.18 Plan for Digital Story Writing

What stories did I like as a child and why?	What are three highly rated books today? Why are they recognized?
What are two story ideas I have now?	What factors should I consider in selecting one story/topic/theme?
How can I learn more about writing a children's book?	What's my first step in writing my story?
What technology can I use to produce it?	How can I learn more about the technology and see examples of it?

Figure 6.19   Peer Review of Digital Story Plan

Rating criteria	Comments (please include specific and constructive feedback)
Is the content age-appropriate?	
Is the story kid-friendly?	
Is the length/difficulty of words appropriate?	
Is the length of the book feasible for the children and the time allotted for its design?	
Do the illustrations fit the story?	
Are the illustrations kid-friendly?	
What do you recommend for software?	

Since Mr. Roy is not an expert in digital publishing software, he invites someone with more knowledge into his classroom. She shows the students free and open source software, including Microsoft Photo Story, which lets the student create slideshows from digital photos and images; iMovie does the same for Apple computers, and Windows Movie Maker is a video editing software application. She also shows them Audacity for adding sound. In addition, some students have taken the school's digital imaging class, so they are familiar with Photoshop and willing to help others use it.

Students then spend several class sessions converting their ideas into a digital story. The story is teacher- and self-evaluated with the rubric in Figure 6.20. Note that this rubric only concerns the technology skills used in the project. Other skills such as writing and presenting are incorporated into the final student rubric.

The importance of assessing technology literacy that is embedded in learning is crucial. Yet, in the real world, every worker does not use the same technologies every day. Technologies are selected and used for

Figure 6.20   Rubric for Technology Application

Skill/ Knowledge	Exemplary	Proficient	Basic	Novice	Score
Knows computer-based technologies	I demonstrate excellence in a wide variety of computer products and technology-based productivity tools and routinely integrate them into my work.	I am competent in using multiple computer and technology products and tools to enhance productivity.	I can use a variety of technology tools and perform basic tasks to support my productivity.	I'm on a learning curve in developing my computer competencies.	
Digital and multimedia products	I confidently use graphic images, video, sound, and other multimedia features to strengthen my story.	I can incorporate digital and multimedia items such as graphics, video, and sound in my work to support the story.	I can add images or other features to my work, but they don't always align with the story.	I'm just learning to use one or two multimedia features and want to be better able to incorporate them in my work.	
Design	My design is truly multimedia and includes a number of well-designed objects and elements.	My design contains some appropriate objects and elements to support my purpose.	My design is limited in several elements, thus compromising its quality and relevance.	I can make few choices of objects and elements to add design elements to my work.	
Selection and use	My use of technology shows deep understanding and proficiency that strengthens my work. I am able to choose the most appropriate technologies for complex, authentic problems.	My routine use of technology shows that I understand it and can incorporate it in my presentations. I can usually select relevant technologies.	I've been using technology more regularly to support my learning and improve my presentations. I sometimes rely on what others tell me to use.	I think if I use just one technology at a time it will improve my presentations, but sometimes I'm not sure which one to use.	

What were your strengths, what worked well, how did technology support your work, what would you do differently next time?

Teacher feedback:

Student self-reflection:

specific purposes. As in the real world, the assessment of technology skills in the classroom also needs to be customized. Some groups are working toward this personalized assessment of technology.

ISTE and the National Assessment of Educational Progress (NAEP) are working together to develop a Technology Literacy Assessment to measure students' ability to understand technology tools and principles, use and design information and communication technology, and connect ethical decisions, social interactions, and their consequences. This interactive test requires students to make decisions, analyze data, and predict outcomes in a variety of content areas and situations.

The Virtual Performance Assessment Center at Harvard Graduate School of Education is designing virtual worlds that assess science inquiry skills and problem-solving abilities. The use of responsive and adaptive technology for assessment is also growing. Students taking tests on the computer can get instant feedback and opportunities for correction. Teachers quickly receive an analysis that highlights strengths and areas in need of improvement. Other assessment programs are being developed that can adjust to a student's knowledge, skills, and test-taking abilities as they take the test.

At the same time that these national, virtual, and adaptive measures are being developed, it is necessary for teachers to use and assess technology in their classrooms. Meaningful, professional development and strong tech support are crucial. The result will be learners who are engaged, self-directed, and take increased responsibility for learning.

Reflection

On a scale of 1 to 10, where are your technology skills now?

1	2	3	4	5	6	7	8	9	10

On a scale of 1 to 10, where would you like your technology skills to be?

1	2	3	4	5	6	7	8	9	10

What are three steps you will take to improve your technology skills?

Describe three ways that you can take an existing lesson plan/learning outcome and embed technology in it.

How would you assess the learning outcomes?

FINAL CONSIDERATIONS

Schools are doing their best to keep up with the rapid changes in the world. This was made real to me recently when I watched a 2-year-old pretend to take a cell phone out of her pocket, press a button in her palm, and say, "Hello, hello?" Then I listened to an 8-year-old complain that the upcoming trip would be boring if he had to watch the same video in the car as his sister. That evening, I attended a school board meeting where visual novels were being adopted for inclusion in the English curriculum. I challenge you to consider how schools will meet the needs of incoming kindergarteners who bring advanced social networking and technology skills to the classroom and expect to use them daily. All of the skills in this chapter build on core knowledge and use that knowledge to be productive citizens of the 21st century. How will you respond to these changes?

Reflection	
For each skill, describe a way you would apply it in your school or classroom.	
Communication	
Collaboration	
Digital Literacy	
Visual Literacy	
Technology Literacy	

(Continued)

(Continued)

Select one or more of the 21st century skills from the chart above and elaborate in the chart below. One example is given to get you started.

Common Core	21st Century	Learning Strategy	Assessment
Literacy/Writing: Produce clear and coherent writings in which the development, organization, and style are appropriate to the task, purpose, and audience.	Communication and technology: write, revise, illustrate and publish original poetry in a particular style.	Write using an ipad, revise with scribble, and post on the web.	Common Core: writing, organization, style, and audience 21st C Skills: learning contract and plan, self- and peer review, applied technology rubric

7

Assessing Skills for Living in the World

> *The illiterate of the 21st century will not be those who cannot read and write, but those who cannot learn, unlearn, and relearn.*
>
> — Alvin Toffler

Think a moment about the skills that students will need for living in the world, not just for today but for a tomorrow that we cannot completely imagine. There are books written about living on your own, but for the most part, they focus on day-to-day routines of managing your money, seeking a job, finding a place to live, and maintaining a car. These are important skills for independent living today, but they are more about personal proficiencies than living in the larger world. Futurists envision many possibilities, from cities in space and robotic homes to futuristic jobs such as nanodecontaminator. While these predictions and proposals are certainly innovative, they generally lack concrete details on the knowledge and skills that will be necessary to live successfully in such a world. Global and civic skills, college and career readiness, and personal responsibility top the list for most 21st century educational thinkers.

Throughout this book, reference has been made to the Common Core and other content standards. It's easy to see how civic skill fits into the social studies curriculum, but most of the other skills for living in the world do not have a clear place in today's schools. The framers of the CCSS acknowledge that they "do not describe all that can or should be taught. A great deal is left to the discretion of teachers and curriculum developers" (Common Core State Standards Initiative [CCSSI], 2011b). They go on to explain that while literacy is critical to college and career readiness, it involves much more complexity than the standards can address.

CIVIC AND CITIZENSHIP SKILLS

> *Only a knowledgeable, empowered and vocal citizenry can perform well in democracy.*
>
> — David Brin

In 2010, the National Assessment of Educational Progress (NAEP; 2011) test in civics was administered to students in Grades 4, 8, and 12. In comparison to 2006, scores rose slightly in the fourth grade, remained flat in the eighth, and went down in Grade 12. Knowledge of the Constitution and the form and function of government was not strong in American's youth. These topics are part of the curriculum but are not universally tested and therefore not highly valued beyond the local curriculum. In general, civics classes follow a curriculum that emphasizes content knowledge over genuine application.

The Center for Information and Research on Civic Learning and Engagement at Tufts University uses data to illuminate trends in adolescent and young adult engagement in civic discourse and issues. Their studies in high schools show the good news that civic understanding can be explicitly taught, resulting in improved civic knowledge and engagement (www.civicyouth.org).

The value of civic engagement has been shown to improve voter participation; to increase understanding, tolerance, and respect for others; and to foster an appreciation that everyone can make a contribution. Role models at home are certainly an important part of this, but schools also have a responsibility to prepare an educated citizenry.

Defining Citizenship

Generic definitions of citizenship generally include the following ideas: Civics is the study of the roles, rights, and duties of citizens. It develops the knowledge and skills necessary to carry out one's role as a citizen. It informs students of civic matters and issues, and encourages and supports participation in civic engagement. It includes education in the theory and practice of government. In some places, it emphasizes the ideals of democracy, but many others believe it is about also understanding multiple forms of government.

Earlier in this book, a compilation and synthesis of ideas on civic responsibility and citizenship identified the following aspects:

- Understands the political structure and process of a democratic form of government
- Compares this to the governmental structures of other countries
- Understands the structure, function, and processes of democratic institutions
- Is willing to participate in and actively participates in the democratic process
- Makes connections at the community, local, state, national, and international levels
- Develops core civic dispositions such as justice, equality, and personal responsibility
- Respects the diversity of perspectives on justice and personal responsibility
- Works toward improving the quality of life for all individuals
- Recognizes the role of institutions in policy making
- Knows how to access and interface with policy-making groups at the local, state, national, and global levels
- Is aware of the connection between local decisions and global implications
- Acts in ways that demonstrate understanding of civic responsibilities
- Accepts responsibility for actions that infringe on other's rights
- Contributes to the well-being of others

In Practice

Mr. Williams begins by asking his students to define citizenship and brainstorm on why it is important for people to know about the government and the responsibilities of citizenship. Afterward, students take a pretest on core civic knowledge. The test results show an average score of 50%—not dissimilar from NAEP scores. Students look up and correct the questions they got wrong. They work in small groups to help each other and also to generate a list of three reasons why this information is important to know.

They then become civic ambassadors and work in groups to research civic information and create a campaign to inform their peers about the importance of civic knowledge and civic responsibility. The campaign must include a technology component. This could be an Edmoto (Facebook-type page), a blog, an electronic poster or brochure, a webinar, or something similar. Required content in the product includes strong defense of the importance of civic knowledge, eight essential talking points, and at least four ways for students to get involved.

Multiple assessments, geared to goals and learning targets, can occur throughout this process. Several examples of assessment of student contracts and written plans that have appeared throughout this book can be adapted to this assignment. Students can maintain learning logs during their work. Feedback and opportunities for revision are typically incorporated. When their products are complete, the class presents its work to an assembly of students taking a civics class. The students in the assembly complete a peer assessment as shown in Figure 7.1.

In response to the research on student civic engagement and studies that show skimpy civic knowledge, the social studies teachers in one school held a roundtable Professional Learning Community in which they brainstormed strategies to engage students in the local and greater community. They came up with many ideas for development and action that were then presented to the students, and the students added some of their own:

- Tweet about current events.
- Design a campaign for a candidate running for public office.
- Meet with government representatives to identify important issues and develop an action plan and, if feasible, follow through with the plan.
- Prepare skits on historic government figures and present them to elementary school students in character.
- Pursue service learning opportunities in the curriculum such as volunteering at the senior center, cleaning up a historic cemetery in town, or raising money for a cause.
- Hold topic days where, in small groups, students research a current civic or political topic and present it to their classmates: services for seniors, health care for poor children, the justice system, etc.

These activities can be assessed in various ways depending on the relevant standards and objectives. Tweets can be assessed for accuracy and conciseness. Political campaigns can be assessed for a knowledge and action component as well as for their use of technology applications. Scripts for skits can be assessed on literacy skills as well as on research and creativity. Activities related to current events can be connected to the CCSS in reading and writing and also be assessed for presentation skills. Informative and persuasive writing, as well as reading for information and evaluating arguments, can all be taken into account in assessment. Teachers can decide which CCSS are the best match for their grade levels and content areas. All of them can use the common civics rubric in Figure 7.2.

Figure 7.1   Peer Assessment of a Civics Presentation

Rate each presentation on a 1–4 scale, with 4 being the best, and explain your answer.

How Did They Do? Explain Your Ratings.	Group 1	Group 2	Group 3	Group 4
I know more now about civics than I did before.				
The ideas presented made sense and were easy to follow.				
The presentation gave me ideas for something that I would like to know more about or even try to change.				
The presentation persuaded me to get involved.				

What I liked best about each group:

1.

2.

3.

4.

Next time I recommend that they

1.

2.

3.

4.

Complete for each group: Two things I learned and/or the two most important facts.

1.

2.

1.

2.

1.

2.

1.

2.

Figure 7.2   Civic and Citizenship Rubric

Skill/ Knowledge	Exemplary	Proficient	Basic	Novice	Score/ Weight
Understands democracy and governments	I can recognize, evaluate, and compare a variety of political forms and structures.	I understand that there are multiple political forms and structures and can explain some.	If I have an outline or a graphic format, I can put together basic comparisons.	I know there are differences between forms of government, but I need help explaining them.	
Participates in the democratic process Contributes to improvement	I make a meaningful contribution to my classroom and community in advancing the democratic process.	I get involved in activities when they are presented and when opportunities become available.	With a poke, I will participate in activities that are part of a democratic action.	I generally prefer to observe rather than get involved.	
Civic dispositions and behaviors	Through my actions I demonstrate my beliefs in equality and personal responsibility and understand the effects of these actions.	I believe in civic involvement and usually am respectful of the rights and differences of others.	For the most part, I believe in equality and generally am respectful of others.	I have a hard time respecting people who are different than me and accepting those differences.	

Reflection

All grade levels and subject areas have occasions for civic learning. Think about your school and jot down potential opportunities and assessments.

Core and Content Standards	Civic Learning Ideas	Assessment

GLOBAL UNDERSTANDING

> *If we are to teach peace and understanding in this world, we shall have to begin with the children.*
>
> — Mahatma Gandhi

Since the beginning of time, groups and cultures have sought to understand each other. When this effort has failed, conflict has frequently been the result. How it came to be that global awareness is equated with the study of world languages is perplexing, but in most schools, that is the area of the curriculum where it is most emphasized. But global understanding involves more than studying another language—it's about using cultural awareness to recognize, respect, and accept the interdependence of all countries and cultures.

Defining Global Understanding

Fernando Reimers (2009) defines *global understanding* as "the knowledge and skills to help people understand the flat world in which they live, integrate across disciplinary domains to comprehend global affairs and events, and create possibilities to address them" (p. 184). Other definitions refer to the attitudes and principles that make it possible to interact with people from around the globe in ways that are intentionally peaceful, respectful, and productive. When students develop global understanding, they recognize that issues span national boundaries and can see that the world is highly interconnected in numerous ways: economically, politically, ecologically, technologically, and more. An important outcome of global understanding is that although cultures view life differently, there are common needs and wants, and when we view the world through the eyes of others, we can better see their views—and they ours.

John Dewey recognized this after his travels to Asia in the 1920s. He expected that teachers and students could use common global perspectives to become more tolerant of similarities and differences. His ideal of a pluralistic society can be maintained through interactions with different perspectives that result in global understanding.

Yong Zhao (2009) is a contemporary spokesman for these ideas when he says,

> A basic truth about living in the global village is that the welfare of all human beings has become so interconnected and interdependent that no individual, organization, or nation can continue to live

prosperously when their fellow villagers live in misery. A major challenge for education is to empower students to start with the genuine difficulty of establishing common ground. (p. 60)

As with other 21st century skills, it is possible to make connections to the CCSS. The reading and writing standards build knowledge of global issues. Communication and collaboration is the foundation for global understanding. The following standards illustrate some of these connections:

- Reading: Consider how and why individuals, events, and ideas develop and interact over the course of the text.
- Reading: Assess how point of view or purpose shapes the content and style of a text.
- Writing: Use technology to produce and publish writing and interact and collaborate with others.
- Speaking and listening: Prepare for and participate in a range of conversations with diverse partners.

From a deeper perspective, it could also be proposed that a student's global understanding should include the following:

- Learns with people from diverse cultures in personal, work, and community settings
- Respects cultural, lifestyle, and religious differences
- Is informed about the global connections in politics, economics, society, history, technology, language, and the environment
- Recognizes, analyzes, and evaluates ongoing and emerging global trends, issues, and challenges
- Participates in and makes a contribution to the global society
- Understands the history, foundations, and traditions of one's own and other cultures
- Appreciates the differences and similarities between cultures and recognizes how each can contribute to progress
- Demonstrates awareness and sensitivity to the way cultural beliefs, behaviors, values, and sensibilities affect the way people think and act
- Values human rights and equality and is sensitive to the issues of bias, racism, prejudice, and stereotyping
- Adopts the perspective of people from other cultures
- Is conversant in languages in addition to English

In Practice

At the big picture level, there is a need to shift from a locally focused curriculum to a globally oriented one. There are numerous opportunities for students to learn about and interact with people from around the globe. Partnerships and exchanges provide opportunities for both cultures to learn. Figure 7.3 highlights some ideas using rubrics and assessment methods from throughout this book.

Figure 7.3   Global Learning

Topic by Grade	Common Core State Standards	Learning Strategy	Assessment
Elementary School			
Children in Other Cultures: Global brochures	Reading, writing (Use technology to publish writing)	Create a paper or electronic "brochure" about children in other cultures.	Research, writing, and technology rubrics
Communicating Around the World: Electronic pen pals (Epals.com)	Write for a purpose. Pick a project (e.g., map reading, storytelling, biodiversity) and align selected standards with it.	Communicate and collaborate with others on the chosen topic.	Content assessment (reading, science. etc.), communication, collaboration with learning logs, peer assessment
Middle School			
Fair Trade Analysis: Who gets how much of the dollar?	Math (calculations, spreadsheet, profit calculations)	Make feasible recommendations for fairer trade practices. Write a letter to Congress.	Math calculations, Checklist for writing: use facts to support a position
Cultural Icons: Place capsules (like time capsules)	Integrate knowledge from diverse sources, research, writing, social studies	Create a place capsule with writings and icons of a culture.	Self-assessment on synthesis of research, accuracy of items, creativity
High School			
Multinational Conference: Food and Culture (globaleducation.ning.com)	Write informative texts, science, research, critical thinking	Display (poster or electronic) on how food science can support the global food chain	Rubrics for technology, research, writing, presentation
Global Summit: Sharing Concerns	Participate in a range of conversations with diverse partners.	Prepare for and present a summit that enlightens the school about global concerns.	Content knowledge, peer assessment of research, collaboration, presentation

Assessment for these activities can include pre- and post-tests, journaling and reflections, logs of participation in community-based multicultural activities, and a portfolio of evidence of learning about cultures.

At the Mandela School, Mr. Carlos begins his global studies unit with an interest survey. Based on these, students search the Internet for more information on topics of interest to them. When they become intrigued by the United Nations Millennium Development Goals (United Nations Development Programme, 2010), they collectively decide that this is of interest to the whole class. In small groups, they explore one of the eight goals, and then each group creates and presents a fact sheet for the other groups. The eight development goals are

- educate every child,
- provide equal chances for girls and women,
- reduce the number of children who die,
- ensure the health and safety of motherhood,
- fight infectious diseases,
- eradicate extreme poverty and hunger,
- clean up the environment, and
- share responsibility for making the world a better place.

Mr. Carlos checks their understanding through a gallery posting. Each student uses sticky notes to post two things learned about each topic. In a second round, students use sticky notes of a different color to give feedback on the postings. The postings are anonymous on the front with names on the back. Mr. Carlos checks these for understanding and gives individual feedback. The class then regroups for a Socratic Seminar. Together, the class picks their top four goals, then divides into study groups on each and prepares for the seminar.

Basic rules of the seminar are as follows:

- Stay focused on the topic and avoid side conversations.
- Read and be prepared to cite text sources to support your statements with logical arguments.
- Reflectively listen and thoughtfully consider all perspectives.
- Take turns when stating your ideas and responding respectfully to others.

The class holds two seminars. The first is with the first two goals that were selected, and members of those groups form a circle of chairs. Around them, in an outer circle, the other two groups are the observers and assessors. In the circle, each group presents its explanations for why its goal is most important and actions that need to be taken to support it. Each team is given questions to respond to and can add its own, such as Why is this the most important? How will it make a difference to the world? What steps will make it happen? The observers record each person's contribution, making notes on the use of text and data, listening skills, questioning, and respect. Mr. Carlos uses a Socratic Seminar rubric as in Figure 7.4 that assesses for reading, speaking, listening, and personal conduct. To assess global understanding, Mr. Carlos adjusts the generic global skills rubric in Figure 7.5. In addition, Students complete a self-assessment checklist/reflection based on these data points as shown in Figure 7.6.

Figure 7.4 Socratic Seminar Rubric

Skill/ Knowledge	Exemplary	Proficient	Basic	Novice	Score/ Weight
Speaking and reasoning	• Clearly responds to the question using evidence from multiple sources that logically connect ideas to actions	• Understands the question, uses at least one source of evidence to make reasonable recommendations	• Responds to the basic elements of a question • Uses data that are somewhat connected to the point	• Reluctant to participate • Contribution does not move the conversation forward	
Listening	• Attentive to others' ideas • Respectfully responds to digressions from the topic	• Generally pays attention to other's ideas and asks questions about them	• Singles out specific points rather than the big picture ideas	• Appears to be inattentive • Comments show misunderstanding of others' ideas	
Conduct and engagement	• Stays focused throughout • Demonstrates a high level of respect for different viewpoints • Moves the discussion forward	• Actively participates • Generally shows composure and respect • Is usually considerate of others' viewpoints	• Expresses own ideas but displays intolerance to others' ideas • Addresses only a few people	• Displays little respect for the learning process. • Unprepared to learn • Statements to others may be inappropriate	
Feedback and Comments:					

Figure 7.5   Rubric for Global Knowledge and Skills

Skill/ Knowledge	Exemplary	Proficient	Basic	Novice	Score/ Weight
Global issues	I can easily explain multiple historical and current issues and how they affect people around the world.	I have a good idea of issues that are happening around the globe and can explain some in detail.	I can name one or two global issues that concern me and others.	I don't pay attention to what is happening in the world.	
Cultural understanding	I am very knowledgeable about multiple cultural beliefs, values, and customs that typically influence the way people act and behave toward others.	I have some knowledge of selected cultures' beliefs, values, and customs that relate to and contribute to others' actions and behavior.	I am aware that culture is part of one's life, but in general my understanding and awareness is slim.	I'm really not interested in learning about and other cultures and prefer to stick to my own.	
Contributes in and to the global society	I have worked constructively with people from other cultures and work hard to learn and understand their experiences and views. I have participated in activities that make the world a better place.	I am able to communicate with people from other cultures. Sometimes I reach out to others beyond my own world.	When urged, I will work with people who are different from me but don't have much interest in contributing to this.	I have difficulty working with people from other cultures and groups and would prefer not to participate in larger initiatives.	
Perspective taking	Understands the complexity of culture and has adequate knowledge to effectively see the viewpoints of other cultures	In the context of history, understands that other groups may have a different perspective on events	Needs some support to see that there are different perspectives and ways of looking at things	Unable to understand that other groups have different views of the same events	
Student Reflection:					
Teacher Feedback:					

Figure 7.6   Checklist With Self-Assessment/Reflection

LEARNING OUTCOME: Rate yourself on a 1–4 scale on each.	
READING: I read at least three sources and used them in my presentations. Rating:	What sources did you use? Describe how you applied what you learned from them.
SOCRATIC SEMINAR: I was prepared, presented knowledgeably, and participated respectfully. Rating:	Explain your rating with specific support for each element.
CIVIC LEARNING: I can show that I understand global issues and other cultures, tried to make the world a better place, and showed respect for other viewpoints. Rating:	What do you think are the two most important global issues and why? What did you learn about other cultures? How will you continue to contribute to making the world a better place? Describe a view or belief that your culture has and explain how it is different from another's.

At the conclusion of the unit on knowledge and skills, Mr. Carlos's students participate in a continuum activity. He puts a string on the floor across the room. He reads a statement and asks students to place themselves on the continuum to indicate their degree of agreement. For example,

- If people were treated more equally, we would have fewer problems in the world.
- I believe that I can make a difference in the lives of others.
- I often think about how my personal decisions affect the welfare of others.

He uses student response as a closing activity to the unit and then reflects on how he might do it differently next time.

Reflection

Select a civic learning outcome that you would like to incorporate in your school or classroom.

- What civic and global topics relate to your classroom, content area, or school?
- How will you learn more about it?
- How will you share what you learned with others and persuade them of its importance?
- What steps will you take to help students develop global understanding?

LEADERSHIP AND RESPONSIBILITY

Leadership is practiced not so much in words as in attitude and in actions.

— Harold S. Geneen

Originally, this section was called just "Leadership." Although every student may not ascend to the highest levels of leadership, it seems reasonable to expect all students to exhibit personal responsibility. Sometimes a student's quietness can be mistaken for lack of leadership, but I have seen many students who are calmly observant in the classroom rather than boisterously engaged. Often, these are excellent students who work conscientiously at learning. They do well on a variety of assessments and produce excellent authentic products. These students are influential during group work and are looked up to by their peers. It is their sense of responsibility, perseverance, and work ethic that sustains their achievement and makes them role models and leaders.

Defining Leadership and Responsibility

Classic definitions of leadership include the terms *visionary*, *relationship building*, *knowledgeable*, *collaborative*, and *tactical*. These attributes are used to move the goals of a group forward as leaders structure the work, delegate, and support their group. In a classroom, student leaders may display some of these characteristics differently. It may be the student who, in a group, gently points out that they are off task and refocus the members. The leader may be the one who celebrates the achievements of others, or it may be the student who is willing to help others master challenging material. They are essentially good role models who work hard, care about their peers, and enable others to succeed.

Leadership and responsibility correlate with other 21st century skills such as communication, collaboration, and problem solving. Additionally, a leader

- recognizes and appreciates the role of the individual in contributing to the greater good;
- sets priorities and goals and takes steps to actively achieve them;
- uses interpersonal skills to work with, guide, and assist others toward a common goal;
- influences others with integrity and ethics;
- makes decisions that improve outcomes for the group;
- takes personal responsibility for success and failure;
- plans strategically and purposefully;
- manages time, resources, and personal skills to maximize productivity; and
- negotiates to seek acceptable outcomes.

In Practice

Opportunities for student leadership arise in the classroom. Young children may have daily responsibilities in the classroom such as calendar organizer or supply manager. In a project-based class, students can be accountable for specific components of the project's design, development, and presentation. Leadership can be incorporated into community service projects in which each student has a role such as researcher, synthesizer, publisher, public relations, or event planner. Students can plant trees, create a community time capsule, cook for seniors, develop a recycling program, or collect items for a women's shelter, the military, or the children of women in prison. When these activities are truly student generated, then leadership opportunities naturally emerge.

Students can also be explicitly taught about leadership. Reading Sean Covey's (1998) book and understanding the concept of win–win builds a strong foundation for leadership. Teamwork activities such as untangling a human knot or building straw structures get students to work together. Afterward they can identify how each person's leadership helped the group achieve its goals. Studying successful leaders and analyzing their beliefs and actions are other learning strategies.

The teachers at Lincoln Middle School decide to teach leadership through literature. Together, the teachers generate a list to choose from. Some teachers decide to have their whole class read the same book, while others differentiate choices or let each student select a book. Titles include

- *Bless Me, Ultima* (Anaya, 1994): Tony is influenced by an old medicine woman, learns about himself, and develops an understanding of the world.
- *The Chocolate War* (Cormier, 2004): Theme of this book is the choice between following a group or exercising personal integrity and leadership.
- *Stealing Freedom* (Carbone, 2002): A young slave girl leads and follows others in her escape on the Underground Railroad.
- *Inkheart* (Funke, 2003): A girl, whose father who can turn fictional characters into real life, is abducted by one of them and must escape.
- *Nory Ryan's Song* (Giff, 2001): A girl helps her family and community survive during the Irish potato famine.
- *Gifted Hands: The Story of Ben Carson* (Murphey, 1996): An inspiration story of neurosurgeon Ben Carson, who overcomes many obstacles to achieves his life goals.

Also available are nonfiction works including biographies of individuals such as Ben Franklin, Amelia Earhart, Nelson Mandela, Sir Edmund Hillary, Winston Churchill, and Eleanor Roosevelt.

During their reading, students keep a log of examples of leadership along with their personal thoughts and connections. They research any misunderstandings or discrepancies between their beliefs and what they have read. They also maintain a vocabulary list of frequently used and new words related to leadership. At the conclusion of the literacy part of this project, they create visual representations of what leadership means to them using a selected technology This part of the project can be assessed using the Common Core literacy standards with conventional measures of

- skill at interpreting texts, identifying central themes, analysing literary characters;
- understanding of meaning of words, structure of texts, and author's purpose;
- ability to convey ideas in writing and to use technology as a publishing tool; and
- ability to analyze accuracy of information and support analysis through credible sources.

The last part of the CCSS, related to the use of technology, leads the way to demonstrations of knowledge. For this part, students select and design an application of what they have learned such as the following:

- Creating a leadership guide for other students based on the readings
- Developing a slide show on leadership including essential knowledge, skills, and examples
- Creating and publishing a blog, a wiki, or a webpage on the topic.

Throughout their work, students keep a leadership log like the one in Figure 7.7. At the end of the unit, students and teachers use the rubric in Figure 7.8 to complete a summative assessment and make recommendations for future learning.

Figure 7.7   Leadership and Responsibility Log

Leadership Skills I Demonstrated	Example
I set goals.	
I developed and followed a workable time plan.	
I took personal responsibility for my work.	
I used resources, skills, and knowledge successfully.	
I worked with others to make decisions, work toward a common goal, make a positive contribution, and listen to others.	
The three most important things I learned about leadership are 1. 2. 3.	

Figure 7.8   Leadership and Responsibility Rubric

Skill/Knowledge	Exemplary	Proficient	Basic	Novice	Score/Weight
Interpersonal skills	Consistently listens to others' viewpoints, responds respectfully, and encourages others to higher achievement	Usually listens respectfully to others' ideas and works collaboratively with a variety of other people	At times listens to other viewpoints but sometimes shows disapproval of others' thoughts and actions	Rarely shows respect and often shows disdain for others' ideas and actions	
Shared goal setting and accomplishment	Routinely demonstrates personal responsibility and collaboration for setting priorities and achieving goals	Usually makes a positive contribution toward shared goals	Sometimes finds it challenging to work with others to establish and achieve goals	Needs support in order to work with others to set and accomplish goals	
Responsibility	Demonstrates sophisticated understanding of personal responsibility for own actions and their effect on others Acts in highly ethical ways	Acknowledges one's responsibility for actions and seeks to act in ethical ways in relation to self and others	Aware of the meaning of personal responsibility and with reminders can accept it and recognize the effect of choices on others	Struggles with the idea of personal responsibility and has difficulty monitoring actions	
Managing	Constructively manages time and resources to boost the productivity of the group	Uses time and resources effectively	When directed, can use time successfully and use selected materials	Confused by how to manage time and use resources effectively	
2 Commendations:					
1 Recommendation:					

Leadership skills build, step by step, over time. Through learning, reflection, and skill development, all students can have an opportunity to become classroom, school, and community leaders and responsible contributors to their world.

Reflection

- How would you rank leadership and responsibility in relation to creativity, technology, and collaboration skills in the 21st century? Put them in rank order from most to least important. With your Professional Learning Community, discuss similarities and differences.
- What are the most significant leadership and responsibility traits and skills for this generation of students? Why?
- How will you incorporate leadership and responsibility in your school and classroom? Describe three specific steps you will take in this direction.

COLLEGE AND CAREER/WORKPLACE SKILLS

Learning is what most adults will do for a living in the 21st century.

— S. J. Perelman

College and career readiness have become part of the national dialogue. Policy makers, school leaders, standards developers, and test makers all call for students to be college and career ready. Certainly, this begins with a good foundation in core areas, but academic knowledge is not enough. The ability to apply this knowledge is an essential gateway skill.

College and career readiness begins with the thinking skills described in Chapter 7. It is students who rise to higher levels of Bloom's taxonomy, solve problems, draw on their creativity, and are insightful into how they think and learn that display the requisite cognitive skills. The activities in Chapter 8—communication, collaboration, and technology expertise—build the workplace skills that employers value. Chapter 9 identifies skills for living in the world that are becoming more and more important in our worldwide economy: civic, global, and personal responsibility, and leadership abilities.

So why doesn't everyone go to college? Some say it is the difficult financial times that cause the high college dropout rate, but most of the literature describes a lack of readiness and a disconnect between skills learned in high school and skills needed in college. As the imperative to pass standardized tests increases, the emphasis on all the other college readiness skills decreases.

The Minnesota Road Map to College and Career Readiness identifies test scores as an indicator of college readiness (Postsecondary and Workforce Readiness Working Group, 2009). At the same time, the Harvard University Pathways to Prosperity study (Symonds, Schwartz, & Ferguson, 2011) points out that we are devoting all our college preparation efforts to the 40% of students who will successfully complete two to four years of college and forsaking those who will follow other career paths. Believing that there should be multiple pathways to success, they advocate providing other ways for young people to develop career credentials and occupationally relevant skills. The bottom line is that college and careers are both important.

Definitions

College ready: having the academic skills, abilities, and attributes to be prepared for any postsecondary education.

Career ready: having the knowledge, skills, and qualities to succeed in a career.

The CCSS for reading, writing, speaking, and listening provide a foundation for all students. As its authors explain, "The standards are aligned with college and work expectations . . . in English Language Arts and mathematics" (CCSSI, 2011a).

Many believe there are additional benchmarks of college and career readiness:

- Develops a plan for personal and professional growth
- Uses models of short- and long-term planning in relationship to life and career plans
- Applies skills, knowledge, dispositions, and capacities to personal and professional roles
- Recognizes that success comes from hard work and perseverance
- Takes personal responsibility for goal achievement
- Manages short- and long-term projects
- Adapts to the changing landscape of daily life, school, and the workplace
- Demonstrates a commitment to development of mastery and ongoing learning
- Contributes and supports others in meaningful productivity
- Works to overcome obstacles and develop expertise
- Commits to continuous change and growth

Workplace skills in the 21st century are changing, yet certain mind-sets and sensibilities necessary for being successful in life have endured. People always have been and will continue to be expected to work with others, communicate successfully, and complete assigned duties. Certainly, global-ization and technology are having a profound effect on skills required in the workplace. Emerging professions, particularly in information-based work require different skills than did more traditional occupations, such as factory work; the pace of change is increasing. Employers are increasingly seeking workers who show mastery of 21st century skills: those who can use technology for a purpose, solve problems, innovate, think critically, and are motivated to achieve. Communication and collaboration are essential. People who can contribute to the workplace through responsibility, time management, and goal orientation will be the most successful.

In Practice

The challenge lies in building these skills in students and assessing how well they've acquired them. The workplace skills of productivity, planning, and self-regulation can be used as instructional wrappers at all levels of schooling. From the early grades, establishing routines builds independence, projects require planning, and group work helps students learn to get along with others. These skills can be assessed with rubrics, feedback, journals, anecdotal records, and student contracts. In the fourth-grade contract-based assessment (Figure 7.9), the student and the teacher both review progress toward 21st century skills.

Student success plans are gaining popularity. Some models are simply a reiteration of test scores and grades, but they can also be more personal and extensive. The Windsor School has decided to start using them at the sixth-grade level and to continuously add to them through middle and high school. The plans are integrated into the weekly advisory program and are intended to support individualized achievement of goals, explora-tions of career pathways, and personal growth.

Content of the success plan include the following:

- Academic records
- Examples of best work
- Student reflections on strengths and areas for improvement
- Course selection that aligns with goals, skills, and interests
- Interest inventories and self-assessment
- Goal setting
- Plan of action for academic success
- Career exploration
- Postsecondary planning
- Internships and mentoring

The assessment of the plan is primarily formative (see Figure 7.10) and helps students and their mentors assess progress and plan next steps. Logs, journals, and reflections are also kept by each student. The success plan can be kept in paper folders or managed electronically.

Figure 7.9   Student Productivity Framework

Personal Productivity

During this week, my goals were _____

During this week, my personal productivity has been (rate from 1 [lowest] to 4 [highest]) _____. Explain why: _____

Something I did well was _____

Something that was frustrating was _____

Something that I can improve is _____

Community Productivity

During this week, my community productivity (includes communicating, collaborating, and contributing), has been (rate from 1 [lowest] to 4 [highest]) _____.

Explain why: _____

A good experience I had was _____

A frustrating experience was _____

Something I want to improve is _____

Student and Teacher Checklist

Rate each on a 1 to 4 scale with 4 being the highest.

Rating		*Evidence and Student Comments*	*Evidence and Teacher Comments*
	Followed plans		
	Used time productively		
	Resolved problems		
	Showed respect to others		
	Worked with others to improve productivity		

Figure 7.10   Success Plan Checklist

My Grades	How did I do this period?
	What am I proud of?
	What will I change next period?
Work Samples	Each sample is accompanied by a reflection that describes the work, summarizes the assignment, illuminates the outcomes, shares success, and makes recommendations for improvement.
Course Selection Work Pages	Final selection of courses Includes input from teachers, parents, mentors, and counselors based on student's goals.
Interest Inventories	Personal and career inventories are reviewed and analyzed.
	Students present how their plans relate to their interests and skills.
Goals	A goal-planning overview is completed.
	Records are maintained on achievement and growth toward goals.
Next Steps	What is my next step?
	What will I do next to reach my goals?

In Ms. Xao's class, students are studying and demonstrating readiness skills as they decide on a fund-raising project that relates to their math standards. One group is researching ideas, evaluating them against a set of criteria, and synthesizing them into a presentation to the class. Another is developing a public relations program to inform the community and engage them in the idea. Another is setting up a spreadsheet to track their finances. And another group is developing a long-range plan for the project. This fund-raiser can be done locally, right in their school, at the community level, or even at a global level as they interface with students in other countries. In addition to assessment of math, reading, writing, and research skills, Mrs. Xao uses a rubric to assess work ethic (see Figure 7.11). These interdisciplinary skills help students find meaning in their work, engage them, and make it real, relevant, and collaborative.

As the pace of change accelerates, as people trade televisions for the Internet and landline phones for handheld devices, the long-term impact will be profound. Education, work, and daily life have been and will continue to be transformed. The consequences for today's children will be significant. In response, our education system also needs to change.

Jobs in emerging fields such as nanotechnology and bioinformation will be mainstream in a few years. In a recent want ad for a Knowledge Deployment Associate, the primary task was to support and trouble-shoot knowledge sharing. To be successful in this new environment, students will need to extend content mastery into planning, productivity, and management.

Figure 7.11   Work Ethic Rubric

Skill/ Knowledge	Exemplary	Proficient	Developing	Rudimentary	Score/ Weight
Accountability	• Punctual, prepared, and organized • Conscientious and independent worker who goes beyond requirements	• Usually on time and ready to learn • Works consistently without supervision to achieve goals	• Assumes minimal personal responsibility • Needs supervision to complete task	• Late and unprepared • Has difficulty working with others and with completing assignments	
Attitude	• Enthusiastic and cooperative • Accepts and acts on feedback	• Positive attitude toward people, process, and product • Accepts feedback	• Somewhat engaged but noncommittal • Listens to feedback	• Negative attitude toward work and others • Ignores feedback	
Work Product and Outcome	• Effectively coordinates time, effort, and resources to ensure completion and quality of work • Final product exceeds requirements	• Uses resources successfully • Final product meets requirements	• Final product is incomplete	• Doesn't demonstrate understanding or interest in final product	
Your strengths/commendations:					TOTAL:
Areas for improvement/recommendations:					

Reflection

• What does college and career readiness mean to you?
• What skills and knowledge did you need at the beginning of your college and career?
• How has this changed?
• What can you do today to support college and career readiness in today's students and tomorrow's workforce?

FINAL CONSIDERATIONS

Although this chapter comes late in this book, some would argue that it is the most important, because these are the traits and abilities that today's students will need to move the world forward in productive and meaningful ways. In a Metlife survey (Metropolitan Life Insurance Company, 2011) the large majority of teachers and parents agree that college and career readiness should be a priority in education. Of course, literacy and numeracy are at the heart of this readiness, but also rated highly were critical thinking skills. Fewer mentioned the softer skills of emotional intelligence and intrinsic motivation, yet they have been shown to be essential for success in life. Education is being pulled in many directions, but the skills for living successfully in the world is a direction that needs additional tugs.

Reflection

For each skill, describe a way you would apply it in your school or classroom.

- Civic and Citizenship
- Global Understanding
- Leadership and Responsibility
- College and Career

8

Multipurpose Assessments

Authentic products measured by alternative strategies are common in classrooms. Less frequently are they assessed objectively against explicit criteria. The guidelines in this chapter explain critical elements of projects and portfolios, show exemplars, and detail strategies for adapting assessments for the 21st century.

PROJECTS

Projects are a medium and a method for 21st century learning. They provide a vigorous and accountable approach to learning that serves as a foundation for teaching, learning, and assessing. Through projects, students explore real-world situations and apply their knowledge to genuine challenges. Projects actively engage students as they combine content knowledge with 21st century skills and shift the responsibility for learning from the teacher to the student.

Definition

Projects are complex student works that generally continue over an extended time. They can be included at any grade level, in any classroom, and in any subject. The use of projects in the classroom presents challenges, but can be managed by following these straightforward guidelines:

- Projects start with a purpose. What do students need to know to complete the project? What will students learn through the project, and what will they know and be able to do at the completion that they couldn't do before?
- Students develop a contract, establish a time frame, and design a work plan in collaboration with the teacher.
- Projects proceed step by step, and the process is transparent. At the start, students describe what they know, then develop leading questions and identify initial resources that will guide them toward what they want and need to know.
- Allow as much self-direction as feasible along with monitoring and guidance along the way. Build scaffolds to support learning.
- Assessments are embedded throughout the project as formative assessments, check-ins, logs, and reflections.

Learning outcomes should be assessed in relation to targets, goals, and standards. The criteria for and means of assessment are made explicit from the beginning, and all parties know how learning outcomes will be measured. A variety of methods can be used. Projects appropriate for the 21st century should involve greater complexity than traditional projects. Figure 8.1 explains the main features of projects in practice.

The Process

There are practical, student-focused steps for the development of projects that can be customized to your class, grade, and subject. These steps have less to do with the topic of the project and the exact nature of the final product than they do with creating a substantial and functional learning process.

There are different ways to begin projects and approach these steps, depending on the students' previous experience with projects. For example, if the project is on a common topic, begin with whole-group brainstorming or collective creation of a KWL chart. For topics on which there are multiple viewpoints, students can place themselves on a continuum of views. For more content-based topics such as digital technologies, students can present their current level of knowledge through a gallery of posted sticky notes on different technologies. This is also a time when plans, purpose, process, and outcomes can be reviewed, group norms established, and exemplars shown.

In the universal process described here, students are first given an overview of the project. Then they start their work by choosing a topic

Figure 8.1   21st Century Projects

Elements of Projects	In Practice
Extended process of learning	An e-zine is completed over several weeks or longer.
Linked to standards	Projects can be done that apply geometric principles to home construction.
Topics can customized	Student selects from genres of music, literature, or poetry.
Process and products can be personalized and student directed	Students can prepare a video/podcast, a Glogster or a Prezi presentation on famous inventors.
Content is embedded	Persuasive essays and letters to the editor must include documented facts and follow writing conventions.
Complex problems and challenges	Students explain why there are divergent views of global warming and recognize the diversity of data.
Rigorous and precise	Students follow their planned strategy and time frame, yet elasticity is built in.
Inquiry-based	Starts with deep, significant questions that continue to emerge throughout the project
Reflects 21st century skills: thinking, acting, and living in the world	A virtual tour displays elements of creativity, collaboration, and applied technologies.
Monitored and managed	Frequent check-ins, conferences, and formative assessments
Results in evidence: product, performance, or multimedia	Grade-level or schoolwide exposition at the conclusion
Use of evidence reflects accuracy and depth of learning	Final project displays content mastery in relevant context through the use of multiple measures
Evaluated using multiple assessment strategies	Rubrics, journals, peer review that reflect and align with a set of common expectations
Assessments include recommendations for improvement	Students reflect on what they would do differently to improve their learning or outcomes.
Guides changes in teaching	Based on assessment, next time the teacher decides to explicitly teach questioning skills.

and recording their ideas in a written proposal or contract that includes the following:

- What do you know about the topic?
- What do you want to learn about the topic? Use a graphic organizer to display your ideas.

- Why is this topic a good choice for you?
- Translate this into actionable learning goals and targets that are customized for you.
- Complete a learning contract that explains how you will proceed, your steps, and a schedule.
- What do you anticipate the final product will look like?
- What skills and knowledge will you gain, and how will you exhibit them?

Knowledge Building

Applied research skills:

- What sources do you think will be relevant?
- Keep an e-portfolio of relevant sources you find.
- Maintain an annotated bibliography or bookmarks of those that you rely on the most.
- Research your topic, applying skills you've learned—use the research skills checklist as needed.
- Reflect on how you proceeded with your research.

The Process

Demonstrations of critical thinking, problem solving, and metacognition:

- Track your learning.
  - Keep records of your steps along the way.
  - Maintain a schedule and progress log of pace and depth of learning
- How will success be demonstrated?
- When will mastery be achieved?
- How will problems be identified and solved?
- How will process and products be monitored along the way?
- How will feedback and synergy be incorporated and built on?

The Product

Applications of creativity and digital and technology literacy:

- What will the final product look like?
- How will it demonstrate your mastery of the topic?
- Consider multiple ways to present your work.
- Select the one that is the best fit for you and your topic.
- Possible ways of displaying learning: written text, poster, presentation, game, simulation, advocacy, multimedia

Presentation

Demonstration of communication skills:

- Plan ahead to incorporate the essentials of good presentation skills.
- Practice and prepare materials.
- Present your best self and your best work in a way that engages with the audience and raises their awareness and understanding.

Assessment

- What methods will be used in the course of the work to help you know and others know that you are learning?
- How will your contract and learning logs reflect your learning?
- How will you display the content knowledge you have mastered and your learning process?
- What is a relevant way for your work to be assessed at its conclusion? For example, would you prefer to reflect on a rubric or write an essay? At the end how will others know what you've learned?.
- What types of reflection and metacognitive activities can reveal your thought processes?
- How will you use your experience to do better in the future?
- Projects also provide opportunities for students and teachers to assess CCSS such as the following:

  o Explains how point of view or purpose shapes the content and style of a text
  o Integrates and evaluates content presented in diverse formats and media
  o Reads and comprehends informational texts
  o Conducts research projects demonstrating understanding of the subject under investigation
  o Presents information, findings, and supporting evidence such that listeners can follow the line of reasoning

Figure 8.2 shows some additional ideas for using projects in content areas.

In Practice

At Tomorrow's Destiny Secondary School, projects are a regular part of the curriculum, but some of the teachers feel that outcomes would be better if they had more organization and structure. The seventh-grade teachers share a common goal of reinforcing digital search skills, especially as applied to researching and synthesizing information, and creating products of learning. Some projects are done individually, others with partners

Figure 8.2   Projects in Content Areas

Content	Project	Assessment
Historical landmarks	Give a guided (virtual) tour of Washington, D.C., explaining the significance of the architecture in relation to historical events.	• Plan: completeness and feasibility • Portfolio of research • Rubric: research, presentation, and technology
Art: Impressionism	Take a field trip to an art museum then prepare a guide to the artwork.	• Analysis and comparison note taking on field trip • Rubric for critical thinking and creativity
Math in action	Throughout the year, compile a portfolio of examples of how math is used in real life.	• Student contract and reflections Feedback on each entry for detail and clarity • Assessment of portfolio for accuracy, depth, completeness
Civics: Create a utopian society	Collaboratively describe the geography, history, politics, citizenry, and economics of your hypothetical society.	• Progress log, feedback, reflection • Rubric for collaboration, problem solving, digital literacy
Cause and effect	With a team, design and create a Rube Goldberg contraption that applies math and physics concepts.	• Checklist on preliminary drawing and revisions • Collaboration, critical thinking, and creativity rubric • Functionality of final product with presentation rubric.

or small groups, depending on the purpose and goals of the assignment and the intended learning outcomes. The teachers have mastered many aspects of project management but recognize that the assessment component still requires attention.

This year, the teachers have decided to have all students in the grade complete a "Great Minds" project. This supports their grade-based goal and also connects to CCSS in reading, writing, and math. Each *kiva*, or team of teachers and students (the term is based on a Native American word), can choose how to approach this assignment. While there are some common components, the plan allows for a degree of flexibility. For example, in one kiva, the teachers and students decide the scope of their project will include great minds in all fields. In another kiva, the teachers decide that researching great minds in math and science is a better fit with their students' identified learning needs and the project's emphasis this year.

From the beginning, students know the process, expected outcomes, and assessment criteria. Overall, they will be assessed on how well they have prepared a multimedia presentation that informs an audience of how great minds throughout history have influenced lives today. Examples of the steps in the process and how each is assessed are shown to the students.

Purpose: Assignment Objectives, Goals, Standards, and Outcomes

The goals the teacher has set for the students are to

- use effective research and digital literacy skills in the selection and evaluation of source material;
- synthesize information into an original product that portrays a great mind and the person's contributions to the world;
- work collaboratively with others to plan, implement, and synergize the project; and
- maintain learning and assessment records including plans, learning logs, and reflections.

Students have added their own goals:

- to use our problem-solving skills to the best of our ability and seek help when needed;
- to work together respectfully;
- to use our knowledge of technology to pick the best way to present our work to others;
- to be as creative as possible with the materials that are available; and
- to thoughtfully reflect on how we are doing and, when done, how we did.

Whole-Group Initiation

The unit begins with the students brainstorming to come up with a list of people who have used their ideas and actions to improve the world. Then, students work in small groups to describe their accomplishments or contributions to the world—and look up those they don't know. They work together in groups to identify the knowledge, skills, and habits of mind each person needed in order to succeed.

Planning for the Project

Teachers review the assignment and show exemplars of successful projects and how they meet the assessment criteria. Some teachers invite a local guest speaker who has made a difference in the world to talk about their experience. This year they decide to include a self-assessment in which students rank themselves on a scale of project skills and knowledge.

	EASY_____explain each_____HARD
Coming up with ideas	_____
Research skills	_____
Working with others	_____
Problem-solving skills	_____
Creating original products	_____
Using multimedia resources	_____
Self-assessment skills	_____
Presentation skills	_____

Knowledge Building and Learning Processes

The project begins with a review of the process and content of the project. They provide a list to guide students' selection of the person to be studied and the strategy for learning and presenting:

- Provide biographical information on the person.
- Explain how their passion and interests developed.
- Describe the thought processes and habits of mind they used.
- Illuminate their important works and contributions.
- Explain how is this used and applied today.
- Think about ways to spread the word about this person: newsletter, website, video, blog, wiki, or podcast

Students then prepare a learning contract as shown in Figure 8.3. As students work they track their progress, reflect on it, and continue to develop their next steps as shown in Figure 8.4. At the conclusion, a multifaceted rubric (Figure 8.5) is used to assess the work. Students use it to self-assess, while the teacher assesses their work against the same criteria. If desired, peer-assessment can also be part of the process.

Projects are complex learning opportunities. Project-based learning requires thoughtful planning and carefully monitored implementation. Standards and learning outcomes must be kept in mind during all activities.

Figure 8.3   Project Contract

Great Minds Project	Learning Contract for:	Date:

Student's Responsibilities:

Teacher's Responsibilities:

I will keep the following records of progress and assessment of my learning in my portfolio and check them off as completed:

- ❑ My preassessment of project skills
- ❑ My learning plan
- ❑ Three leading questions to guide my work
- ❑ My journal and progress reports where I track my steps, note progress, record findings and make plans
- ❑ Checklist of research strategies that I learned and used
- ❑ A metacognitive reflection on the research process
- ❑ Small-group consults where I give and receive feedback from peers
- ❑ Record of meetings with my teacher
- ❑ First draft and dry run of presentation with feedback from class using a rubric
- ❑ Revisions with a self-assessment
- ❑ Preparation of final product and presentation
- ❑ Final reflection and rubric

Timeframe	
Work to Do	*By (Date)*

Student's Signature	Teacher's Signature
Parent's Signature	

Figure 8.4 Progress Report

DATE	PROGRESS MADE SINCE LAST REPORT: *Describe specific accomplishments and outcomes. Show evidence.*	PLANS: *Short- and long-term goals. What needs to be done tomorrow, next week, next month?*	NEXT PERIOD: *Describe specific strategies and steps.*
ACTIONS What actions did you take? What steps were successful?			
COLLABORATIONS Who did you work with? What did you accomplish?			
HABITS What habits of mind did you use and how did you use them?			
PLANS What part of your plan was achieved? Explain what, where, and how.			

Figure 8.5 Project Rubric

Skill/ Knowledge	Exemplary	Proficient	Basic	Novice	Score/ Weight
Identification of problem/ topic	• Selected a feasible person with 3 strong leading questions to guide research	• Selected someone of interest and wrote 3 clear questions to answer	• Picked someone with help • Could only think of 2 questions	• Needed substantial help selecting a person and identifying what to learn	
Planning	• Used skills and priorities to thoughtfully and accurately build a practical yet flexible plan	• Designed a plan that was feasible and realistic to follow	• Some of the steps in the plan weren't clear or actionable.	• Plan was missing steps, and the process didn't follow the plan.	
Research skills and strategies	• Developed a workable strategy, and selected appropriate resources that were most relevant	• Used some of the research skills learned in class to pick multiple resources to use	• Had difficulty finding sources and determining which ones were relevant	• Used the website that came up first and didn't search or consider other sources	
Analysis and synthesis	• Thoughtfully analyzed and synthesized multiple sources	• Used some learned strategies to review information and organize it	• Understood most sources and combined parts of each	• Found a few understandable sources and cut and pasted parts of each	
Organization, accountability, and record keeping	• Prepared, organized, and conscientious student who independently goes beyond requirements	• Usually maintains records and works consistently without supervision	• Assumes minimal personal responsibility; needs supervision to complete task	• Disorganized and unprepared; needs help completing assigned tasks	
Problem solving	• Accurately sequences and applies problem-solving skills in multiple ways	• Generally able to solve problems in a thoughtful sequence	• Able to discern parts of the problem but needs help achieving resolution	• Finds it challenging to follow the problem-solving steps and generate solutions	

(Continued)

175

Figure 8.5 (Continued)

Skill/ Knowledge	Exemplary	Proficient	Basic	Novice	Score/Weight
Creativity	• Consistently shows flexibility and originality • Produces many new ideas and ways to do things	• Generally able to demonstrate and apply components of creativity in the course of work	• Tries to think creatively but sometimes needs help coming up with new ideas	• With support, can generate some creative ideas	
Metacognition	• Uses metacognitive abilities to improve learning and productivity • Routinely applies them in daily practices	• Typically applies ability to think about thinking during learning and uses this to perform better	• Sometimes able to think about thought processes but doesn't routinely apply them	• Tries to understand thinking but has difficulty applying the concept	
Multimedia	• Highly knowledgeable and capably uses multiple media to strengthen demonstrations of learning	• Competent in the selection and use of appropriate media to incorporate in a presentation	• Able to use a few selected media to support a presentation	• Selecting media and incorporating them appropriately can be done with support	
Collaboration	• Worked well with others; efficient use of time and equality of participation	• Generally stayed on task and participated; used time well	• Tried to work with others but did not consistently do their part	• Had difficulty working with others respectfully	
Presentation	• Poised and professional style that engages audience and conveys message	• Good stage presence; audience listens and seems to understand information	• A little nervous and fidgety; follows planned presentation notes	• Needs extensive notes, support, and encouragement to present information	

Reflection

What did the student learn (3 personal, 3 factual)?

What worked well?

What could be done differently?

The assessments can be complex also, but most teachers who use projects in their classrooms would say that the learning outcomes are worth the time.

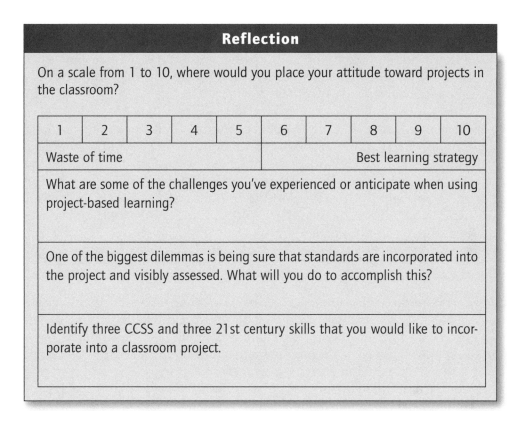

Reflection

On a scale from 1 to 10, where would you place your attitude toward projects in the classroom?

1	2	3	4	5	6	7	8	9	10
Waste of time					Best learning strategy				

What are some of the challenges you've experienced or anticipate when using project-based learning?

One of the biggest dilemmas is being sure that standards are incorporated into the project and visibly assessed. What will you do to accomplish this?

Identify three CCSS and three 21st century skills that you would like to incorporate into a classroom project.

PORTFOLIOS

Portfolios are used routinely in other professions. In nursing, they are used to develop and demonstrate proficiency. The United States Navy uses them to prepare recruits for submarine operations. Education has been a little slower in getting on board. An interest in alternative assessments and portfolios emerged in the 1980s and 1990s in response to an increased emphasis on large-scale multiple-choice tests.

A study by the Center for Research on Evaluation, Standards, and Student Testing (CRESST; 1990) found that portfolios have positive consequences for teaching and learning. With them, teachers raise the expectations for learning and spend more time on higher-level thinking and problem solving with students. The authors went on to say that early research suggests that portfolio assessment, when well designed, leads to improvement in student skills, achievement, and motivation to learn. Consistency across teachers as well as clear criteria and thoughtful planning were identified as benefits of the use of student portfolios.

In relation to electronic portfolios, Joan Herman and Lynn Winters (1994) state,

> Professional literature extols the potential benefits of electronic portfolios for teaching, learning, and assessment—particularly when compared with traditional multiple-choice tests. Although initial findings favor portfolio assessments, the challenge lies in ensuring technical quality, equity, and feasibility for large scale assessment purposes. (p. 55)

Elizabeth Hartnell-Young (2008) recommends using a joint teacher/ student approach and being thoughtful about using selected materials at various times for selected purposes. She advises teachers to consider storage, planning, and tools for communication before starting. She praises portfolios for being able to support the abilities and needs of a wide range of students because teachers can scaffold learning until a student is confident enough to work independently.

Definition

Portfolios are collections of student work that represent their knowledge, skills, and learning outcomes. Their purpose is to provide evidence of growth and achievement. A dynamic portfolio can be updated regularly so that it serves as an ongoing collection of work. Portfolios can be formative in nature and show sequences of work, work in progress, and growth. Alternatively, they can be summative and display final results and attainment of standards. Teachers can use them to collect examples of student work by classroom, grade level, content area, or overall school. In doing so, they generate a picture of student work over time. Students can collect and manage their work individually or in collaboration with their teachers.

Considerations in designing portfolio include clarity of purpose, availability of technology, training and support, and structures for their development over time. In terms of assessment, it is essential that they align with targets, that the artifact selection is purposeful, and that there is consistency between learners and among teachers.

A wide range of artifacts can be incorporated in a portfolio, including student writing, examples of problem solving, in-progress and completed projects, group work, analysis of information, observations, reading logs, and summaries. All of these can provide evidence of core knowledge, higher-level thinking, problem solving, creativity, and student reflection.

Assessment of portfolios involves two considerations. From the start, the purpose, process, and use of portfolios need to be absolutely clear to students and teachers. Second, the assessment strategy must align with the content and purpose of the portfolio. Alternative assessments such as rubrics, checklists, and reflections are well suited to portfolios. Individual artifacts can be assessed as well as the complete portfolio.

In relation to the first requirement, the following should be considered:

- Alignment with objectives and standards (national, state, content area, local) must be considered in the design and use of a portfolio.
- Clarity of purpose: Why is the portfolio being developed? Is it for formative or summative purposes? Will all work be displayed or just a sampling?
- Purposeful selection of materials: Portfolios rarely include all of a student's work. Materials representative of all stages of the process will be selected differently from those that represent the final achievement. Decide who will select the materials and what criteria will be used.

Considerations involving assessment strategy may include the following:

- Identify a process and requirements for reflection and assessment.
- Assessment criteria: Standards and assessment criteria need to be preestablished. This helps students understand what good work is and how their effort can make a difference in their learning.
- Procedures for assessment: Select the strategy that best matches the standard, purpose, and materials in the portfolio.
- Consider how the assessment will inform future instruction and portfolio design.

In Practice

Mr. Amid and Ms. Rouge combined their math and art classes for an interdisciplinary assignment on mathematical applications in interior design. To start, students are given a preview of the goals and assignments in the unit, their sequence and purpose, the requirements for their final portfolio, and grading criteria. Both geometry and design standards are reviewed. Working in pairs, they began by selecting two to four rooms in a house. They use a design program to graph it and add furniture, and begin their work with a thumbnail sketch. They keep a portfolio of work in progress. During the project, they share their work with the class on the electronic board and get feedback from other students and teachers. (See the portfolio checklist in Figure 8.6.) The mathematical applications are graded in a more traditional manner that measure whether the dimensions were drawn accurately, proportions are correct, and items in the room are drawn to scale. The more creative aspects of the design, such as use of space, color, line, and proportion, will by nature be more subjective and are better suited to a rubric or reflection. The teachers decided that although the formative work will count for a portion of the grade, a

Figure 8.6   Portfolio Checklist

Quality Indicators	Student Notes	Teacher Notes
Clarity of purpose		
Accuracy: room dimensions and total square footage		
Craftsmanship: neat and understandable		
Skillful use of technology		
Accuracy of math		
Evidence of collaboration		
Time management		
Recommendations for improvement:		

Figure 8.7   Math and Design Portfolio

Standard	Advanced	Proficient	Basic	Novice	Score/ Weight
Mathematical precision	We used correct formulas, and all our calculations were accurate.	We had a few small errors in use of formula or calculations.	A few mathematical errors affected our final calculations.	We had difficulty using math, so our design wasn't as good as it could be.	
Elements of design such as line, space, color, and proportion	We used multiple elements of design to make our work the best possible.	We used some elements of design that you could see in our work.	We included one or two design elements.	We thought we had design in our work, but our audience needed them explained.	
Collaboration	Everyone contributed, did his or her best work, and worked respectfully.	For the most part, we made good use of our time and resources and worked together well.	Some people didn't do their part or were bossy.	We really didn't work together; people disagreed, so everyone did his or her own things.	
Functional design: rationale for arrangement, explanation of choices, traffic flow	Our final product was very practical and could easily be turned into a real place.	Our final product was reasonable and could conceivably be a real place.	We had an interesting design, but it needs more work to be realistic.	There's no way anyone could live in our design, but we have some ideas to fix it.	
Presentation	Our presentation was well organized, easy to understand, and clearly displayed, so the audience could easily connect to our design.	We gave a good presentation that had a clear sequence and accurate information for the audience.	We shared some information on our design, but it seemed that there were questions on the steps we followed and the information we used.	It would have helped to plan a little better to make sure we were clear and organized before we began.	

summative portfolio containing each student's final work would be more relevant to the goals and purposes of the assignment.

Electronic Portfolios

As the use of technology in the classroom expanded, electronic portfolios emerged in the late 1990s and early 2000s. These portfolios can contain the same written material as in earlier portfolios, but in a digital format. They can also include electronic products and evidence of work. PowerPoint presentations, photographs, videos, voice recordings, web pages, blogs, interactions, collaborations, experiments, simulations, performances, and exhibits can all be part of the portfolio. Electronic portfolios are dynamic in that they can change continuously and seamlessly with the learner. Connections between the examples of work and selected standards can be shown through hyperlinks. Students can post written work, multimedia, audio, and projects that can be cross-references to other projects. Such electronic portfolios can demonstrate content knowledge as well as 21st century skills such as critical thinking, problem solving, and creativity.

According to Helen Barrett (2009), the benefits of electronic portfolios for students and teachers are

- the minimal storage space requirements;
- the ease of creating backup files;
- their portability;
- their long shelf life;
- their learner-centered orientation;
- the opportunity to increase technology skills;
- the increased ability, through hypertext links, to illuminate and align standards; and
- their ability to be accessed by different audiences through multiple media.

Other advantages that have been attributed to the use of portfolios include their ability to

- show student growth over time, both short term and long term;
- build content knowledge while engaging students in the learning process;
- support skill-building in self-assessment;
- show achievement, strengths, and weaknesses;
- give students control over learning;
- support intrinsic motivation through engagement and control;
- illuminate the link between learning and assessing;
- develop skills in planning, reflection, and assessment;
- support a range of learning outcomes from content to creativity and communication; and
- supports a range or learners, abilities, and needs.

Just as 21st century assessment requires effective assessment practices, quality portfolio development practices should be applied to 21st century portfolios. Students can demonstrate proficiency in thinking, acting, and living skills through a range of portfolio components.

The two examples included here show the range and diversity of portfolio programs. The first one shows an elementary gradewide electronic program.

At the Maya Angelou School, teachers have scheduled Fridays as Writing Workshop days. Every two weeks, students take a high-quality piece of their writing and publish it in an electronic magazine. Different styles, genres, and themes are explored throughout the year. During the writing process, the themes are introduced, rough drafts are written, peer and teacher feedback guides revisions, and final products are produced. During the year, students record readings of their work in audio and video format. They also collect pictures and other icons that relate to their favorite authors and genres. Teacher feedback and reflections on each entry are included, and journal entries are analyzed for growth in learning.

At the end of the year, they hold a writers' celebration which students attend in the role of their favorite authors and present their work to parents and other members of the school community. Throughout the unit, writing is assessed with standards-based measures. The portfolio is holistically graded using the rubric in Figure 8.8.

Paper Portfolios

Paper portfolios are relatively easy to use in that they don't require any special training for students and teachers and no additional equipment is needed. On the other hand, they do require physical storage space, and there are limits to the type and amount of content that can be included.

Mrs. Chou teaches seventh-grade social studies and is using student portfolios during a unit on government. There is only one computer lab in the building, and access to it is limited, so students keep paper folders in the classroom. Students are given a learning tracker and overview of the unit that includes an explanation of purpose, guiding questions, learning activities, a vocabulary builder, and a preview of assessments.

In this unit, it is expected that students will

- be able to describe the history of and amendments to the U.S. Constitution,
- compare and evaluate loose and strict interpretations of the Constitution,
- analyze the role of the three branches of government in relation to constitutional decisions, and
- defend a position on interpretation of the Constitution.

Figure 8.8 Portfolio Rubric

Standard	Expert	Capable	Developing	Beginner	Score/ Weight
Required items	All items are included and strongly relate to the purpose of the portfolio.	Most items are evident in the portfolio and relate to its purpose.	Some are visible, but several are missing, making the purpose unclear.	Very few of the required items are included. The purpose is not evident.	
Quality of work	My portfolio includes my highest-quality work.	Most of my work is of high quality.	My work shows a mixture of quality.	I think I need some help to do better	
Clarity of purpose	The items I selected obviously match the purpose of my portfolio.	Most of the items I put in my portfolio are relevant.	I put in some things that were required and others that I just felt like.	My portfolio is a collection of work that's not always related to the purpose.	
Ease of navigation	My portfolio is easy to review and follow. Sections are labeled and are in the required sequence.	A reviewer can follow the path of my portfolio through my main headings.	Some of my items are grouped together and labeled, but others are more haphazardly organized.	All my materials are just put into the portfolio.	
Reflection	I was able to accurately evaluate my portfolio, thoughtfully, reflect on my work, and make recommendations for improvement.	I think I was pretty close to matching the evaluation criteria for the portfolio. I had a few ideas for making it better.	I reflected on my portfolio but wasn't sure how precise my work was and didn't have too many ideas for making it better.	I wrote a few comments about my portfolio but probably need some help with this.	

Mrs. Chou begins with a preassessment that she uses to guide her plans, inform her instruction, and group students. Students are expected to keep their first writings and products and their final or best work in the portfolio.

Activities embedded in the unit that support 21st century skills include the following:

- Prioritize the Amendments to the Constitution and defend your list to others (critical thinking, metacognition).
- Create a visual representation of the three branches of government and the role of each in relation to the Constitution (ICT).
- Write campaign speeches advocating both views on gun control (decision making, communication).
- Compare these two quotes (analysis):
  - Thomas Jefferson: "The natural progress of things is for liberty to yield and government to gain ground."
  - Henry David Thoreau: "That government is best which governs least."

A variety of assessments are used throughout the unit. The formative assessment and first drafts are given less weight than the final products. Writing and content standards are graded in more traditional ways for accuracy of content and adherence to writing standards. The portfolio rubric in Figure 8.8 is used, and students also complete a reflection on the final portfolio as shown in Figure 8.9.

Figure 8.9 Student Portfolio Reflection

- How does your portfolio show growth along the way?
- What are the three most important things you learned?
- What is one thing you want someone to notice about your portfolio?
- What do you like most about your portfolio
- What would you change if you had the opportunity to do the project over again?

Portfolios can show growth over time and help students learn organizational skills that are important for daily life. Their flexibility allows for an emphasis on a range of student skills and knowledge from content to metacognition. Portfolios are a constructive and active tool for learning and for tracking learning. Think of them as reservoirs for 21st century skills.

Reflection

A few portfolio ideas are described here. Add you own in the empty boxes.

Subject/Grade/Standard	Portfolio Possibilities
Reading: Character development	Characters I've met this year: A collection of character studies based on books and stories read this year.
Science: Seasons	Tracking the seasons: Each season of the year has scientific observations and experiments associated with it. Student select their best example of each and at the end blog their summary.
Elementary: Mixed subjects	Recording my neighborhood: After several local field trips to look for new vocabulary, symbols of culture, mathematical angles, and other grade level standards, work is assembled and organized.

9

Moving Assessment Into the 21st Century

> *Assessment efforts should not be concerned about valuing what can be measured but, instead, about measuring that which is valued.*
>
> —Banta, Lund, Black, and Oblander (1996, p. 5)

Changes to assessment that are made thoughtfully, selectively, and progressively will best serve today's students. These complex changes should be built on a durable core of beliefs and actions that improve teaching and learning for every student. The assessment fundamentals in Chapter 3 are informed by and in turn inform these core beliefs, which then inform practice, leadership, and policy.

PRACTICE

Students in today's classrooms require a different set of skills than in the past. The factory model has been replaced with a nonlinear knowledge-building model. Thus, assessments in today's classrooms should be multi-modal, multimethod, inclusive of the whole child, and applied. Digital immigrants are rarely without some form of technology as they interface with information from multiple sources. This doesn't mean that all teaching and learning are grounded solely in technology, but rather emphasizes the importance of aligning teaching and learning with the ways of using technology and learning styles that are characteristic of these students.

Despite the complex changes in students and their world, traditional education has moved toward a more standardized model of assessment in which every student in every grade takes the same test at the same time. These tests drive instruction, but to know whether students are prepared for this century, we need to assess the knowledge and skills we value. Yong Zhao (2011, p. 1) makes clear that current policies "threaten to turn American children into robotic test takers, narrow and homogenize our children's education, and value testing over teaching and learning."

Twenty-first century learning starts with intentional teaching and robust learning at the classroom level. Classroom instruction and assessment begins with an agreed-on set of common beliefs that are collaboratively and deliberately explored and developed. By balancing core knowledge with 21st century skills, teachers can create classrooms that are centers for authentic learning and assessments in which core standards are brought to bear on the outside world. A teacher may know that students are expected to understand slopes and angles, but designing a staircase to their dream room will turn that standard into a real-world application.

The one-size-fits-all model of teaching needs to evolve into a model of the differentiated classroom, with different sizes and styles of learning and assessing. Assessment must be flexible, adaptive, and multifaceted. National standards may be the canopy, but they are not the ground floor of practice.

LEADERSHIP

School leaders begin with a vision—not merely for reforming but for transforming schools. It's not just students who need 21st century skills and knowledge; leaders too must learn to work collaboratively, use technology, be efficient problem solvers, distribute leadership tasks and roles, and maintain a global perspective. Developing a curriculum that is both rich with content and focused on skills will be a challenge. Designing schedules that provide adequate time for both knowledge building and applied learning will require flexibility and creativity. Classrooms that are problem- and project-based will not be quiet places, and learning may be messy.

District leaders can take large and small steps to move schools into the 21st century, starting with the incorporation of 21st century skills in every curriculum. Updated assessments should align with and reflect the new outcomes we want. We can gain a better understanding of the standards by examining them in the light of enduring principles and essential questions. We can start to integrate them with 21st century criteria by ensuring that students are exposed to selected 21st century skills in every content area and at each grade level. This doesn't require a 180-degree change, but it does require steering our boat through new waters.

POLICY

Mission

Policy, leadership, and practice go hand in hand and are built on reciprocal relationships. When diversity in schools increased, policies were written to address world language instruction and multicultural awareness. After Columbine, school safety and antibullying policies and programs were developed. When Elementary and Secondary Education Act (ESEA) was reauthorized in 2002, it wasn't long before No Child Left Behind began redirecting curriculum and instruction. Global competitiveness requires adapting the best practices of the world's education systems to our needs. Doing so is essential to shifting schools from the factory model of education to a more forward-thinking model.

Can you remember the last district mission you read? Most educators would have a hard time reciting it. Which of the following statements is more meaningful and inspiring? Use your 21st century skills of comparing and contrasting to draw conclusions about how they are alike and different, and in what ways they reflect 21st century values and beliefs.

MISSION 1: Inspire, engage, and educate each student to become a contributing citizen and a responsible, independent, and critical thinker through a world-class education that

- challenges each student to meet and exceed high expectations through a rigorous curriculum that prepares them for lifelong learning;
- enables each student to think critically, work collaboratively, communicate effectively, and act with integrity in a complex society;
- prepares each student to develop and adapt their knowledge, skills, and talents to meet the demands of a rapidly changing world;
- develops interdependent skilled future leaders and independent thinkers who are able to resolve problems of the next generation; and
- encourages each student to be an active local, national, and global citizen.

MISSION 2: Provide each student with the highest-quality education in a safe environment. In recognizing the diversity of our town, we will provide each student the opportunity to develop to his or her maximum potential and to be a lifelong learner and critical thinker. Each student will develop self-discipline and become a self-fulfilling and responsible member of society. This will be accomplished through

- monitoring student achievement outcomes and results through indicators that demonstrate progress,
- providing the necessary resources (time, personnel, and materials) to raise achievement levels,
- selecting school leaders who are a "good fit" for the community,
- providing a healthy and safe learning environment,

- communicating with the public on educational needs and accomplishments, and
- educating district leadership on trends and innovations in education.

If you looked carefully, you noticed that the first statement describes many of the 21st century skills that have been emphasized in this book. It is future oriented, student focused, and skills based. The second one is focused on the present, with a strong emphasis on what leadership will do for students. If we are to move toward the first model, then the mission of teaching, learning, and assessment will need to change.

Standardized Testing

Tom Loveless (2011) at the Brookings Institution explains that each type of standardized assessment is different, making it difficult to prepare students for all of them. He reports that "The publicly released items on the eighth-grade NAEP are, on average, two to three years below the eighth-grade mathematics standards recommended by the Common Core" (p. 5). PISA, the international performance measure, also tests a different set of knowledge and skills, with an emphasis on critical thinking. As the challenges of teaching content for a multitude of tests becomes greater, doesn't it make more sense to teach the thinking skills that will serve all students? Elena Silva (2008) notes that we are developing the ability to test and measure thinking skills, and as the reliability of these tests improve, they will become a more important accountability measure. In the past, the emphasis has been largely on preparing students for standardized tests. In the future, we must direct our efforts to devising tests that emphasize preparation for the real world.

Grading and Reporting

Current grading practices and report cards are not always accurate reflections of what students know, understand, and can do. In the future, assessment will be less a matter of grading against basic standards and more a report on the skills the student has acquired. A photo album of applied thinking skills, interpersonal communication, and global citizenship is more informative than a snapshot. Routine checking and feedback are more important than a final grade in improving outcomes. Models of growth in student learning are more informative than static measures. Reporting systems that connect learning to multifaceted goals and targets and provide clarity and fairness for all teachers, students, and constituents will set the standard for assessment.

Professional Development

Professional development has been identified as one of the weak links in educational reform. Adequate time and resources must be dedicated to this aim. The highest quality preservice training and continuous in-service training and mentoring are essential to the implementation of best practices. Ongoing professional development must keep teachers up to date on current research and scientifically based practice. Marc Tucker (2011) points out that to compete globally, teachers need to be chosen from the top ranks of college students, develop solid content mastery, have strong pedagogical skills, and be provided with compensation competitive with that of similarly degreed professions.

It's not only new teachers who can benefit from mentoring. Even experienced teachers who may not be familiar with a particular strategy can develop skills by observing and learning from others. Other professions have mandatory training, mentoring, and recertification. The teaching profession needs to adopt such rigorous practices also.

Teacher Evaluation

Evaluations of teachers in 21st century settings will be different from those in a traditional test-based setting. School leaders must encourage teachers to stretch beyond their boundaries and take risks with alternative types of assessments and strategies for reporting them. Evaluation and wages tied primarily to standardized test scores impair teachers' ability to embrace 21st century skills. New evaluation criteria must include 21st century skills, alternative assessments of student learning, frequent dipsticking, and student ownership of learning.

REFOCUS

Common Core State Standards (CCSS) may be the new foundation of education, but the importance of 21st century skills cannot be ignored. When 21st century skills are incorporated in every goal, unit, lesson, and assignment, then 21st century assessment will need to follow, and teachers, schools, and districts will need the courage and persistence to say that they are no longer giving only assessments that are miniature versions of national measures.

Many voices are calling for a fairer and more balanced system of assessment. Succinctly stated,

> It is our contention that a number of new developments—including research on how children learn, advances in assessment, and innovations in accountability systems—afford us an opportunity to retool assessment systems to create a new paradigm for measuring the skills and knowledge graduates need to succeed— while at the same time improving instruction so students actually acquire the necessary knowledge and skills for the 21st century. (National Association of State Boards of Education [NASBE], 2009, p. 4)

Assessment is most powerful when there is clear alignment of the processes and products of learning through students, teachers, classrooms, schools, districts, and states, on both the national and international levels. This alignment is horizontal when students and teachers at a given grade level see the standards flowing and connecting throughout all content areas; it is vertical when they see the connections between standards from grade to grade.

In an ideal world, robust 21st century skills would be built on a strong foundation of core skills. Technology would be infused throughout teaching and learning. Assessment would be based on growth models in which responsibility for student success is shared across a comprehensive support system. Here are some suggestions for achieving this:

- Learn more, become informed, and understand the 21st century imperatives.
- Discuss and reflect with others: What's important? Why is change necessary?
- Decide on an actionable goal. Become united in your convictions and establish priorities to begin to move forward.
- Consider how your goal fits in with standards-based reforms.
- Create consensus and momentum. Build collaborations between teachers, schools, and community leaders.
- Reflect on ways to fit the new practices into your community, culture, and educational philosophy.
- Commit to a starting point. What will you do first, and where will you begin? Establish specific steps.
- Identify the resources you need.
- Try pilots and exemplars to implement small-scale change at first.
- Honor and respect the hard work of teachers and leaders in making this transformation.
- Design and provide ongoing professional development, and inform your community.
- Use Professional Learning Communities to align curriculum, instruction, and assessment.

Reflection

What are your 21st century educational priorities?

In your school or classroom, how can you weave the CCSS and 21st century skills together?

With your colleagues, select one or two 21st century skills and resolve to incorporate them into teaching and learning. Explain how you will do this.

What kind of professional development will support these changes?

What policy changes do you recommend?

ENDINGS AND NEW BEGINNINGS

To be prescient requires a combination of much insight, a good amount of knowledge, and the power of intuition. Many of our best leaders have led from instinct and perception; other have used sweat equity for their greatest achievements At least two well-known innovators have relied on both of these: Thomas Edison said, "Genius is 10% inspiration and 90% perspiration," and Bill Gates said, "Sometimes you have to rely on intuition." Being a visionary means building on a foundation of knowledge combined with instinct that is used to produce the desired results.

In the past, many educational reforms did not come to full-scale fruition (nongraded classrooms), and others have failed dismally (open classrooms). Using the lessons of history is an essential first step to bringing about 21st century reforms. Balanced reforms have shown greater potential for success—for example, schools that incorporate the best strategies for teaching and learning, and are balanced in meeting the academic, developmental, and psychosocial needs of today's students.

> If there is anything to be learned from the river of ink that was spilled in the education disputes of the 20th century it is that anything in education that is labeled a "movement" should be avoided like the plague. (Ravitch, 2000, p. 453)

A movement is just that; a short-term change in location or position. A reform is a transformation in patterns and models: The new blueprint is different in design, structure, and results.

There's an old adage that says what once was old is new again. Every generation dusts off and polishes the jewels of a prior generation. Vintage becomes chic. We don't need shabby chic, but we do need real reform that changes ideas and actions in fundamental ways. Over 2,000 years ago, the sages understood how children learn. Socrates peppered his students with questions as a way to judge their understanding, engage them, and spur their learning. Plato, an early supporter of intrinsic motivation, noted that children would never learn unless they wanted to learn. John Dewey was also a harsh critic of what he considered dead knowledge—that which has no application or usefulness—and praised learning that was useful and applied in the real world.

Oddly enough, as there has been better research and more rapid change, some recent reforms appear to fit into the ambit of the fashionable, factional, and fleeting. Since the 1960s, the pace and range of these movements has been mind-boggling, each purporting to be life changing Be careful of falling into the trap of thinking that we are scientifically up to date with 21st century skills and assessment. Newer technologies may provide better reliability, but this can change on an almost daily basis.

The imperative is to separate wheat from chaff and core ideas from educational appendages. The need for a common voice and a consistent focus on what works in education is essential. A good starting place is clear and consistent targets and intentions Then delineate the skills and use the data to build reflective and informed designs. The result will be a balanced model that combines content with context throughout education. I urge you to continue to keep up with the research on 21st century skills and knowledge; propose and advocate the changes we need rather than the ones we want; commit to moving forward on this course; and always monitor, assess, and celebrate success. Stay focused on the goal, start with small steps, extend existing practices, and build change from the ground up.

Lingering Questions

Assessment will continue to have a key role in learning. Our task is to ensure that its role will be as constructive and meaningful a role as possible in our future. While new questions will arise, some fundamental questions will continue to be asked. For now, here are some to ponder:

- What is really important to test, measure, and assess in the 21st century?
- How do we develop assessments that encourage students to carry forward their learning?
- How do we use large-scale assessment to support deep thinking?
- How do we teach students about learning to learn? How will we know that they have mastered those skills?
- How do we do all this while improving content knowledge?
- How do we build assessments that are responsive to continuous change?
- How do we think globally, yet act locally?

What lingering questions do you have?

> *Small changes can produce big results. When the underlying problem is too difficult to fix, people address the symptoms with easier fixes, leaving the underlying problem to grow worse until it is much more difficult to fix.*
>
> — Peter Senge (1994, p. 63)

Appendix A

21st Century Rubrics

Rubrics gained popularity in the 1980s and 1990s, coinciding with the growth of authentic assessments. Early rubrics, often expanded checklists, were improved and elaborated through the addition of levels and descriptors. Today, rubrics are defined as scoring guides that organize and clarify the rating criteria for a specific assignment or target. They describe a range of quality indicators from exemplary/superior to substandard/inferior. Four point rating scales have been found to have the most interrater reliability, and clearly written descriptors contribute to a rubric's validity.

Rubrics serve as teaching tools when they make explicit the expected learning outcomes. They also support learning as students work toward the defined levels of achievement. An advantage of rubrics is that they blur the distinction between teaching, learning, and assessing. They can be used formatively to display goals and targets, as an interim assessment during the course of an assignment, and as a summative assessment.

Barbara Moskal and Jon Leydens (2000) explain that assessment validity relates to the appropriateness and correctness of evidence that is used to make interpretations of student learning. In this respect, a rubric is valid when it reflects the selected content and is used to inform teaching and learning. Reliability relates to the consistency of the assessment scores across teachers, various populations, and different types of measures. This is more of a challenge with rubrics than with traditional tests. To ensure that scores are consistent between teachers and that the rubric scores are consistent with other measures is a challenge because the metrics for measuring 21st century skills are just being developed. For rubrics, reliability is best accomplished when teachers develop them collaboratively and use levels and descriptors effectively to make clear what knowledge and skills are being assessed.

Mrs. Mack uses rubrics to help her students in the planning process for a long-term assignment. After the students write the first draft of their project proposal, they receive feedback from the teacher that shows how their work aligns with the scoring rubric. Revisions are a routine part of her classroom practice. After revisions are made, the revised plans are then subjected to the same rubrics, but this time through a peer review process. When the final touches are put on the proposals, they are submitted to Mrs. Mack with a self-assessment and reflection using the same rubric. At this point in the process, Mrs. Mack asks students to color code their work to align with the rubric criteria. For the standard of synthesizing the ideas of others, they highlight those sections in blue. The parts that show the planned steps in the project are highlighted in yellow. Mrs. Mack tracks progress on the scores throughout this process and uses these data to continue to provide feedback to students on their work. When the final plan is complete, the final grade almost completely supersedes the earlier formative grades. A small score indicating compliance with the process, time management, and consistent effort contributes to the final grade.

The most effective rubrics are those that have descriptors that are understandable to all users, focus on and align with the learning outcomes, and are used to measure important knowledge and skills that aren't easily measured with selected-choice questions. A classic teacher-focused research rubric might say "Student selects and synthesizes relevant resources." One that is more student focused might be rephrased to read, "I found three sources and explained how each related to my topic." Rubrics can be flexible for the assignment and can even include a category of "Met the requirements of the assignment."

The four levels are broadly described in Figure A.1 using typical terminology for the levels. Teachers and districts can select one consistent descriptor or be more flexible and adjust them as needed for a specific assignment. I've seen rubrics that fine-tune the value of each level to allow for A, B and C grade conversion. Since a 3 automatically gives the

Figure A.1   Rubric Terminology

Level 4	Level 3	Level 2	Level 1
Top Tier = 3.6 to 4.0	Skilled Tier = 3.2 to 3.5	Able Tier = 2.8 to 3.1	Emerging Tier = 2.0 to 2.7
• Exemplary • Advanced • Excellent • Goes beyond requirements • Fully complete	• Accomplished • Proficient • Good • Meets requirements • Mostly complete	• Developing • Basic • Fair • Some misconceptions • Partial	• Beginning • Novice • Poor • Serious errors • Incomplete

student 75% and a 1 is the equivalent of 25%, the conversions shown in Figure A.1 more accurately align with typical formats for reporting achievement.

20th century rubrics measure traditional skills and knowledge such as reading, writing, numeracy, and research. Teachers will continue to integrate these with 21st century rubrics. In this section, you'll find ideas for assessing 21st century skills and knowledge: thinking, acting, and living. These rubrics reflect newly emerging understandings of what forward-looking teaching and learning looks like. Figure A.2 is a global rubric and incorporates the main principles of 21st century learning. Some items are directed to students and others to teachers to show how simple changes in phrasing can change the type of rubric.

Figure A.2 Universal 21st Century Rubric

Skill/Knowledge	Exemplary	Proficient	Basic	Novice	Score/Weight
THINKING Critical Thinking (Teacher-focused)	Consistently demonstrates multiple skills in evaluation, analysis and, synthesis	Routinely applies two components of critical thinking	Developing multiple types of critical thinking skills	Struggles to evaluate and analyze information	
THINKING Problem Solving (Teacher-Focused)	Accurately sequences and applies problem-solving skills in multiple situations	Generally able to solve problems in a thoughtful sequence	Able to discern parts of the problem but needs help achieving resolution	Finds it challenging to follow the problem-solving steps and generate solutions	
THINKING Creativity (Student-focused)	I show flexibility and originality in my projects all the time and come up with many new ideas and ways to do things	I can create new things with a few suggestions and ideas from my teacher	I like to think creatively but sometimes don't come up with a lot of new ideas	It's really tough for me to come up with something new and original by myself	
ACTING Communicating Collaborating (Student-focused)	I get excited and engaged when I work with others to share ideas and learn together	I'm a good team member—I listen to other's ideas and explain mine clearly	I like to be part of a team but get confused when there are too many ideas or people disagree.	Sometimes it's hard for me to work with others and accept their ideas. I just like to do it my way	
ACTING ICT (Teacher-focused)	Strong information access and applied technology skills in multiple media	Understands and uses information and media to create good quality products	Developing skills in accessing information and using technology	Has difficulty in selecting information and using technology to manage it.	
LIVING Citizenship/Responsibility (Teacher-focused)	Enthusiastically fulfills the responsibilities of good citizenship. Sets goals and independently acts on them	Participates in the democratic process on their own accord. Works consistently to fulfill responsibilities	Demonstrates citizenship when requested. Sometimes needs help to work to set and achieve priorities	Minimally contributes to the democratic process in the classroom and community. Not sure how to establish goals	
LIVING Global Understanding (Teacher-focused)	Aware of, sensitive to, and celebrates cultural diversity in a global context	Familiar with multiple aspects of cultural diversity and appreciates various global viewpoints	Understands that people around the world have different experiences and beliefs	Disrespectful of cultural differences	
LIVING College, Career, and Workplace (Teacher-focused)	Utilizes multiple 21st century skills to plan and manage one's life	Has a direction in life and uses some skills to reach it	Developing skills needed for planning and managing one's life	Minimal focus and actions in relation to goals and productivity	
Comments:					Total:

198

Figure A.3 is a tool that can be used in the classroom to synthesize this information into a grade-book format. W. M. Smith School, a third- to sixth-grade community-based school, uses it along with the traditional report cards to report progress on students' 21st century skills. The scores align with their common rubrics that are based on a one to four scale. Trackers can be used either for a specific project or over the long term.

Figure A.3 Student Tracker

Period or Unit					Class		
					Teacher		
Student	Thinking Critical Thinking	Thinking Creativity	Acting Collaborating	Acting Technology	Lifelong Civic	Lifelong Leadership	Summary
Willoughby	4	2	3	4			
Hinckley	3	3	3	4			
Desiderata	2.5	4	4	3			
Chatyra	3	3	4	3.5			
Stockton	3.5	2	3	4			

21ST CENTURY RUBRICS

The following rubrics are proposed for adaptation by students, teachers, and schools. They are by no means meant to be complete. It is possible to create a customized rubric for specific assignments by selecting and combining items from several individual rubrics. For example, for her third-grade class, Ms. Harbinger compiles her own rubric for an immigrant experience project in which students are required to do research, collaborate, synthesize, use ICT, and present what they learned. An example of this type of project rubric is shown at the end of this section.

Thinking

Critical Thinking

Skill/Knowledge	Exemplary	Proficient	Basic	Novice	Score/ Weight
Apply	Purposefully seeks and uses information and data from multiple sources and prior experience in relation to real-world situations.	Finds and uses a few selected facts, sources, and evidence to understand the present and make plan.	Uses selected data and pieces of information that are provided in relation to learning in the present.	Misunderstands facts, data, and principles and needs help to meaningfully utilize them.	
Evaluate	Adeptly appraises evidence. Compares and contrasts multiple criteria and perspectives and thoughtfully connects them to the present object, setting, and performance.	Understanding of the evaluation criteria is evident but not fully utilized and explained. Able to make some connections to learning.	Has difficulty demonstrating that they understand the evaluation criteria and accurately using them.	Evaluation of the object, setting, or performance doesn't clearly relate to given criteria or standards.	
Uses Data to Develop Critical Insights	Uses accurately selected data to draw conclusions that are aligned with facts.	Demonstrates the use of data to draw conclusions and form insights.	Tries but has difficulty selecting data and using them to draw conclusions.	Unable to apply and use data independently in a meaningful way.	
Analyze	Identifies main issues, establishes priorities among details, and sees unstated implications. Comprehends complex ideas and multiple perspectives.	Identifies and understands the main issue but reasoned judgments are undeveloped.	Describes the main issue inaccurately. Unable to thoughtfully scrutinize it in an objective manner.	With help, can grasp a straightforward issue and draw simple conclusions.	
Synthesize	Identifies and compares components of arguments to generate a new and cohesive summary. Skilled at combining parts into wholes.	Able to put together two divergent ideas, see straightforward patterns, and summarize them.	Can see the ideas related to one viewpoint and uses them to generate a summary.	Relationships between ideas are elusive except at a rudimentary level.	

Problem Solving

Skill/Knowledge	Exemplary	Proficient	Basic	Novice	Score/Weight
Identifies the Problem	I clearly described a problem with supporting details in relation to the situation.	I described the basics of the problem with some supporting information.	I explained parts of the problem but not the complete problem.	I had difficulty defining the problem.	
Applies Problem-Solving Steps	I used the full range of steps and strategies I learned to solve problems.	I was able to use most of the problem steps and strategies.	I used a few of the problem steps that I learned.	I think I missed some of the steps in problem solving.	
Identifies Solutions	I came up with at least four feasible and clearly described solutions.	I offered two to three plausible solutions.	I described one or two possible solutions.	I was unable to give any solutions.	
Evaluates Solutions	I was able to thoughtfully evaluate and analyze all the possible choices before selecting the most feasible one.	I was able to make a reasoned judgment about the choices and pick one that makes sense.	I was able to compare my options and pick one to start with.	I picked one, but I wasn't sure it was a good choice.	
Defends Solutions	I analyzed all the solutions and picked one that shows my understanding of the problem and the outcomes.	I evaluated the solutions and explained why I picked one that seems to be feasible.	I gave a simple explanation for one choice.	I wasn't able to explain my solution. I just thought it was a good one.	
Real World Applications	I can demonstrate my problem-solving skills successfully even when they are not part of school assignments.	I try to use my problem solving skills outside of school and usually I'm successful.	I sometimes think about how I would solve a problem away from school.	I do best at school when there is a structured format and someone can help me.	
Inductive Reasoning	I can accurately identify and interpret relevant facts and information that helps me to draw logical conclusions.	I can select relevant information that will lead me to reasonable conclusions.	I can use selected information and facts to draw some conclusions.	I'm not sure what information to use and how to use it to draw conclusions.	
Deductive Reasoning	I can work with fundamental principles of a topic and use relevant generalizations to draw logical conclusions.	I can use basic principles and generalizations to draw a conclusion and predict outcomes.	I think I draw logical conclusions but I'm not sure I understand the core principles.	The conclusions I draw don't have direct bearing on the generalizations and principles I chose to use.	

Creativity

Skill/Knowledge	Exemplary	Proficient	Basic	Novice	Score/Weight
Curiosity	I am intrigued by novel elements and ideas and actively seek them out.	I'm curious about some things and usually am willing to explore new ideas.	With some help I will explore new ways of thinking and doing.	I hardly ever wonder about ideas and things.	
Fluency	I can look at things in various ways and describe multiple and diverse purposes for them.	I can usually come up with some alternative ways of looking at things.	If I work with someone else I can find other ways of looking at things.	Usually I just see things from my own perspective.	
Originality	I can come up with many new ideas and products on most topics and can bring something new to fruition.	I can come up with some new ideas on my own and, if it's easy, work toward using it.	If I have some guidelines I can usually come up with new ideas.	I need help thinking of new things.	
Elaboration	It's easy and fun to add details to something to make it better.	I can usually come up with ways to add details to something to make it better.	Maybe a few ideas come to me if I think really hard.	Sometimes I just can't think of ways to make something better.	
Flexibility	I adapt well to new situations and can see many possibilities in my everyday learning and living.	I can work effectively even when things change and notice the potential of some things as I learn.	Sometimes it's hard for me to adjust to change. When someone reminds me to think differently, I usually can do so.	I am unable to be productive when things change. It's hard for me to "think outside the box." I like things as they are.	
Divergent	It easy for me to combine ideas, modify and adapt them, and rearrange them to improve the outcomes.	I can do two or three of these to change a product or process: combine, modify, adapt, or rearrange.	I can do one or two but my ideas are relatively simple.	This is hard for me to do because I tend to see things as they are rather than how they could be.	
Messiness/Risk Taking	I know that creativity can be messy but still strive to try new things. I don't worry much about my mistakes, because I learn from them.	I'm willing to try to projects and don't worry too much about making mistakes.	Sometimes I hold myself back because I might make mistakes and it won't come out right.	I feel nervous and try to avoid the messier aspects of creativity.	
With Others	I'm most creative when I use the synergy that comes from working with others.	My ideas get better when I work with others to improve on something.	I'll usually watch and listen before sharing my creative ideas, but then I add a few.	It's hard for me to tell if any of my ideas are worth sharing with other, so usually I don't.	

Metacognition

Skill/Knowledge	Exemplary	Proficient	Basic	Novice	Score/Weight
Reflective	I can review my learning with precision and insight. This helps me learn and improve my skills and knowledge.	I am able to consider my actions in a way that helps me do better in the future.	With prompts and reminders to guide my reflection I can improve on my learning.	I need a visual or verbal structure to help me think about my learning. With help, I can build on it.	
Aware of Thinking	I am very aware of my thoughts, use them to improve skills and knowledge, and can explain how they influence my learning.	I think about my beliefs and ideas, can express them, and can use them to help me learn.	Sometimes my thoughts are mixed up and it takes me time to sort through them.	I can explain a few of my thoughts and with assistance can connect them to my learning.	
Strengths and Styles	I recognize the importance of knowing my learning strengths and styles, monitor them, and utilize them routinely.	I have a pretty good idea of how I think and learn and know that I should incorporate it in my work.	I'm not always sure how to use my strengths and learning styles to improve my work.	It doesn't really matter how I think and learn as long as I do some of my work.	
Using Metacognition	I use my metacognitive abilities to improve my learning and productivity. I routinely apply them in my daily practices.	I routinely apply my ability to think about my thinking as I learn and work and generally they help me perform better.	Sometimes I can stop and think about my thought processes, but I don't find it very helpful in my daily routines.	This is really hard to do. I try to understand how I think but I have difficulty applying it to my life.	

Acting

Communicating

Skill/Knowledge	Exemplary	Proficient	Basic	Novice	Score/Weight
Oral Communication	Clarity, pace, volume and articulation are all strong and enhance Communication.	Clarity, pace, volume, and articulation are acceptable for the purpose of the communication.	One significant part of oral communication may be compromised.	It is difficult to hear and follow the communication.	
Receptive Communication: Listens, Reads, Views	Distinguishes facts from opinions, recognizes intent of messages, summarizes main ideas, identifies support for viewpoint.	Determines facts and recognizes persuasion. Identifies and summarizes the main ideas.	Can identify facts in a message. Skills are developing in interpreting messages.	Restates facts. Partially understands the purpose of a message.	
Discerns Intent	Identifies and interprets overt and nuanced messages. Draws logical conclusions.	Decodes most messages but better with overt than nuanced.	Can understand main ideas in a message but needs help with the nuanced ones	Understands most facts but unable to grasp nuance.	
Uses Communication Strategies	Produces communications that are clear, accurate, and reflective.	Communications are usually understandable, with a few minor errors.	Able to produce basic communications		
Communicates Clearly for a Purpose	Recognizes the purpose and then organizes and presents information to meet it.	Aware of the purpose. The information and presentation serves the intended purpose.	Somewhat unclear on the purpose, thus compromising the quality of information and the presentation.	Confused about the purpose of communication and has difficulty focusing on content and process.	
Presentation Skills	Poised and precise. Responds to audience cues by adjusting tone, depth, and pacing.	Exhibits poise. Usually aware of the audience and makes effort to respond to their cues.	Tries but has difficulty being poised, professional, and responsive.	Presentation is missing professional components. Unaware of audience reaction.	

Debate

Standard	4 Exceeds Expectation	3 Meets Expectations	2 Working Toward	1 Below Standard	Score
Content: Opening Remarks, Rebuttal	Strong argument with clear views. Logical, specific and on target.	Perspective is clear. Arguments are mostly convincing and focused.	Viewpoint is a little nebulous. Remarks are neutral and somewhat vague in detail.	Focus is not established. Unconvincing statements.	
Support	Support is fact-based, detailed and compelling.	Support contains facts and data and is purposeful.	Support is incomplete in facts, purpose, and focus.	Support is not evident.	
Organization	Fluent, clear, and logical process. Effective use of time.	Sequential progression of topic that demonstrates good use of time.	Sequence is difficult to follow. May not meet time requirements.	Limited sequence and organization that doesn't meet time requirements.	
Research	Topic is strongly supported with relevant data.	Includes analysis and synthesis of research.	Resources are inadequate or inadequately analyzed and applied.	Resources are limited, resulting in substandard product.	
Presentation	Poised and professional, resulting in high audience attention.	Effective style that engages the audience.	Needs further practice in presentation skills and audience engagement.	Disengaged from presentation and audience.	
Contribution to Team and Debate Process	Prepared for role. Energizing, respectful, and encouraging of others.	Contributes to teamwork and adheres to guidelines. Respectful of others.	Inconsistent use of preparation, respect, and teamwork.	Lack of respect and responsibility affects the learning environment.	

Collaborating

Skill/Knowledge	Exemplary	Proficient	Basic	Novice	Score/Weight
Works Productively	We used all our time efficiently to stay focused on the task and produce the required work. Everyone did their assigned duties and sometimes more.	We worked together well and for the most part stayed on task until we completed our work. Each person performed nearly all their duties.	We worked together sometimes, but not everyone contributed or did their job, making it hard finish our work.	We really didn't work together very well. Everyone wanted to do their own thing and tell others what to do rather than focus on the task.	
Demonstrates Respect	Everyone respectfully listened and discussed ideas that were shared.	Members listened and interacted respectfully most of the time.	Some people had difficulty being respectful of other's ideas.	Members were unwilling to listen to others and were argumentative with teammates.	
Compromises	Everyone was flexible in working together to achieve a common goal.	We usually were able to compromise in order to move our work forward.	If more people compromised we would have moved forward faster.	There was a lot of disagreeing and some individuals wanted it only their way.	
Shared Responsibility; Everyone Contributes	Everyone did his or her best work and followed through on assigned tasks.	Most people followed through on their part.	It was hard to get everyone to do his or her part.	We really couldn't depend on everyone to do his or her part.	

Digital Literacy

Skill/Knowledge	Exemplary	Proficient	Basic	Novice	Score/Weight
Finds	Able to sort through options and independently find information that is relevant to the problem	Can find most of the necessary information adequately and make relevant choices	Able to access some information but typically misses key issues	Practical knowledge of what to search for and how to find it is minimal	
Uses Multiple Sources	Skilled at just about all forms of text, video, music, simulation, and more	Skilled in at least 3 different types/sources of information	Able to use at least one source capably and may have rudimentary abilities with others	Most of the sources are new and require learning	
Selects	Exceptional ability to understand partiality of sources and thoughtfully makes relevant choices from a wide range of options	Sufficient understanding of source bias is used to select credible sources relevant to objectives	Able to select a few sources, but strategies are inefficient in selecting relevant one for a purpose	Difficulty in independently selecting sources and understanding their relevance	
Evaluates	Accomplished at verifying author and source and recognizing bias in information	Good skills in checking authors' credentials and checking consistency of information	Accept sites at face value but with a checklist can identify discrepancies in information	Needs help distinguishing fact from fantasy on a website	
Considers Source, Message Effect	Sensitive to the persuasive nature of electronic sources and can explain each one's methodology	Aware that sources may have a bias that influences personal decisions	Generally accepting of digital information. Aware of blatantly incredible information	Trusts website to provide information in their best interests	
Uses to Produce Original Work	Uses strong analysis and evaluative skills to use digital information to create an original product	Good skills in synthesizing digital information into a new product	Developing skills, and with practice will apply digital information to an original product	Uses digital information for learning purposes but not yet ready to produce original work	

Technology Literacy

Skill/Knowledge	Exemplary	Proficient	Basic	Novice	Score/Weight
Knows Computer-Based Technologies	I demonstrate excellence in a wide variety of computer products and technology-based productivity tools and routinely integrate them into my work.	I am competent in using multiple computer and technology products and tools enhance productivity.	I can use a variety of technology tools and perform basic tasks to support my productivity.	I'm on a learning curve in developing my computer competencies.	
Digital and Multimedia Products	I confidently use graphic images, video, sound, and other multimedia features to strengthen and display my learning.	I can incorporate digital and multimedia items such as graphics, video, and sound in my work to support my main ideas.	I can add images or other features to my work but they don't always align with my purpose.	I'm just learning to use one or two multimedia features and want to be better able to incorporate them in my work.	
Technicality	When I use technology in my work, the applications run flawlessly.	My applied use of technology is generally good, with only minor technical problems.	I frequently have technical problems when I use it in my work.	I'm very challenged in using technology in my learning and it usually doesn't work right.	
Design	My design is truly multimedia rather than linear and includes a number of well-designed objects and elements.	My design contained some appropriate objects and elements to support my purpose.	My design is limited in several elements, thus compromising its quality and relevance.	I can make few choices of objects and elements to add design elements to my work.	
Selection and Utilization	My use of technology shows deep understanding and proficiency that strengthens my work. I am able to choose the most appropriate technologies for complex authentic problems.	My routine use of technology shows that I understand it and can incorporate it in my presentations. I usually can select relevant technologies.	I've been using technology more regularly to support my learning and improve my presentations. I sometimes rely on what others tell me to use.	I think if I use just one technology at a time it will improve my presentations, but sometimes I'm not sure which one to use.	
Legal/Ethical	I have in-depth knowledge of legal and ethical issues such as copyright.	I'm familiar with legal and ethical issues such as citing sources.	I have a basic understanding of some legal and ethical issues in technology.	I haven't heard much about the legal and ethical issues around technology.	

Living

Civics and Citizenship

Skill/Knowledge	Exemplary	Proficient	Basic	Novice	Score/Weight
Understands Democracy and Forms of Government	I can recognize, evaluate, and compare a variety of political forms and structures.	I understand that there are multiple political forms and structures and can explain some.	If I have an outline or a graphic format I can put together basic comparisons.	I know there are differences but I need help explaining them.	
Participates in the Democratic Process; Contributes to Improvement	I make a meaningful contribution to my classroom and community in advancing the democratic process.	I get involved in activities when they are presented and when opportunities become available.	With prodding, I will participate in activities that are part of a democratic action.	I generally prefer to observe rather than get involved.	
Civic Dispositions and Behaviors	Through my actions I demonstrate my belief in equality and personal responsibility and my understanding of the effects of these actions.	I believe in civic involvement and usually am respectful of the rights and differences of others.	For the most part I believe in equality and generally am respectful of others.	I have a hard time respecting people who are different than me and accepting those differences.	

Global

Skill/Knowledge	Exemplary	Proficient	Basic	Novice	Score/Weight
Global Issues	Can explain multiple historical and current issues and how they affect people around the world	Has a general idea of issues that are happening around the globe and can explain some in detail	Identifies one or two global issues and makes one or two connections to people	Isn't aware or doesn't pay attention to what is happening in the world	
Cultural Understanding	Highly knowledgeable about multiple cultural beliefs, values, and customs that routinely influence the way people act and behave toward others	Some knowledge of selected cultures beliefs, values, and customs that relate to and contribute to their own behavior	Aware that culture is part of their life but in general knowledge, understanding, and awareness are superficial	Ignorant and uninterested in learning about and recognizing other cultures	
Contributes in and to the Global Society	Works constructively with people from other cultural groups and seeks to learn and understand their experiences and views. Participates in global initiatives to improve the world	Communicates and works with people from other cultures. Sometimes reaches out beyond their own world to make a contribution	When urged, will work with people who are different from them, but has minimal interest in contributing to the collaboration	Has difficulty working with people from other cultures and groups and chooses not to participate in larger initiatives	
Perspective Taking	Understands the complexity of culture and has adequate knowledge to effectively see the viewpoints of other cultures	In the context of history, understands that other groups may have a different perspective on events	Needs some support to see that there are different perspectives and ways of looking at things	Unable to understand that other groups have different views of the same events	
Equity and Equality	Supports and promotes fairness and equality for all members of the class	Treats everyone equally. Recognizes when someone is not being treated fairly	Understands about equality but sometimes forgets proper conduct	Has a hard time identifying and accepting the basic rights of others	

Leadership and Responsibility

Skill/Knowledge	Exemplary	Proficient	Basic	Novice	Score/Weight Weight
Interpersonal Skills	Consistently listens to other's viewpoints, responds respectfully, and encourages others to higher achievement.	Usually listens respectfully to other's ideas and works collaboratively with a variety of other people.	At times listens to other viewpoints but sometimes shows disapproval of others' thoughts and actions.	Rarely shows respect and often shows disdain for other's ideas and actions.	
Shared Goal Setting and Accomplishment	Routinely demonstrates personal responsibility for setting and achieving goals.	Usually makes a positive contribution toward shared goals.	Sometimes finds it challenging to work with others to establish and achieve goals.	Rarely is able to independently work with others to set and accomplish goals.	
Responsibility	Demonstrates sophisticated understanding of personal responsibility for own actions and their effect on others. Acts in highly ethical ways.	Acknowledges their responsibility for their actions and seeks to act in ethical ways in relation to self and others.	Aware of the meaning of personal responsibility and with reminders can accept it and recognize the effect of their choices on others.	Overwhelmed and confused by the idea of personal responsibility and has difficulty monitoring actions.	

Work Ethic

Skill/Knowledge	Exemplary	Proficient	Basic	Novice	Score/Weight
Accountability	Punctual, prepared, and organized. Conscientious and independent worker who goes beyond requirements.	Usually on time and ready to learn. Works consistently without supervision to achieve goals.	Assumes minimal personal responsibility. Needs supervision to complete task.	Late and unprepared. Does not work with others or complete work.	
Participation	Actively involved and highly productive.	Attentive and generally involved and productive.	Present but minimally involved and productive.	Doesn't participate. Off task and/or disruptive.	
Attitude	Enthusiastic and cooperative. Accepts and acts on feedback.	Positive attitude toward people, process, and product. Accepts feedback.	Somewhat engaged but noncommittal. Listens to feedback.	Negative attitude toward work and others. Ignores feedback.	
Communication	Communicates directly and clearly. Listens thoughtfully to others.	Speech is clear and eye contact is made. Listens respectfully to others.	Speaks but doesn't always listen. May be unclear in expressing ideas.	Needs to be reminded to listen to others. Speech is difficult to follow.	
Teamwork	Values and synthesizes individual contributions and utilizes them for goal achievement.	Contributes to group discussions and tasks. Works with others toward goal.	Contributes knowledge and skills to the group. Interpersonal skills are emerging.	Doesn't demonstrate interest in the ideas of others. Distracts others.	
Individual Contribution	Accepts responsibility and takes a leadership role. Frequently helps others.	Accepts responsibility and fulfills individual role within the group. Sometimes helps others.	Sometimes participates the group but prefers to work independently.	Participates in the group but contribution is limited.	
Work Product and Outcome	Effectively coordinates time, effort, and resources to ensure completion and quality of work. Final product exceeds requirements.	Utilizes resources successfully. Final product meets requirements.	Final product is incomplete.	Doesn't demonstrate understanding or interest in final product.	

College/Career/Workplace

Skill/Knowledge	Exemplary	Proficient	Basic	Novice	Score/Weight
Planning/Goal Setting	Uses priorities to set realistic short-term and long-term goals and actionable plans for life and work.	Able to set goals and develop the core elements of a personal and professional growth plan.	Sets a few realistic goals and has some plans for life and work.	Requires a scaffold to set goals and develop plans.	
Management of Plans and Goals	Effectively and purposefully works toward goal achievement and attentively implements plans.	Typically follows the plan to achieve goals.	Sometimes sets goals but generally focuses on short-range execution of them.	Rarely sets and manages goals.	
Commitment to Mastery	Persistently works toward giving the best effort and producing the best outcomes possible.	Steadily works toward higher levels of mastery and productivity.	Work is produced with undistinguished quality and effort.	There are few indicators of motivation to produce one's best.	
Productivity	Routinely coordinates time, effort, and resources to ensure the highest quality work.	Appropriate use of resources results in a final product that meets requirements.	Sometimes forgets to check time and pacing, resulting in an incomplete product.	Needs support to select materials and use time appropriately.	
Accountability	Punctual, prepared, and organized. Conscientious and independent worker who goes beyond requirements.	Usually on time and ready to learn. Works consistently without supervision to achieve goals.	Assumes minimal personal responsibility. Needs supervision to complete task.	Late and unprepared. Does not work with others or complete work.	

213

Flexibility/Adaptability

Skill/Knowledge	Exemplary	Proficient	Basic	Novice	Score/Weight
Flexibility	Replaces old beliefs and strategies with proven new ones that will improve outcomes. Open to and adjusts to feedback	Adopts many new ideas that are perceived as helpful to goal attainment. Accepts and acts on feedback	Willing to change direction and strategies when encouraged or through targeted feedback	It's a challenge to trade old beliefs and ways for ones that may be more productive. Rarely listens to feedback	
Adjusts to Change	Embraces change for a purpose. Uses novelty as an opportunity for growth	Unconcerned about change. Willing to do what is required and adapts as needed	Uninterested in change or changing. Accepts status quo and may need coaxing to adjust	Easily confused and overwhelmed by change	
Resolves Challenge	Remains determined to complete tasks and achieve goals and works to overcome obstacles	Persists in pursuing goals and completing tasks with a little encouragement	Considers giving up when faced with challenges but may keep on with significant support	Abandons tasks and goals in the face of adversity	

Initiative/Motivation

Skill/Knowledge	Exemplary	Proficient	Basic	Novice	Score/Weight
Priorities	Consistently sets challenging goals and establishes realistic priorities to achieve them.	Sets achievable goals and determines feasible priorities to achieve them.	Sets some goals with plans that are actionable, but not always complete.	Able to set reasonable goals and priorities with assistance.	
Self Direction	Develops a thorough action plan and follows through with it.	Creates a plan and generally acts on it independently.	Composes part of a plan but needs reminders to act on it.	Does best when someone collaborates on the plan and provides frequent direction.	
Monitors and Perseveres	Actively monitors work and thoughtfully adjusts to prevent impending problems.	Keeps track of how things seem to be going but doesn't always think ahead or consider possible problems.	Is aware that things are moving forward but not attentive to necessary adjustments.	Oblivious to the process and outcomes of actions and choices.	
Continuous Growth	Excited about and actively manages continuous growth and learning.	Takes pleasure in learning and growing and generally directs its course.	Waits for direction and generally takes the path that is offered.	Resists growing and learning. Prefers for things to remain as they are.	

Appendix B

21st Century Lesson Plan

Effective teaching, meaningful learning, and quality assessment are enduring.

Subject/Class:	Teacher:
Unit:	Grade:
Topic:	

Common Core State Standards

State/Local/Content Standards	
Enduring Understandings/Essential Questions	
Learning Objectives; "Students will . . ." (include 20th and 21st c. outcomes)	
INITIATION Expectancy Connections to prior learning	
PREASSESSMENT	

INSTRUCTIONAL STRATEGY
Acquisition of Content
    • Direct/Self Directed
    • Instruction
    • Modeling/Coaching
    • Digital/Electronic	

LEARNING PROCESS and ARRANGEMENTS
    • Engagement
    • Application
    • Grouping	

21ST CENTURY SKILLS	
FORMATIVE ASSESSMENT Response to FA	
RESOURCES and MATERIALS	
ASSESSMENT	
CONTENT Summative knowledge	
PROCESS OF LEARNING Skills developed	
PRODUCTS OF LEARNING Demonstrations of authenticity	
Grading/Reporting	

IN PRACTICE

Rachael Carson, *Silent Spring* (1962)

In 1962, the environmental movement was introduced to the public via this book that documented the effects of pesticides on the environment. The book claimed that the use of DDT to kill mosquitoes was also killing birds, harming humans, and affecting the larger ecosystem. The book generated much controversy and criticism, some of which endures today.

Subject/Class: *English, Science, Social Studies, Interdisciplinary*	Teacher:
Unit: *Protecting Our Environment*	Grade: *8*
Topic: *Solving Environmental Problems*	

Common Core State Standards

- Determine central ideas of a text and analyze their development; summarize the key supporting details and ideas
- Acquire and use a range of content—specific words and phrases
- Evaluate the argument and claims in a text including the validity of the reasoning as well as the sufficiency of the evidence: Evaluate a speaker's point of view, reasoning, and use of evidence and rhetoric
- Write informative/explanatory texts to convey complex ideas
- Write arguments supporting claims, using valid reasoning
- Participate effectively in a range of conversations and collaborations with diverse partners, building on other's ideas and expressing their own clearly and persuasively
- Use digital media strategically to present information and evidence
- Add as relevant to your state, district, school, and content area

Enduring Understandings/Essential Questions

- Recognize the impact that one dedicated person can have on our environment
- Make connections between the environment and personal/community quality of life
- Evaluate the interdisciplinary connections of current issues

Learning Objectives; Students will (include 20th and 21st c. outcomes)

- Describe primary concerns of scientists in protecting the environment using topical vocabulary
- Explain and analyze the challenges and controversies involved (past and present) in being a good steward of our environment
- Research and produce a digital/web2.0 product that informs and persuades others

| INITIATION Expectancy Connections to prior learning | • Based on the chapter titles, write or illustrate what you think will be the main idea of one chapter and the challenges that Rachael Carson will describe in her book Silent Spring. Make connections to prior learning in science and social studies. Post chapter titles around the classroom. Students stand at one chapter and discuss it with others who picked the same chapter. Report out on learning expectations

Alternative Initiation

• Quotes: Display these quotes and have students predict the main idea of the text based on these quotes.
• This can be done individually or collaboratively with an entrance slip.
• "Man has lost the capacity to foresee and to forestall. He will end by destroying the earth." — Albert Schweitzer
• "I am pessimistic about the human race because it is too ingenious for its own good. Our approach to nature is to beat it into submission." — E.B. White |
| --- | --- |
| PREASSESSMENT | Five Selected choice questions and three response questions about main ideas and connections between literature, science, and social studies |
| Instructional Strategy Acquisition of Content

• Direct Instruction
• Modeling/ Coaching
• Digital/Electronic | • Watch selected videos of Rachel Carson. Complete an empty outline form.
• Compare/contrast Rachel Carson's research methods to the scientific method.
• Produce an electronic/web 2.0 product for promoting environmental awareness. Distribute written assignment/ grading rubric. Show exemplars of electronic projects. |
| LEARNING PROCESS and ARRANGEMENTS

• Engagement Structure
• Making Meaning
• Collaboration | Teams prepare, through reading, viewing, and collaborative planning, for a Socratic Seminar or debate on the use of pesticides. |
| 21ST CENTURY SKILLS | • Global Connections: Skype with a school in Brazil on the current status of deforestation and agricultural development in relation to the environment. |

(Continued)

(Continued)

	• Chapter 17 proposes alternatives to pesticides that were being used at the time. Research current methods and create a blog to inform and persuade the community to use gardening techniques that protect the environment. • 21st C. Skills: Analysis, problem solving, communication, collaboration, technology literacy, work ethic.
FORMATIVE ASSESSMENT • Response to FA	Throughout the learning process strategies such as • Preassessment as noted • During Instruction: Empty outlines, exit slips • Post assessment: ABC review. Students write test questions and use in a Q and A mix-up • In response, content is differentiated, groups are formed/reformed, assessments are adjusted
RESOURCES and MATERIALS	Silent Spring (online reading of selected chapters, videos)

ASSESSMENT	
CONTENT	• Summative data analysis of the use of pesticides then and now • Vocabulary—Accurate use of selected terms in the context of writing a press release or letter to a legislator about the environment
PROCESS OF LEARNING	Skills and knowledge developed: Student journals
PRODUCTS OF LEARNING	Demonstrations of authenticity: Electronic and print products/presentations

Appendix C

Questions and Answers

THE CHALLENGES TO
21ST CENTURY ASSESSMENT

1. The Term *21st Century Education* Is
Everywhere I Turn, But No One Seems to Agree on
What It Is? Why Is That?

That's an astute observation. There is a need to do a better job of defining the skills, determining how they fit into teaching and learning, and illuminating ways to assess them. At the present time, the 21st century initiatives are coming from many sectors: educators, policy makers, test makers, and the business sector. It is likely that they each have a unique perspective and agenda. The purpose of this book is to synthesize this variety of perspectives into a flexible view on educational inputs and learning outcomes. Multiple sources are reviewed and organized in a way that reflects the broader purposes of education.

There is growing consensus on the need to change education, There is general agreement on the skills and knowledge today's students need to be successful. There is a growing lexicon of common and shared definitions, but it will take time for this all to coalesce. Proposals for how schools can respond to this new paradigm are still in the early stages, as are strategies for teaching these skills. What is least available are ways to measure and assess the 21st century learning outcomes.

In the meantime, as the ideas unfold, it would definitely help to more clearly define the skills, be more specific about what they look like, and determine reproducible strategies for incorporating them in teaching, learning, and assessment.

2. What's the Difference Between 20th Century and 21st Century Learning and Assessing?

If you are over 30, most of your education took place in the 20th century. There were lots of books and maybe a few videos. If you created things, they were probably made from paper, plastic, and recycled materials. You read from books and periodicals and sometimes from handouts that the teacher copied for you. There was a strong emphasis on content mastery, and selected choice tests were the norm.

Students born during the 1990s or later grew up with technology. Computers and cell phones are merely extensions of themselves. Information is available 24/7, and there is more of it than ever. Social connections are instantaneous, and free time is often spent with electronic devices, games, and social networking. Thus, what's changed is how information is accessed and used. Students don't take a test before using technology. They demonstrate proficiency through its use.

Twenty-first century learners need to know how to find, use, and manipulate information. They need to be able to employ it to generate new ideas. In the workplace, teamwork and communication are routine. Employers are seeking people who are self-motivated, have a positive attitude, and demonstrate leadership and people skills.

These are the changes that are driving transformations in teaching, learning, and assessing in our classrooms and schools.

3. Is There Any Scientific Basis to This?

In one respect that that an accurate challenge. It is one that NASA could have used before launching the Hubble telescope. Despite initial faltering, the scientists and engineers at NASA utilized their problem-solving skills, worked collaboratively, and applied technology to resolve the problem. They had no prior experience in meeting this challenge nor research-based solutions to this particular incident, yet they were successful.

Applying similar reasoning to 21st century skills: It is possible to explore the array of research in many related areas and domains to find relevant connections. The work of Bob Marzano and John Hattie has shed light on the most effective teaching strategies, many of which overlap with 21st century skills. The research on motivation done by Edward Deci and Carol Dweck reveals that motivation is built on choice, control, and engagement. Neuroscience is helping us understand how brain functioning relates to learning and revealing how, developmentally, students acquire and apply higher-level thinking.

Studies on students' use of technology show that they live in two different worlds; one in school, with limited use of a few selected technologies, and their lives outside of school, in which they are continuously immersed in technology. There is increasing evidence that digital technologies are changing learner's brains (Carr, 2010). If education is to keep up with this, then assessing learning also needs to keep pace.

While the research on 21st century learning is just emerging, there is supporting evidence for it in related fields. A stretch, maybe, but so was Galileo's theory of the solar system.

4. The Skills Seem Soft and Vague and Therefore Harder to Assess.

It certainly is easy to assess whether student can add 27 and 54 or to define the word *hypothesis*. Many tests ask students to recall historical events or find the main ideas in an article on such topics as the effects of lack of sleep on student achievement. It is harder to measure a student's ability to solve a construction problem using mathematical principles. It is equally difficult to assess a student's analysis of the results of a lab experiment or ability to work with others to create a campaign to help those in need, or the quality of a student's reflection on his own podcast.

Progress has been made in designing valid and reliable assessments. We are developing the ability to objectively assess 21st century skills. That doesn't mean it is easy. Portfolios can document growth, and rubrics can be used to assess selected criteria for products and performances. It will be harder to assess the ability to work collaboratively with others; to do so will require assessing such factors as ability to contributing meaningfully to the group, to listen to the ideas of others, to work together to create a new product, and to develop plans to solve a problem. In the long run, though, these types of assessments will be an important part of preparing students for the future. Therefore, strategies and metrics to assess them are essential.

5. There is Already More Content Knowledge Included in the Curriculum Than There Is Time to Master. How Can We Possibly Find the Time for These 21st Century Skills?

Content knowledge is the foundation of any 21st century application. Certainly, it would be impossible for a doctor to perform surgery without the requisite knowledge and skills. An auto technician can't fix a car just because he hears a noise. Students too, need to master core knowledge. This can be done independently of the application of that knowledge; better, it can be done in the context of 21st century skills. Content knowledge should be assessed through practice, as it is with doctors and technicians.

Research shows that engagement and enjoyment contribute to a love of learning. Motivation is increased when students have choice and control (Deci & Ryan, 2006; Dweck, 2006; Pink, 2009). So, while content is important, student engagement is equally important. Teachers can put content in the context of problem solving, product development, creative applications, and relevant technologies. It is time to move beyond the core subjects to fostering learners who can work productively with content in real world settings. Knowing whether students have mastered these skills will, by necessity, lead to alternative ways of assessing. This won't take more time, just different priorities

6. Will It Work for Lower-Achieving Students Who Need Common Core Mastery First?

All students need to master basic literacy and numeracy. As a result, instruction at the lower grades may have a strong emphasis on mastery. As students develop core knowledge, 21st century skills can be integrated more routinely into daily practice. There are some who advocate the integration of applied learning and critical thinking from the early grades on. There's also evidence that some portions of the brain need to mature before certain types of higher-level thinking can be utilized. Basically, it is a chicken-or-egg dilemma; for each student and classroom, decisions can be made to best meet the needs of the learners.

When used thoughtfully, applied learning and authentic assessment can serve to embed knowledge in memory. Learning becomes more meaningful when students apply it in real world situations. Interpreting Internet text, creating graphic designs, and synthesizing information into new products have applications in all content areas.

Students who drop out of high school cite a lack of interest and a lack of engagement. Their academic achievement becomes stagnant as they find themselves less drawn in to learning. What better way to appeal to these students than with projects, problem solving, creativity, and technology grounded in a strong core of content knowledge? Instructional strategies can incorporate all of these.

7. What About the Developmental Basis for Them: How Do We Know When Students Are Ready for 21st Century Skills?

All students can learn to use 21st century skills. For some, teachers may need to provide extra scaffolding and support. Very young children can learn to work together and share jobs on a common task. Comparing can be done at various levels of complexity from animal groups to ambiguous global issues.

And it doesn't take much to add creative thinking to most units of learning by asking questions about how else something may be used or what it may look like in the future. When 21st century skills are incorporated into the curriculum in developmentally appropriate ways, then all students benefit.

8. What Will These New Tests Look Like?

They may not be tests. Tests are static measures that provide a snapshot of a child's knowledge at one moment in time. Assessments that are informative and display student thinking are more important in the 21st century. It is relatively easy to start developing and using such assessments on a small scale in classrooms; it will be much harder to develop large-scale measure that will require new psychometrics. If we are looking for visible thinking and encouraging divergent responses, then single answer tests should not be the primary measurement.

Computerized adaptive testing is being developed and may have potential for 21st century skills. Computers are also being programmed to follow keystrokes to determine sequences of thinking. It may be easier to apply these techniques to some subjects than others, such as collaboration and citizenship. In the meantime, there are emerging strategies such as having skilled human readers categorize completion items and then enter the category into the computer. The challenge lies in developing tasks, assessments, and scoring systems that meet the conditions of validity and reliability.

9. It Seems Like We Are Giving One More Task to Already Overburdened Teachers.

It's true that teachers have more and more responsibilities added to an already complex stack. Consider this list of 21st century acronyms: RTI, PLC, NCLB, NAEP, PISA, IEP, 504, ESOL, GLE, and CRISS. In addition, teachers are confronted with new grading and reporting programs, smartboards, new standards, and more. Doug Reeves (n.d.) refers to this as initiative fatigue and explains that over extended periods, emotional energy and time become drained.

Twenty-first century skills are more like the wrapper to support initiative integration It's not difficult to apply the acronyms to 21st century skills. For example, with a vocabulary drill, ask students to create funny sentences with the words. Send students in search of real-world applications of a newly learned math concept. Rather than initiative fatigue, consider it initiative reconstruction and use it to revitalize teaching, learning, and assessing.

10. Is This Just Another Passing Initiative?

There are both supporters and critics of the movement to introduce 21st century skills into education. Some see it as akin to fads that faded quickly, like Total Quality Management (TQM) and Edison Schools, while others see it as more similar to more enduring movements such as Montessori education. Critics argue that taking time away from content knowledge is not a good idea in these times of high-stakes outcomes, while supporters believe that 21st century skills must be integrated with core knowledge. Some concerns have been expressed about lower-performing students and whether these changes will serve to dilute an already overflowing standards-based curriculum.

Some say these are not new skills. They are right. Socrates believed in questioning and reason. Plato's ideas on abstract thinking and Aristotle's work on sorting and organizing knowledge continue today. The work of Dewey, Vygotsky, and Glaser was not widely embraced during their times, but their basic ideas have endured. The ideas are not new; it is the world that has changed, making these theories more relevant than ever.

Thinking skills, personal actions, and lifelong competencies cannot be ignored by today's teachers and learners. These are what the knowledge workers of the future need to master. Twenty-first century skills will be a passing fad unless the skills are explicitly included in the curriculum. Many discussions and proposals describe the aims and goals of 21st century learning in general terms with little thought to how they will be taught and how they will be measured. Until policies for teaching 21st century skills are formulated at the national and state level, it is unlikely that they will be included routinely in curriculum, teaching, and learning. Without valid and reliable assessments at all levels, it will be difficult to persuade schools and educators to move in this direction.

11. Why Now?

Many factors flow into the current vortex of 21st century education. Standardized testing hasn't changed education for the better. Teaching to the test has made only a slight change in educational outcomes in the United States. Other countries are improving on international measures, while U.S. students are no longer competitive. The rapid proliferation of knowledge and the brisk pace of change require modifications to teaching and assessing. Educators can no longer ask simply what students know, but also need to ask what they can do with that knowledge. Critical thinking, planning, problem solving, communication, collaboration, and technology skills are essential and need to be interwoven with factual knowledge. We can no longer afford to teach and test only discrete content.

12. What Is Important to be Asking as We Prepare for the Future?

Over a decade ago, William Spady (1999) listed the important questions to ask about any school reform. Rather than asking how many classes a student should take, what content should they know, or what tests should measure this, he suggested that more enduring outcomes be considered. A clear understanding of what our students will be facing when they complete their education and how to prepare them for that is a reasonable starting point. He asked educators, "What performance abilities and qualities do students need in order to face those conditions successfully and what kinds of learning experiences will develop them?" (p. 5). He suggested that educators then need to determine what teaching and learning practices will best support those learning outcomes and develop high-level applied learning. Commitment to a long-term process, shared expertise, and a clear direction will move us forward on that question: What is important to know and do, and how can we help students achieve it?

13. Myths and Truths About 21st Century Teaching, Learning, and Assessing

Myths	Truths
It's not for everyone.	Students all ages, grades, subjects, genders, cultures and achievement levels can benefit from it. This is learning that is relevant to life.
It's only for older students.	Some types of higher-level thinking are easier for more mature brains, but all can benefit from it when used thoughtfully and appropriately.
It's too hard for some students.	As with all learning and assessing, there must be a good match to a learner's developmental abilities.
Classrooms will become chaotic.	There may be some messiness, but much learning occurs in a nonlinear fashion. There may be more activity because of higher levels of engagement.
It's more important to teach core content.	Core content and 21st century skills must be integrated—each supports the other, and they must be assessed together.
It makes more work for teachers.	It's a change that requires a different approach to teaching and assessing. It's not an add-on that makes more work.
It will replace tests.	It will increase the spectrum of assessments that are used to determine learning.
It changes everything.	Yes, some arrangements, routines, and resources will be adapted, hopefully for the better.
It's not real life.	Life is not a multiple choice test.

References

Ananiadou, K., & Claro, M. (2009). *21st century skills and competencies for new millennium learners in OECD countries.* (OECD Education Working Papers, No. 41). Paris: OECD Publishing. Retrieved from http://www.oecd-ilibrary.org/education/21st-century-skills-and-competences-for-new-millennium-learners-in-oecd-countries_218525261154

Anaya, R. (1994). *Bless me Ultima.* New York: Grand Central Publishing.

Anderson, L. W., & Krathwohl, D. R. (Eds.). (2001*). A taxonomy for learning, teaching and assessing: A revision of Bloom's taxonomy of educational objectives: Complete edition.* New York: Longman.

Banta, T. W., Lund, J. P., Black, K. E., & Oblander, F. W. (1996). *Assessment in practice: Putting principles to work on college campuses.* San Francisco: Jossey-Bass.

Barrett, H. (2003). Electronic portfolios. In A. Kovalchik & K. Dawson (Eds.), *Educational technology: An encyclopedia.* Santa Barbara, CA: ABC-CLIO. Retrieved from http://electronicportfolios.org/portfolios/encyclopediaentry.htm

Binkley, M., Erstad, O., Herman, J., Raizen, S., Ripley, M., & Rumble, M. (2010). *Defining 21st century skills* (Draft White Paper 1). Melbourne, Australia: University of Melbourne, Assessment and Teaching of 21st Century Skills. Retrieved from http://www.act21s.org/wp-content/uploads/2011/11/1-Defining-21st-Century-Skills.pdf

Blakemore, S., & Choudhury, S. (2006). Development of the adolescent brain: Implications for executive function and cognitive development. *Journal of Child Psychology and Psychiatry, 47*(3), 296–312. Retrieved from http://www.icn.ucl.ac.uk/sblakemore/SJ_papers/BlaCho_jcpp_06.pdf

Bloch, S. (2008). *Butterflies in my stomach.* New York: Sterling.

Bloom, B. S. (1956). *Taxonomy of educational objectives: The classification of educational goals. Handbook I: Cognitive domain.* New York: David McKay.

Bridgeland, J., Dilulio, J., Jr., & Morison, K. B. (2006). *The silent epidemic: Perspectives of high school dropouts.* Washington, DC: Civic Enterprises. Retrieved from http://www.sswaa.org/userfiles/file/2012handouts/B13/The%20Silent%20Epidemic%20(44%20pages).pdf

Bronson, P., & Merryman, A. (2010, July 10). The creativity crisis. *Newsweek.* Retrieved from http://www.thedailybeast.com/newsweek/2010/07/10/the-creativity-crisis.html

Cakir, M. P., Zemel, A., & Stahl, G. (2009). The joint organization of interaction within a multimodal CSCL network. *International Journal of Computer-Supported Collaborative Learning, 4*(2), 115–149. Retrieved from http://gerrystahl.net/pub/ijCSCL_4_2_1.pdf

Carbone, E. (2002). *Stealing freedom.* St. Paul, MN: Elisa Emc Publishers.

Carr, N. (2010). *The shallows. What the Internet is doing to our brains.* New York: Norton.

Carson, R. (1962). *Silent spring.* Boston, MA: Houghton Mifflin.

Center for Research on Evaluation, Standards, and Student Testing. (1990). *Portfolio assessment and high technology.* Los Angeles: University of California at Los Angeles. Retrieved from http://www.cse.ucla.edu/products/guidebooks/hightech.pdf

Common Core State Standards Initiative. (2011a). About the standards. Retrieved from http://www.corestandards.org/about-the-standards

Common Core State Standards Initiative. (2011b). Frequently asked questions. Retrieved from http://www.corestandards.org/frequently-asked-questions

Cormier, R. (2004). *The chocolate war.* New York: Robert Ember, A Random House Imprint.

Costa, A., & Kallick, B. (2000). *Habits of Mind.* Retrieved from http://www.instituteforhabitsofmind.com/

Covey, Sean. (1998). *7 Habits of highly effective teens.* New York: Touchstone Press.

Deci, E. L., & Ryan, R. M. (Eds.). (2006). *The handbook of self-determination research.* Rochester, NY: University of Rochester Press.

Dede, C. (2009a). Comparing frameworks for "21st century skills." Retrieved from http://www.watertown.k12.ma.us/dept/ed_tech/research/pdf/ChrisDede.pdf

Digital literacy. (n.d.). In *Wikipedia.* Retrieved from http://en.wikipedia.org/wiki/Digital_literacy

Dweck, C. (2006). *Mindset: The new psychology of success.* New York: Random House.

Elder, L. (2007) *Another brief conceptualization of critical thinking.* Retrieved from http://www.criticalthinking.org/pages/defining-critical-thinking/766

Enzensberger, H. M. (1997). *The number devil: A mathematical adventure.* (M. Heim, Trans.) New York: Henry Holt.

Flanagin, A. J., & Metzger, M. J. (2010) *Kids and credibility: An empirical examination of youth, digital media use, and information credibility.* Chicago: The MacArthur Foundation. Retrieved from http://www.macfound.org

Flavell, J. H. (1979). Metacognition and cognitive monitoring: A new area of cognitive-developmental inquiry. *American Psychologist, 34*(10), 906–911.

Friedman, T. (2005). *The world is flat: A brief history of the twenty-first century.* New York: Farrar, Straus and Giroux.

Fuller, R. B. (1982). *Critical path.* New York: St. Martin's Griffin.

Funke, C. (2003). *Inkheart.* Somerset, UK: The Chicken House.

Gibson, C. J., & Lennon, E. (1999). *Historical census statistics on the foreign-born population of the United States: 1850–1990* (Population Division Working Paper No. 29). Washington, DC: U.S. Bureau of the Census.

Giff, P. R. (2001). *Nory Ryan's song.* Waterville, ME: Thorndike Press.

Glaser, E. M. (1941). *An experiment in the development of critical thinking.* New York: Teachers College, Columbia University.

Glass, I. (2010). Speech and interview given at KQED in San Francisco.

Glasser, W. (1968). *Schools without failure.* New York: Harper and Row.

Goleman, D. (1995). *Emotional intelligence.* New York: Bantam Books.

Greenstein, L. (2005). *Classroom assessment: Teacher's knowledge and practice.* Unpublished doctoral dissertation, Johnson and Wales University.

Greenstein, L. (2010). *What teachers really need to know about formative assessment.* Alexandria, VA: ASCD.

Hattie, J. (2008). *Visible learning: A synthesis of over 800 meta-analyses relating to achievement.* New York: Routledge.

Hattie, J., & Timperley, H. (2007).The power of feedback. *Review of Educational Research, 77*(81). Retrieved from http://rer.aera.net

Hart, W., & Albarracin, D. (2009). The effects of chronic achievement motivation and achievement primes on the activation of achievement and fun goals. *Journal of Personality and Social Psychology, (97)*6, 1129–1141.

Hartnell-Young, E. (2008). *Impact study of e-portfolios on learning.* Nottingham, UK: Nottingham University. Retrieved from http://research.becta.org.uk/index .php?section=rh&catcode=_re_rp_02&rid=14007

Herman, J. L., & Winters, L. (1994*).* Portfolio research: A slim collection. *Educational.*

Jacobs, H. H. (Ed.). (2010). *Curriculum 21: Essential education for a changing world.* Alexandria VA: ASCD.

Jacobsen, E. R. (2011). Average SAT scores of college-bound seniors (1952–present). Retrieved from http://www.erikthered.com/tutor/historical-average-SAT-scores.pdf

Jerald , C. (2009). *Defining a 21st century education.* Alexandria, VA: The Center for Public Education. Retrieved from http://www.centerforpubliceducation .org/Learn-About/21st-Century/Defining-a-21st-Century-Education-Full-Report-PDF.pdf

Johnson, L., Levine, A., Smith, R., & Stone, W. (2010). *The 2010 Horizon report,* Austin, TX: New Media Consortium.

Kanevsky, L., & Keighley T. (2003). To produce or not to produce? Understanding boredom and honor in underachievement. *Roeper Review, 26*(1), 20–28.

KnowledgeWorks Foundation. (2008). *The 2020 Forecast: Creating the Future of Learning.* Cincinnati, OH: Author.

Lapkoff, S., & Li, R. M. (2007). Five trends for schools. *Educational Leadership, 64*(6), 8–15.

Lawrence, I., Rigol, G. W., Van Essen, T., & Jackson, C. A. (2002). *Research Report No. 2002–7: A historical perspective on the SAT: 1926–2001.* New York: College Entrance Examination Board.

Lemke, C., Coughlin, E., Thgadani, V., Martin, C. (2003). *enGauge 21st century skills: Literacy in the digital age.* Culver City, CA: Metiri Group.

Lengler, R., & Eppler, M. (2007). *Towards a periodic table of visualization methods for management.* IASTED Proceedings of the Conference on Graphics and Visualization in Engineering (GVE 2007). Clearwater, Florida. Retrieved from http://www.visual-literacy.org/periodic_table/periodic_table.html

Leu, D. (2010, October*).* *New literacies of online reading comprehension: Preparing all students for their reading future.* Presentation to the Connecticut Alliance of Regional Service Centers.

Loveless, T. (2011). *The 2010 Brown Center report on American education: How well are American students learning?* Washington, DC: Brookings Institution. Retrieved from http://www.brookings.edu/~/media/Files/rc/reports/2011/0111_naep_loveless/0111_naep_loveless.pdf

Lovett, M. (2008). *Teaching metacognition.* Retrieved from http://net.educause .edu/upload/presentations/ELI081/FS03/Metacognition-ELI.pdf

Lyman, P., & Varian, H. (2003). *How much information?* Retrieved from http:// www2.sims.berkeley.edu/research/projects/how-much-info-2003/

Marzano, R. (2007). *The art and science of teaching.* Alexandria, VA: ASCD.

Macaulay, D. (2010). *The new Way Things Work*. New York: Houghton Mifflin.

Metiri Group. (2003). *enGauge 21st century skills*. Culver City, CA: Metiri Group, Author. Available at www.unctv.org/education/teachers_childcare/nco/documents/skillsbrochure.pdf

Metropolitan Life Insurance Company. (2011). *MetLife survey of the American teacher: Preparing students for college and career readiness*. New York: Author. (ERIC Document Reproduction Services No. ED 519278)

Moore, G. E. (1965). *The Moore's Law website*. Retrieved from http://www.intel.com/technology/mooreslaw/

Morse, S. (2006). *The school dropout crisis: Why one-third of all high school students drop out and what your community can do about it*. Richmond, VA: The University of Richmond Pew Partnership for Civic Change. Retrieved from http://www.pew-partnership.org/pdf/dropout_overview.pdf

Moskal, B., & Leydens, J. (2000). Scoring rubric development: Validity and reliability. *Practical Assessment, Research, and Evaluation, 7*(10). Retrieved from http://pareonline.net/getvn.asp?v=7&n=10

Murphey, C. (1996). *Gifted hands: The Ben Carson story*. Grand Rapids, MI: Zondervan.

National Assessment of Educational Progress, National Center for Education Statistics. (2011). *NAEP Civics Report*. Retrieved from http://nationsreportcard.gov/civics_2010/summary.asp

National Association of State Boards of Education. (2009). *Reform at the crossroads: A call for balanced systems of assessment and accountability*. Retrieved from http://nasbe.org/index.php/downloads/study-groups/developing-the-21st-century-educator-study-group-2010/meeting-materials/280-reform-at-a-crossroads-chapter-4

National Center for Children in Poverty. (2012). *Data tools*. New York: Columbia University, Mailman School of Public Health. Retrieved from http://www.nccp.org/tools

National Center for Education Statistics. (2009). *Comparing NAEP, TIMSS, and PISA in Mathematics and Science*. Retrieved from http://nces.ed.gov/timss/pdf/naep_timss_pisa_comp.pdf

National Commission on Excellence in Education. *A nation at risk: The imperative for educational reform*. (1983). Washington, DC: U.S. Department of Education. Retrieved from http://www.ed.gov/pubs/NatAtRisk/title.html

National Governors Association Center for Best Practices, Council of Chief State School Officers. (2010). *Common core state standards for English language arts and literacy in history/social studies, science, and technical subjects*. Washington, DC: National Governors Association Center for Best Practices, Council of Chief State School Officers. Retrieved from http://www.corestandards.org/assets/CCSSI_ELA%20Standards.pdf

National Governors Association Center for Best Practices, Council of Chief State School Officers. (2010). *Common core state standards for mathematics*. Washington, DC: National Governors Association Center for Best Practices, Council of Chief State School Officers. Retrieved from http://www.corestandards.org/assets/CCSSI_Math%20Standards.pdf

Nielsen Company. (2012). *The Australian online consumer landscape*. Retrieved from http://au.nielsen.com/site/documents/AustralianOnlineLandscapeExecSummReport2012FINAL.pdf

Organisation for Economic Co-operation and Development, Centre for Educational Research and Innovation (2008). *21st century learning: Research innovation, and policy.* Retrieved from http://www.oecd.org/dataoecd/39/8/40554299.pdf

Parish, P. (1963). *Amelia Bedelia.* UK: Harper Collins.

Partnership for 21st Century Skills. (2010a). *Review of CCSSI Language Arts Standards.* Retrieved from http://www.p21.0rg/documents/P21%20CCSSI%20Comments%20ELA%20FINAL%2004.02.10.pdf

Paul, R., & Nosich, G. (2009). *A national model for the assessment of higher order thinking.* Tomales, CA: The Foundation for Critical Thinking. Retrieved from http://www.criticalthinking.org/assessment/a-model-nal-assessment-hot.cfm

Pink, D. (2009). *Drive: The surprising truth about what motivates us.* New York: Riverhead Books.

Postsecondary and Workforce Readiness Working Group. (2009). *The road map to college and career readiness for Minnesota students: Final report and recommendations presented to the Minnesota P-16 Partnership.* Retrieved from http://www.massp.org/downloads/readiness.pdf

Project Tomorrow. (2010). *Creating our future: Students speak up about their vision for 21st century learning.* Irvine, CA: Project Tomorrow, Author. Retrieved from http://www.tomorrow.org/speakup/pdfs/SU09NationalFindingsStudents&Parents.pdf

Ravitch, D. (2000). *Left back: A century of failed school reforms.* New York: Simon and Schuster.

Ravitch, D. (2002). A brief history of testing and accountability. *Hoover Digest* (4). Retrieved from http://www.hoover.org/publications/hoover-digest/article/7286

Reeves, D. B. (n.d.). Overcoming initiative fatigue [Video file]. Leadership and Learning Center. Retrieved from http://www.leadandlearn.com/multimedia-resource-center/videos/overcoming-initiative-fatigue

Reimers, F. (2009) *Educating for global competence.* In J. E. Cohen & M. B. Malin (Eds.), *International perspectives on the goals of universal and basic secondary education* (pp. 183–202). New York: Routledge

Rideout, V. J., Foehr, U. G., & Roberts, D. F. (2010). *Generation M2: Media in the lives of 8 to 18 year olds.* Menlo Park, CA: Henry J. Kaiser Family Foundation. Retrieved from http://www.kff.org/entmedia/mh012010pkg.cfm

Robinson, K. (2006, February). Ken Robinson says schools kill creativity [Video file]. Retrieved from http://www.ted.com/talks/ken_robinson_says_schools_kill_creativity.html

Rogers, C. R. (1967). *On becoming a person.* London: Constable.

Schmoker, M. (2011). *Focus: Evaluating the essentials to radically improve student learning.* Alexandria, VA: ASCD.

Senge, P. (1994). *The fifth discipline.* New York: Doubleday.

Shekerjian, D. (1991). *Uncommon genius.* New York: Penguin.

Silva E. (2008). *Measuring skills for the 21st century.* Washington, DC: Education Sector Reports. Retrieved from http://www.educationsector.org

Silva, E. (2009). Measuring skills for 21st century learning. *Phi Delta Kappan, 90*(9), 630–634.

Sizer, T. (1997). *Horace's school: Redesigning the American high school.* New York: Houghton Mifflin.

Small, G. (2009) *New technology and the brain.* Retrieved from http://www.today .ucla.edu/portal/ut/081015_gary-small-brain.aspx

Spady, W. G. (1999). School reform: Rushing backward toward the future. *On the Horizon 7*(2), 1–7.

Sternberg, R. J. (1985). *Beyond IQ: A triarchic theory of intelligence.* Cambridge, UK: Cambridge University Press.

Stevenson, A. (1952, October 8). Speech at the University of Wisconsin, Madison.

Stevenson, H. (1990). Mathematics achievement of children in China and the United States. *Child Development, 61,* 1053–1056.

Symonds, W. C., Schwartz, R. B., & Ferguson, R. (2011) *Pathways to prosperity: Meeting the challenges of preparing young Americans for the 21st century.* Pathways to Prosperity Project. Boston: Harvard Graduate School of Education.

Tan, S. (2007). *The arrival.* New York: Arthur A. Levine.

Torney-Purta, J., & Wilkenfeld, B. (2009). *Paths to 21st century competencies through civic education classrooms: An analysis of survey results from ninth-graders* (Technical Assistance Bulletin). Chicago: American Bar Association Division for Public Education.

Trilling, B., & Fadel, C. (2009). *21st century skills: Learning for life in our times.* New York: Jossey-Bass.

Tucker, M. (2011). *Standing on the shoulders of giants: An American agenda for school reform.* Washington, DC: National Center for Education and the Economy. Retrieved from http://www.ncee.org/wp-content/uploads/2011/05/ Standing-on-the-Shoulders-of-Giants-An-American-Agenda-for-Education-Reform.pdf

United Nations Development Programme. (2010). *Millennium Development Goals.* New York: Author. Retrieved from http://www.undp.org/content/undp/ en/home/mdgoverview.html

U.S. Department of Education. (2008). *A nation accountable: Twenty-five years after A Nation at Risk.* Washington, DC: Author.

Yang, G. L. (2006). *American born Chinese.* New York: First Second.

Zagursky, E. (2011, February 3). The numbers show it: American creativity has been declining since 1990. *Ideation.* Williamsburg, VA: William and Mary University. Retrieved from http://www.wm.edu/research/ideation/ professions/smart-yes.-creative-not-so-much.5890.php

Zhao, Y. (2009). Needed: Global villagers. *Educational Leadership, 67*(1), 60–65.

Zhao, Y. (2011). *A nation at risk: Edited by Yong Zhao.* Retrieved from http://zhao learning.com/wp-content/uploads/2011/03/anationatrisk.pdf

Index

CORWIN

A SAGE Company

The Corwin logo—a raven striding across an open book—represents the union of courage and learning. Corwin is committed to improving education for all learners by publishing books and other professional development resources for those serving the field of PreK–12 education. By providing practical, hands-on materials, Corwin continues to carry out the promise of its motto: **"Helping Educators Do Their Work Better."**